D1066345

EDUCATING *the* DISFRANCHISED *and* DISINHERITED

EDUCATING *the* DISFRANCHISED *and* DISINHERITED

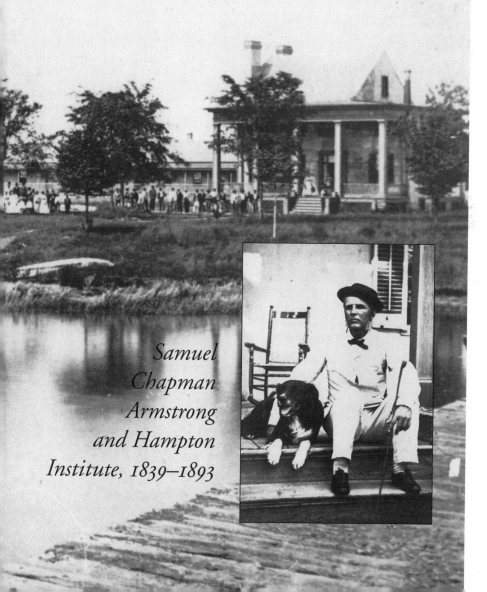

Samuel Chapman Armstrong and Hampton Institute, 1839–1893

ROBERT FRANCIS ENGS

Library of Congress Cataloging-in-Publication Data

Engs, Robert Francis.
Educating the disfranchised and disinherited : Samuel Chapman Armstrong and
Hampton Institute : 1839–1893 / Robert Francis Engs.
—1st ed.
   p. cm.
ISBN 1-57233-051-1 (cl.: alk. paper)
   1. Armstrong, S. C. (Samuel Chapman), 1839–1893. 2. Hampton Normal and
Agricultural Institute (Va.)—Biography. 3. Hampton Institute—History. I. Title.
LC2851.H313 .A764 1999
378.1'1'092—dc21
   [B]   98-58089

For my mother and in memory of my father

Contents

Illustrations

PREFACE

Samuel Chapman Armstrong (1839–1893) is one of the most intriguing figures of nineteenth-century American history. "The General," as he loved to be called, was founder and first principal of Hampton Normal and Agricultural Institute, the premier school for industrial education of African Americans in the postbellum South. Here was a unique man who embodied all the conflicts and contradictions of race, religion, class, and gender that characterized postbellum America. On the one hand, he was genuinely committed to the uplift of the freed people, women as well as men. He envisioned African Americans as becoming—ultimately, if not immediately—like himself. He designed his institute for that purpose, and, over the ensuing twenty-five years, achieved considerable success toward his goal. He even openly designated his protégé, Booker T. Washington, a black man, as his spiritual and philosophical heir. On the other hand, Armstrong was very much a member of some of the most elite white circles in late-nineteenth-century America. A confidante of United States presidents and industrial moguls, he was the major conduit through which northern philanthropy was channeled to southern black schools.

The remarkable story of Samuel Chapman Armstrong strikingly illuminates his genius in manipulating multiple constituencies and balancing myriad roles. At the same time, it provides extraordinary insight into the convoluted struggle to accommodate new realities about race and gender in postbellum society and the role of education in that process. American life in the late nineteenth century has been much analyzed, but often in a fragmentary way that has obscured the whole. Through Armstrong, we may grasp connections and themes that previously have eluded students of the era.

Despite Armstrong's importance and the stellar reputation he enjoyed during most of his adult life, no scholarly biography of him has been written, and for nearly a century no biography of any sort has been published.[1] Such neglect seems peculiar, for Armstrong appears as a major actor in studies of black education in the late nineteenth century, and in Booker T. Washington's writings. In the biographies written by friends and relatives, and in Washington's fawning celebration of Armstrong in *Up from Slavery,*

General Armstrong emerges as a hero. The turn of the century, however, marked the beginning of an inversion of Armstrong's reputation. When W. E. B. DuBois, in *Souls of Black Folk* (1903), harshly criticized Washington and his accommodationist educational philosophy, he implicitly condemned Washington's deceased teacher, Samuel Armstrong, as well.[2]

Recent studies of Armstrong have also been quite critical. In his *Schooling for the New Slavery,* Donald Spivey, as the title forewarns, paints Armstrong as a consummate villain. In more scholarly and dispassionate studies, as in August Meier's *Negro Thought in America* and Louis Harlan's masterful two-volume biography, *Booker T. Washington,* Armstrong is portrayed as a crucial orchestrator of the directions that black education would take in postbellum America. My treatment of Armstrong in *Freedom's First Generation* viewed him primarily from the perspective of the emerging black community of Hampton, Virginia. James Anderson, in *The Education of Blacks in the South, 1860–1935,* draws upon the wealth of new research on black education after the Civil War to produce a compelling study. Based upon an exegesis of Armstrong's writings in Hampton Institute's *Southern Workman*, Anderson sharply criticizes Armstrong for seeking to limit black aspirations and for advocating black passivity in the struggle against unrelenting oppression.[3]

Neither sanctification nor vilification will lead to an understanding of the complex and often contradictory man who was Samuel Armstrong. A much more rewarding approach is to utilize the myriad heretofore overlooked sources that illuminate Armstrong's heritage, education, and life's work. These sources paint an intriguing picture of the intricate and conflicting patterns of postbellum life among northern philanthropists, embittered white southerners, and, most of all, among northern white teachers and the African American students they sought to educate.

Each period of Samuel Armstrong's life helped to determine how he sought to shape his world. As the son of American missionaries to Hawaii, Armstrong was imbued with a deep religiosity characteristic of many in antebellum reform movements. Such sentiments began to wane among some segments of the elite in the aftermath of war and reconstruction. This was not true of Armstrong and many of his allies, however.

Armstrong was born to American parents abroad and therefore legally was a subject of the Kingdom of Hawaii. Consequently, when he came to America for the first time in 1860, to attend Williams College, he did not fully comprehend the sectional conflicts that were about to tear the United States apart. His education and ensuing military service as an officer in the Union army paralleled those of his schoolmates, including one—James Garfield—who later would become president of the United States. Armstrong was a member of the generation of men so effectively portrayed by George Fredrickson in his *Inner Civil War.*[4] Their wartime experiences persuaded them that they had transcended the work of the Founding Fathers. The Civil War had demonstrated that the original design for union had been flawed. This new generation, at the cost of lives and limbs, had rectified those errors. Moreover, they had discovered a specific role for themselves. They were to serve as guides for those who made up the vast lower class, just as they had commanded its members as officers during the Civil War. These postbellum northern men thought a good deal about how to restore the nation, how to make the South a place safe for Yankee investment, and what to do with the freed slaves. The future of America was in industry, and the agrarian South somehow had to be brought into the process.

Samuel Chapman Armstrong embraced much of this vision, but he also differed from his contemporaries in many ways. Most notably, his missionary upbringing impelled him to serve others. His Hawaiian childhood had left him not without racial prejudice (as will be seen especially in his disparaging remarks about the Chinese and his fondness for the term *darkie*) but largely without the antipathy toward African Americans that characterized racism in America. In consequence, he cast his lot with the evolving freed people of the South, first as a commander of black troops during the war, then as a superintendent in the Freedmen's Bureau, and ultimately as founder and principal of Hampton Institute. Armstrong believed that the freed people should not be ciphers in the process that would reconstruct the New South; rather, they should be active participants and contributors.

In espousing such views, Armstrong clearly formed part of the generation James McPherson portrayed in *Abolitionist Legacy.*[5] These men and women McPherson aptly describes as "the children of the abolitionists." During and after the Civil War, this group gave up the comfort and safety of homes in New England and the Midwest to become teachers, preachers, and caretakers of the freed slaves. Among such types also were men who had pursued military careers. Samuel Chapman Armstrong was one of them. His involvement with southern blacks began as a commander of the 9th and 8th regiments of United States Colored Troops.

Although he shared the motives and goals of civilian missionaries, Armstrong's strategy and tactics for black "uplift" frequently diverged from those of his allies. First, his military experience, and his success in it, had persuaded him that blacks needed a more rigid, disciplined educational environment than other missionaries advocated. Second, his upbringing as his father's assistant in organizing schools for indigenous Hawaiians had wedded him to the idea of "industrial education" as a primary means of advancement for "backward peoples." Third, that same background had inspired in him a grandiose notion of "saving races." Thus he set out to design a system that would give the black masses at least a rudimentary education. He refused to make Hampton

Institute into even a nascent college. It was to be a teacher training school whose graduates were to go out into the countryside and teach their "brothers and sisters." In taking this stance, Armstrong placed himself on a collision course with other missionary educators who were advocating a more idealistic and open-ended course for African American education—albeit for *fewer* African Americans, given their educational deficiencies. His conflict with these other advocates of freedmen's education provides considerable insight into the national debate over how black people were to fit into postbellum American society, or if they were to fit at all.

Once Armstrong had established Hampton Institute and gained firm control of it, more of his character and his methods were revealed. It is for these aspects of his life and work that he has been both praised and condemned. While genuinely dedicated to serving others, he seldom doubted that he was the person best qualified to decide how that service should be provided. His provincial upbringing in Hawaii and his considerable ego compelled him to seek and enjoy acclaim, especially from members of the northern elite, with whom his mother's family was well connected.

At the same time, circumstances in the post-Reconstruction South forced Armstrong to become a consummate educational politician. He somehow had simultaneously to placate an increasingly assertive and anti-Negro white South and elicit funds from northern philanthropists concerned about the worsening plight of the southern Negro. Most important, he had to persuade his primary constituency—freed African Americans—that his educational program and its underlying philosophy of self-help, agricultural self-sufficiency through land ownership, and abstinence from politics constituted their best course of action.

In order to keep all these disparate groups working toward the realization of his foremost goals—the growth and security of Hampton Institute—Armstrong had to become a master prevaricator. This surely is part of what has so frustrated those (including the author of this book) who have attempted to study the man. It also may be one of the character flaws emulated by his protégé, Booker T. Washington. There are enormous inconsistencies in Armstrong's public statements. Statements were skillfully modulated to satisfy the particular audience being addressed. There were similar inconsistencies in his private correspondence. In some letters he appears to be a consummate racist; in others he seems an educator deeply devoted to the ultimate equality of African Americans.

His actions likewise evince a pattern of contradiction. On the one hand, his design for education at Hampton was authoritarian and paternalistic in the extreme. On the other hand, he rapidly incorporated the best of his black graduates into the staff (if not the faculty) of the institute. In 1878, he immediately seized the opportunity to bring Native American students to Hampton. A government stipend was assured for each such student, and adding this group to the student body would enable the school to raise money from groups or individuals who had little concern for African American education. Fragmentary surviving financial records indicate that Armstrong used such private funds for the general expenses of the institute, as well as for the Indian students. Nevertheless, the intensity with which Armstrong publicized Indian education at Hampton gave blacks legitimate grounds for questioning the school's commitment to serving their needs. Such examples suggest what a circuitous and often treacherous route educators of black folk in the late-nineteenth-century South had to follow to continue providing even a modicum of opportunity for aspiring students.

The two facts most crucial for understanding Samuel Chapman Armstrong are that he was raised as a missionary child, and that he grew up in a multiracial, predominantly non-European society. His unique background made him significantly different from most Americans, even his allies, in the struggles for black advancement in the late nineteenth century.

Past analyses of Armstrong, which insist upon viewing him within the context of Booker T. Washington's life and forced submission to "accommodationism," may miss much more instructive and salient points. For example, how did a European American imbued with the missionary obligation function in postbellum America? And what does a missionary do if his or her enterprise is successful?

American Christian missionary efforts among "heathens" always were two-tiered enterprises. First was the task of saving souls, converting unbelievers to the "true" faith. Second was "civilization," enabling the converted to become participants in the culture that, in the eyes of the missionaries, embodied Christian virtues. Armstrong's life epitomizes the dilemma of a missionary who accomplishes the first goal and then achieves the second as well.

Before they met him, Armstrong's "clientele," the freed slaves, already considered themselves Christians. Indeed, often they thought that they were better Christians than the missionaries who came to aid them. Armstrong, through the education he provided at Hampton Institute, prepared them for incorporation into the larger society. Then Armstrong faced the inevitable dilemma: how can demeaned people be incorporated into a society that, in part, defines itself by its persecution of those very people? This is not a problem unique to Armstrong and his fellow missionaries after the Civil War. It has ever been the albatross of white Christian "home" missionaries. How can their converts be integrated into the missionaries' own racist society?

Armstrong struggled to realize his missionary obligation while participating in a society that was increasingly racist and was unashamed of that. His struggle offers insight into the nature of late-nineteenth-century American racism, the potential and limitations of missionary vision, and the resilience of black people, whether they are trying to cope with their foes or their allies.

In the life and work of Samuel Chapman Armstrong are revealed the processes by which some white Americans became dedicated to the advancement of black Americans who had become their fellow citizens. Also illuminated are the strengths and weaknesses of those who meant well but were severely constricted by their own personalities and by their visions of society and of race. Most important, perhaps, Armstrong's successes and failures provide benchmarks by which we can measure our own progress in resolving those problems of race and class with which we continue to struggle. Sam Armstrong still may have some lessons to teach. This volume may help us learn some of them.

ACKNOWLEDGMENTS

I must thank, first of all, the John Simon Guggenheim Foundation for financing the leave that enabled me to do the majority of research for this study. Second, the National Endowment for the Humanities enabled me to initiate this research. Most of all, however, my own institution, the University of Pennsylvania, provided the time and funds needed to complete this project.

As deeply indebted as I am to those who helped fund this enterprise, I am more profoundly grateful still to those who helped make it possible by sharing their resources with me. The staffs of the National Archives, the Library of Congress, and the libraries of Harvard University were most gracious. Two groups of individuals were the best partners in research that I have ever had. One group was the staff supervising the Williamsiana Collection at Williams College. The other were the men and women of Hampton University.

What follows in this book may not always be to the liking of my Hampton partners, but it could not have been created without their guidance. President William Harvey gave me unrestricted access to the institution's archival holdings. University Museum Director Jean Zeidler and former University Archivist Fritz Malval guided me through Hampton's enormously rich collections. But it was the assistance of the staff in the archives—Donzella Wilford, Cynthia Poston, and Deborah Richardson—upon which I most depended. These individuals permitted me and my assistants more than ordinary access to their collections. I did not just "sample from" the Armstrong Collection at Hampton; I sat in the midst of it, and each of those staff members would bring, or point me to, a new box when she thought it would help. My debt to them, and to all at Hampton who were so kind to me, never can be repaid.

The inspiration to write a biography I owe to my teachers, William McFeely, C. Vann Woodward, and James McPherson, who instilled in me the conviction that I could overcome the challenges that this biography might present. I wish especially to acknowledge my earliest research aides: Robert Waters, who traveled with me to Williams College; and Robert

Gregg, who, along with Waters, helped to transcribe the voluminous records gathered at Williams. Eric Balaban not only helped me sort through Library of Congress records, but also conscientiously sought out new sources that he thought would be of value to me.

As graduate students, Lorenzo Griffin and James Johnson were most helpful readers and critics. Their common sense and critical questioning have much improved this manuscript. My brother, Michael Engs, took time from his Hawaiian vacation to research in Honolulu libraries at my behest. My students, Lisa Hiyakawa and Richard Lau, did the same during their Christmas breaks. I owe a special debt to Brandon Hirsh, who acted as researcher, typist, and soothsayer; and to Jason Busch, who proofread the final manuscript. Most of all, I thank Rubin Sinins, whose work as my primary research assistant surpassed the highest expectations any professor might formulate. His energy, commitment, and efficiency compelled me to work far harder than I thought myself capable of doing.

There are many others to whom I incurred great debts in the accomplishment of this task. Drew Faust and Richard Beeman, my valued colleagues; Baird Tipson; Leon and Evelyn Higginbotham; and Mary Berry took time from their busy schedules to make critical readings of drafts. Jane Bryan, head of reference at the University of Pennsylvania's Van Pelt Library, has been irrepressibly cheerful and unfailingly helpful in ferreting out sources and obscure references. Jeff Kerr-Ritchie and I shared resources and ideas, as well as the anguish that accompanies research, writing, and publication. His insights and suggestions were particularly valuable in bringing this project to its conclusion.

It is traditional and, in this case, entirely appropriate to reserve one's deepest thanks for one's family. My "extended" family, the Olivers and the Engs, have nurtured and encouraged me; they have read draft chapters and endured boring explications of Armstrong and southern black education. My "nuclear" family cheerfully has suffered even more. My son, Robert, a genuine "computer whiz," guided me through the intricacies of word processing; my wife Jean has been an unfaltering supporter and frequent reader of the words that follow. She will be even happier than I, however, to get Samuel Chapman Armstrong out of our home and back into the larger world he so enjoyed.

Robert Francis Engs
Philadelphia
July 1998

INTRODUCTION:

April 6, 1868

On a bright spring day in Elizabeth City County, Virginia, young Brevet Brigadier General Samuel Chapman Armstrong pronounced his Hampton Normal and Agricultural Institute open to students. "I stand now where I have long aimed to stand," Armstrong exulted; "I can say to any noble, aspiring, whole-souled colored youth of either sex in the South—'Here you can come ragged and poor as you are, and become the men and women you wish to become.'"[1] It was the climactic moment of Armstrong's career and life. In hindsight, it seems that everything he had done in the first half of his life led inexorably toward that day. Everything he was to do thereafter, for better and for worse, resulted from it.

In 1868, the new Hampton Institute was not much to look at. It consisted of some old army barracks, the remnants of Chesapeake Army Hospital, and the decrepit mansion house of the former Little Scotland plantation. Nevertheless, the new school represented a remarkable, albeit temporary, convergence of one man's vision with a fleeting national consensus on societal rebuilding and racial readjustment in the aftermath of the Civil War. The freedmen had gained the vote. The possibility remained that substantial numbers of them might acquire land as well. They needed to be educated in how to use both. In pursuit of that goal, an alliance of not entirely compatible forces emerged. On the one hand were antebellum abolitionists and evangelical Christians, together with advocates of postbellum freedmen's aid and missionary uplift. These joined, on the other hand, Republican politicians scheming to insure national Republican hegemony through the southern black vote, and Yankee entrepreneurs seeking to create wealth by exploiting southern land and labor, especially *black* labor.

It was a portent of future difficulties that young Armstrong seemed to embody all these potentially conflicting agendas. He did not merely *believe in* the missionary enterprise and racial uplift. Rather, he *was* a missionary, born the son of missionaries to Hawaii and raised helping his parents Christianize and educate indigenous Hawaiians. His father's primary strategies for Hawaiian "civilization" were land redistribution and mass education, which included training in agriculture. Samuel Armstrong had been his father's secretary during those endeavors. Better still, the younger Armstrong had been a commander of black troops during the recent war and an agent in the Freedmen's Bureau at the beginning of Reconstruction. He embraced the Republican party and believed that an economic renaissance in the South, based on scientific agriculture and moderate industrialization, was the proper course for both men of property and striving laborers. Together they would make the South prosper again. Hampton Institute was designed to facilitate this process. Its activities would benefit not merely the hundreds trained on its campus, but also the thousands of impoverished and ignorant freedpeople in the countryside who would be taught by Hampton graduates.

The national consensus that had facilitated Hampton's creation lasted barely longer than it took Hampton's first class to graduate (three years). After 1872, it became apparent that Republican hegemony could be sustained without the southern black vote. Northern defense of freedmen's rights gradually faltered and by the 1890s ceased almost entirely. Yankee businessmen found the freedmen and their allies either too honest or too innocent to be reliable partners in their get-rich schemes. Southern landowners—former slavemasters—exhibited neither honesty nor innocence. Those who had the power to make such decisions quietly decided that the freed blacks would become sharecroppers, bound to the land through debt. Even some proponents of black education began to argue that purpose of that education was to reconcile the freedpeople to their inferior status, rather than to instill in them aspirations for upward mobility and social equality.

Although ultimately unsuccessful, Samuel Armstrong's struggle to maintain the clarity of his April 1868 vision in the face of this betrayal of black freedom from every direction, provides special insight into the man, his class, his time, and the African Americans and Native Americans whose lives he touched.

I

The Armstrong Legacy

Richard Armstrong and His
Hawaiian Mission

In a sense, Samuel Armstrong's path to Hampton started in County Fermanagh, Corporation of Enniskillen, Northern Ireland. There Samuel's grandfather, James Armstrong, began traditions among the family's men that would continue for at least three generations. He took care to ingratiate himself with the well established of his community so that he might move on to a new world and a new career. He also chose as his wife a woman who shared his faith and his commitment to a plain, hardworking, Christian life.

James was of Presbyterian, Scotch-Irish descent. He had worked as both a teacher and a surveyor before emigrating. When he decided in 1786 that better opportunities might await him in America, he took care to secure letters of recommendation from the County Burgesses, his tutor and vicar at Ennis McSaint Parish, and from the curator of that same parish. The curator assured the recipient of his letter that James Armstrong had served him for seven years and had "acquitted himself with as much honesty and integrity as I could expect or wish for."[1]

With such credentials in hand, James Armstrong sailed for America, arriving in the fall of 1786 and settling in Northumberland County, Pennsylvania. He became a teacher at a local academy and soon married Eleanor Pollack, a woman described as "kindly" but with a "force of character . . . above average."[2]

James did not long remain a schoolteacher. He purchased a large farm in Northumberland County, and there, on 13 April 1805, his last child, Richard, was born. Young Richard was raised in a secure, devoutly Presbyterian environment, but in his childhood there were few clues to his missionary future. When he was deemed too sickly for the life of a farmer, his older sisters took on the farm work, while he was sent off to Milton Academy in Milton, Pennsylvania.[3] From there he proceeded to Dickinson College in Carlisle, Pennsylvania. He graduated in 1827 with high praise from the college's President William Neill. About Armstrong, Neill wrote, "We believe him to be a young gentleman of unblemished morals and sincere piety." Neill's expectation was that Richard would become a teacher because of his knowledge of Latin and Greek.[4]

Richard, however, already felt a different calling. He entered Princeton Theological Seminary and graduated in 1831.[5] In March of that year, Richard wrote to his older brother. He planned to "go to the heathen to preach . . . the Gospel." He added, "[T]he choice is not of my own, it appears to be marked out by Him who I am bound to serve forever. . . . The work of the missionary, it is true, is self-denying and laborious, but I must remember that he who does not love Christ more than houses or lands . . . cannot be his disciple."[6] In the twenty-nine years that followed, Richard Armstrong would have many experiences that caused him to question the wisdom of those idealistic sentiments.

The agency through which Richard sought to achieve his goals was the American Board of Commissioners for Foreign Missions. The American Board had been created in 1810 to spread evangelical Christianity to the "colored" races across the world. Among its founders was the prominent New England divine, Lyman Beecher, who later would become father of Harriet Beecher Stowe. Unlike his daughter, but much like his colleagues on the American Board during these years, Lyman Beecher took an ambiguous stance on the morality of slavery. The board saw its task as extending the "reach of Christ's Kingdom." The worrisome topic of human bondage, be it among white southerners, Native Americans, or peoples abroad, was secondary to the establishment of the "true" religion throughout the world.[7]

In 1831, the debate over slavery had not yet been fully joined. Of more concern to the American Board and to Richard Armstrong was the remote Kingdom of Hawaii. In that year, the board was assembling its fifth contingent of missionaries to these islands. Richard Armstrong was determined to be among them. He even managed to spend a few months at the University of Pennsylvania Medical School, learning rudimentary health care for use in his missionary work.[8]

Richard solicited a letter from President Archibald Alexander of Princeton Theological Seminary, which testified to Armstrong's "pure zeal for the glory of God and . . . salvation of the heathen." Alexander also observed that Richard "would be a kind and attentive husband to any lady whom he would choose as a companion in entering on this important enterprise."[9]

Those last lines by President Alexander were no mere afterthought; the American Board required that all their missionaries to foreign lands be married. Richard met, courted, and married a devout young woman from Russell, Massachusetts, Clarissa Chapman. Despite the requirement that Richard marry someone in order to go abroad, all observers claimed that the Armstrong-Chapman wedding was truly a "union of the heart" and not merely a "religious marriage of convenience."[10] Like his father, James, Richard had garnered recommendations from respectable men who were supportive of his goal. Also like James, he had chosen a wife well suited to him and to the tasks that lay ahead for them both.

Clarissa Chapman Armstrong, born in May 1805, was but a month younger than her new husband. She, too, was the youngest in her family, and from a "staunch Presbyterian" background. Like Richard, she had grown up on a farm and—like Richard's sisters—had had to carry out many of the farm chores, because her father had been crippled with rheumatism. Clarissa's family was notably more distinguished than Richard's. Her brother, Reuben Chapman, eventually became chief justice of the Massachusetts Supreme Court and was of considerable assistance to his nephew, Samuel, early in his career at Hampton Institute.[11]

Clarissa's mother was a woman advanced for her time, insisting that her daughters receive more education than just good lessons in housewifery under her tutelage. Clarissa attended a female academy, learning the rudiments of reading as well as of spinning and weaving. She attended other academies where she acquired the skills needed to become the district schoolteacher. Early on, Clarissa demonstrated a willingness to seek adventure that would serve her in good stead later in life. She gave up her position in New England to work with Divie Bethune in New York. There Mrs. Bethune was organizing one of the first "infant schools," precursors of the modern kindergarten.[12]

Since Clarissa told this story long after the events, she may have been rationalizing what occurred, but she claimed that she also felt a call to do missionary work in Hawaii and fortuitously met young Richard Armstrong, who had the same vision. She also claimed to have had the same doubts as her future husband: she was unsure of her faith and "fitness" for such work.[13]

Whatever the motivations for their alliance, Clarissa Chapman and Richard Armstrong were joined in wedlock at the First Congregational Church of Bridgeport, Connecticut. on 25 September 1831. They made a handsome couple, she tall and slim, with "a pleasing face, fine presence, and attractive manner"; he "spare and wiry, every fibre of which was alive," with "penetrating blue eyes" and "attractive smile."[14]

The young couple had a busy two months in the fall of 1831. Richard was ordained on 27 October, a month after the wedding; they bid hasty farewells to both their families, and, on 26 November, they sailed from New Bedford, Massachusetts, aboard the American whaling ship *Averick*.[15]

The six-month, ten-thousand-mile journey was an arduous one. Although the Board of Commissioners for Foreign Missions had not designed the trip to test the mettle of their novice missionaries, the voyage served that purpose. Richard Armstrong found himself in constant distress, both physically and spiritually. The nine missionary couples and one bachelor were constantly seasick.[16] Their cabins were below deck in steerage. These tiny rooms were crowded with all their worldly goods, as well as bodies. Richard had to climb over their freight simply to get on deck. Clarissa was too ill to make the effort. When Richard finally recovered somewhat, he proved to be almost as concerned about the well-being of the digestion as of the soul. In his diary for that period, he argued, "Persons going to sea for the first time, I think, had better always have a little wine."[17]

But it was his soul and the souls of his missionary companions and the sailors aboard that caused Richard the most anguish. The missionaries tried their best to convert the crew, whom Armstrong described as "generally very dissipated and thoughtless men. Some of them deeply and dangerously tainted with Universalism—that horrible doctrine which gives licentiousness loose rein, and leaves men secure in their sins."[18]

Primarily, though, Richard worried about the health of his own soul and the physical well-being of his wife. Of himself, he said, "[A]m I prepared for the worst? I feel doubtful about it: my hart [sic] is so cold, and my faith so weak, that I cannot but fear. But I will try to cast all my cares for the future upon Him who careth for me, and Who has promised that His grace shall be sufficient for me."[19]

Other experiences while journeying aboard the *Averick* also were morally agonizing. The ship made port calls at Rio de Janeiro and at the penal colony of Juan Fernandez, off the coast of Chile. It was in Rio that both Armstrongs had their first encounter with slavery, and both were appalled. "O, Slavery!" Richard lamented, "that scourge of the poor African. How my soul hates thee! What heart will not bleed over the condition of the poor slave who is bought and sold, . . . condemned to ignorance and oppression and ignominy, just because his color is black, and he has not the power to resist oppression."[20]

Clarissa later recalled her experience visiting Rio: "It was indeed a paradise, but the trail of the serpent was there. On an open road I saw a long train of black men, miserably clad, chained together. . . . From that day my sympathies went out to the poor slaves everywhere, but little did I think that I should live to rear a son who would lead Freedmen to victory in the great contest which in future years should come in my native country."[21]

Happily for both Armstrongs, the passage around Cape Horn was unusually tranquil. Then, in the southern Pacific, Richard experienced the high point of his journey. The whaling ship found and killed several whales. His meticulous description of the process (including diagrams) would have informed Herman Melville, had he required it. A man of his times, Richard had no qualms about the killing of whales, and he observed, "Now, at last, we have decent oil for our lamps."[22]

Finally, on 21 May 1832, the *Averick* came to anchor in Honolulu harbor. "We . . . beheld for the first time the sable heathen among whom we so long expected to live and labour."[23] But Richard's soul was not at rest.

Doubts about his own adequacy remained: "I feel today as though [for] some time I had made no progress in the divine life. . . . My heart has been stupid. . . . I have neglected the word of God and secret prayer too much and perhaps this is my reward, barrenness."[24]

Very soon, Richard had a more tangible problem with which to deal. On 17 July 1832, Clarissa gave birth to the first member of the next Armstrong generation, Caroline Jane.[25] It is no wonder that Mrs. Armstrong was so ill during their voyage from New Bedford—she had been pregnant throughout. Naturally, reflecting the modesty characteristic of the Victorian era, neither she nor Richard mentioned that fact in their journals during the period.

The Armstrongs and their companions were welcomed warmly by the earlier American missionary residents. Richard found their "simplicity and apparent godly sincerity" encouraging.[26] Still, he had not overcome his own doubts about his capabilities. Assigned at first to the mission on Molokai, the next island east from the principal settlement at Honolulu on the island of Oahu, Richard complained that he could not feel "for the perishing sinners" among his indigenous charges.[27] It was not those "gentle" Hawaiians about whom he should have worried. The senior missionaries in Honolulu had a task in mind for the Armstrongs that would far more seriously burden Richard's faith and stamina.

These veteran missionaries in Hawaii in the 1830s seem to have embraced the same expansionist vision that preoccupied their countrymen back home. In the missionaries' case, it was all those "heathens" further west in the Pacific who "did not yet know Christ" who attracted their concern. They proposed to send some of their own number to the Marquesas Islands some 740 miles northeast of Tahiti. British missionaries claimed that region as their bailiwick, but the Americans petitioned for the opportunity to send some of their workers, and the British agreed.[28] The English claimed that "these islands were in a favourable state for the reception of missionaries."[29] Given the events of the next year, one wonders if the British were having a bit of dangerous—even unchristian—fun with their American cousins.

In mid-July 1833, the Armstrongs, accompanied by their infant daughter and two other missionary couples, arrived in the Marquesas and made landfall on the island of Nukuhiva. From the missionary perspective, the people of that land were far more "savage" than the natives of Hawaii. They were "naked, cannibalistic, and warlike." Moreover, they had created mean-spirited and vengeful gods, reflective of the harsh quality of their own lives.[30]

Like European and American missionaries wherever they traveled in tropical lands, the first thing which they found offensive was a striking difference in dress codes. Armstrong and his companions were appalled by the "naked and noisy natives who (men, women, and children) came swimming up to us in multitudes, as soon as the anchor was cast." "To think," Richard continued, "of spending my days among these wild, naked, rude and fierce barbarians. But I found consolation in the Gospel, whose truths never [were] more cheering in my mind."[31]

It is true that, by New England standards, the inhabitants of Nukuhiva were scandalously underdressed. Adult men and women wore the briefest of loincloths, while the children went entirely naked. Tragically, these and other missionaries never made the connection between dress and illness. Their excess of clothing led them to catch chills once they became wet, leading to colds and pneumonia. The indigenous inhabitants, who could dry quickly in the tropical sun, stayed quite healthy—until they began to be infected by European diseases, that is.

The loquaciousness of the natives, and the decibel level at which they expressed their opinions, also distressed the missionaries. They were used to the somber, softer conversations of their brethren back in the northeastern part of the United States. But these matters paled in comparison to the missionaries' concern about the Nukuhivans' dietary habits.[32]

Cannibalism, as far as the missionaries could discern, was a by-product of the constant warfare among the residents of different islands and even among the different villages on Nukuhiva. War threatened throughout the nine-month life of the mission, and its members survived only because of the intervention of the powerful local chief, Hape.[33]

Chief Hape found the white missionaries fascinating but, like his followers, refused to embrace their Christian God. Instead, he suggested that the missionaries acquire island customs. He proposed to Richard that he exchange Clarissa for one of his (Hape's) wives. He added an offer to exchange children when Clarissa gave birth to her first son, a "lovely, golden haired infant" whom they named William Nevins Armstrong.[34] Richard, in an effort to mollify the chief after refusing this offer, also gave his son the name Hape.[35]

Finally, after nine months of struggle, the missionaries' position on Nukuhiva became untenable. The local clans were about to embark on internecine warfare. This situation came about, in large part, because Hape, the peacemaker and protector of the Americans, had died. His body lay putrefying several yards from the missionaries' homes. (The Nukuhivans did not bury their great chiefs; rather, they allowed them to rot in their huts and vied for the honor of being as close to them as possible.) The Armstrongs and their tiny band managed to gain berths on a passing American whaler, appealed to their British colleagues on Tahiti to "continue in the effort" (hopeless though it must have seemed), and set sail back to Hawaii.[36]

The Hawaii to which the weary refugees from the Marquesas returned was a society in turmoil. The islands' past greatly resembled the current reality of

Nukuhiva, from which the Armstrongs were fleeing. Long prior to European discovery of the islands by Britain's Captain James Cook in 1778, the inhabitants of what Cook named the Sandwich Islands had a history of warfare among different clans and inhabitants of the several islands. They were as "savage" as their cousins further west in Polynesia. Indeed, Captain Cook himself may have been a victim of cannibalism. His rescuers in November 1778 could find only some of his bones.[37]

The Hawaiian Islands finally were united in 1810 under the rule of King Kamehameha I. Hawaii soon became a vital resupply station for whaling ships and merchant vessels crossing the Pacific. The Americans, British, and French all claimed special access to that kingdom. Kamehameha II (who succeeded his father in 1819) struggled to accommodate these competing foreign demands. Then, in 1820, the American Board of Commissioners for Foreign Missions sent its first workers to the islands in an effort to "save the natives" from their heathenism *and* the "corruption" engendered by others of European descent.[38]

The native Hawaiians were desperately in need of help. The indigenous population was falling victim to European diseases, alcoholism, and a general ennui that historically has afflicted traditional societies encountering more "modern" cultures. The native population of the islands had dropped from an estimated 300,000 when Cook first visited Hawaii to 108,000 in 1836. By 1853, there were only 73,000 native Hawaiians left.[39] Armstrong recorded in his journal in 1838, "Civilization sends the heathen, life in one hand and death in the other: the *Bible* and the *bottle*."[40]

Given such dire circumstances, it is perhaps understandable that the American missionaries quickly incorporated into their role as "Christ's Advocates" the task of ensuring the physical survival of the Hawaiian people. They were remarkably successful in converting a majority of the Hawaiian people, including the royal family, to Christianity. But in taking on that second, more secular role, they simply became advocates for Western "civilization" as they understood it. Through their influence over the Hawaiian royalty and the government's ministers, they attempted to create a Protestant theocracy on the islands.[41] One of the American missionaries' least successful maneuvers in this regard occurred in the 1830s, when they orchestrated the government's expulsion of French Catholic missionaries. When the commander of a French frigate threatened to bombard Honolulu unless religious freedom for Catholics were restored, the government and the American missionaries conceded. Under the "Laplace Convention" in 1839, Catholic and Protestant schools were put on an equal footing. It is likely, however, that only the presence of American and British warships in Pearl Harbor prevented an attempted French takeover of the kingdom in the interim before reconciliation was achieved.[42]

These were the circumstances to which Richard and Clarissa Armstrong, along with their two little children, returned in 1832. They arrived while the Annual Conference of missionaries was in session in Honolulu. The group was deeply divided, in part because of the increasingly secular activities of some of its members. Richard Armstrong already was beginning to share the view that it did little good to save souls if the bodies containing them were dying in disastrous numbers. He may have become a victim of that dispute within the missionary group. In any case, the conference strongly disapproved of his party's return from Nukuhiva without permission. Each couple was assigned to isolated outstations, with little time to recover from their ordeal and without adequate supplies. The Armstrongs were sent to Haiku on the island of Maui. Their new post could be reached only by a week-long journey via schooner, canoe, and, finally, ox-cart.[43]

Once again, Richard and Clarissa nearly perished—in this instance, due to a hostile environment rather than hostile natives. At Haiku, however, they lost their older son, who had survived even the hardships of the Marquesas and the arduous journey back. They gave Hape's Christian name, William Nevins, to their second son, who was born a week before Hape's death.[44]

During the next seven years, Richard Armstrong worked diligently on Maui. He became fluent in Hawaiian and preached his sermons in that language. He established mission churches, taught the natives to read, and doctored the ill. The hardships surpassed even those he had envisioned as a young man back in Pennsylvania. Traveling was vital to his work but often nearly impossible. Several times he nearly drowned trying to handle Hawaiian canoes.[45]

The rigors of his work often left Richard ill and despondent. In 1838, he complained of an ongoing illness that had lasted two months. "I have been compelled to stop . . . and consider my ways, search my heart and think of death."[46] On other occasions, he doubted the efficacy of his work. He wrote: "Have been preaching [here] more or less for more than a year and know not that I have been the instrument of converting one soul. . . . O Lord! Help me to feel my responsibilities; help me to feel for perishing sinners."[47]

Richard often was his own harshest critic. In 1837, he described himself as having a "passionate temper" and being guilty of such faults as "earthly mindedness, unbelief, sloth, pride, anxiety, and selfishness."[48] In the years that followed, his critics would accuse him of some of these same faults, but none are recorded as accusing him of *sloth*.

Even as Richard Armstrong went through these years of physical affliction and self-doubt, he was developing his views concerning Hawaiians and their needs. He also was becoming one of the most effective missionary preachers in the islands. Richard became devoted to the Hawaiian people and they to him. Of course, he never considered them his equals. To Armstrong, they were children entrusted to his care. But their inferiority he ascribed to their lack of Christianity and "civilization." The gravest threat to their advancement, he felt, came from "unscrupulous and immoral white men." However, they could not save themselves unaided. They required God-fearing and well-intended white helpers for that task.[49]

Richard grew more fully into manhood and his ministry during his years on Maui. There, three more of his children—Mary Jane, Richard Baxter, and Samuel Chapman—were born. There, too, he began to overcome his doubts about his adequacy in the roles he had undertaken. Upon his departure from Maui in 1840, he agonized: "Severe is the trial of parting with the people whom I had adopted as my fellow-travellers to the grave, with whom I have spent five years of toil, solicitude, and felicity, in the midst of whom I have seen more of the glory of God's grace than in all my life before. . . . When I came here there were only ten or twelve church members; now there are seven hundred. . . . Unto Thee I commit the sheep and the lambs, knowing they are safe in Thy keeping."[50]

Richard had been called to Honolulu. He was to take charge of the largest native church on the islands. His new church, "Kawaiahao," the completion of whose construction Richard oversaw, had a congregation of three thousand. Armstrong's relocation also placed him in the seat of government and in close proximity to those missionaries with whom he had been sparring for years. Now, eight years after his return from the Marquesas, he was more than ever persuaded that the key to Hawaiian Christianization and survival was intervention in their secular, as well as religious, lives. Feeling as he did, Richard found himself involved in the disputes among missionaries, secular American immigrants, indigenous Hawaiians, and representatives of European powers—particularly the British and the French. The turmoil resulting from increased immigration from Asia, America, and Europe, combined with the growing dissipation of Hawaiian royalty, made Armstrong ever more anxious about the future of his native charges. "Never have I been more depressed in regard to the natives," he lamented in 1848, "It would seem to be the design of God to blot [the Hawaiians] from the face of the earth. Almost the entire population has been prostrated; great numbers die daily."[51]

Richard's dedication to the Hawaiians and their survival led him deeper and deeper into the quagmire of national politics. His first major effort in government was a land reform act, the "Great Mahele" or land division, which gave one-third of the islands' land to common Hawaiians (the other two-thirds were retained by the chiefs and royal family).[52] What most troubled Richard Armstrong was not the unfairness of this distribution, but the fact that the few remaining Hawaiian commoners had little idea how to utilize their new land. This concern led him to develop the notions about manual labor education that he would refine over the next two decades.[53]

In the course of his fight for land reform, Richard became a "Counselor to the King." Thereafter he was appointed a member of the Privy Council; minister for public instruction; and, finally, president of the Board of Public Education.[54] Throughout his public career, Richard's strength and stubbornness sustained him but also occasionally got him into trouble. He successfully fought an ongoing battle with the French consul, who was determined to undermine the English-language public schools. He also changed his opinion about the possible utility of wine on certain occasions.

Richard tried to remain apolitical while pursuing a very activist moral agenda and became absolutely vehement about abstinence from alcohol. In 1849, a French admiral once again tried to seize control of the Hawaiian government, sending troops to sack state offices and stealing the royal yacht. The coup attempt was turned back, but the French retained their right to sell wine and spirits in the islands. After dining with American and Hawaiian officials at the palace in 1849, perhaps for a review of the recent crisis, Richard observed in his journal, "All passed off pleasantly, though I should have been much better pleased to have seen no wine on the table."[55]

On the question of temperance, Richard Armstrong knew no fear. As part of his duties, he preached to the royal family each Sunday evening. When informed that the king, Kamehameha III, had been drunk for days and would not listen to his white advisors, Armstrong delivered a blistering anti-drinking sermon, condemning the king by name. Kamehameha was outraged and threatened to have Richard beheaded. Members of the Privy Council urged Armstrong to go into hiding. Finally they managed to calm—and sober up—Kamehameha. Richard was restored to his duties.[56]

For seven years, Richard Armstrong combined his ministry with service to the king and the promotion of new schools. Finally, in November 1847, he was asked to take the position of minister of public instruction, the incumbent having died.[57] Richard hesitated at first. His missionary colleagues left no doubt as to their feelings: "Each of [us has] devoted himself to the teachings of religious truth. . . . Acceptance of any secular occupation, however much it might facilitate mission work, would be an abandonment of the cause."[58]

The missionaries had become most sensitive to the often accurate complaint that they "came to do good and ended doing very well indeed." Former missionaries or their offspring had become the leading political, mercantile, and agricultural figures in the islands.[59] Richard Armstrong, however, did not see his work as an effort for personal gain nor an "abandonment of the cause." His efforts would enhance the larger missionary effort. Like his son thirty years later, he had little patience with those who put orthodoxy before practical necessity. He wrote to William Lee of the Privy Council, "No sphere of labor . . . [N]o branch of government seems to me of more vital importance to the welfare of the Hawaiian race than this. Education, intellectual, moral, and physical, is the great lever by which philanthropists of every land are seeking to redeem and elevate the masses of the people." He continued, "If depopulation here is to be arrested; if the vices which are consuming the natives are to be eradicated; if an indolent and thriftless people are to become industrious and thrifty; if Christian institutions are to be perpetuated, the work must be accomplished . . . in the education of the young."[60] Having said that, Armstrong resigned his pastorate and took up the work that would occupy the rest of his life. He also was compelled to move from the missionary compound and took up residence in the splendid "Stone House," owned by the Kingdom of Hawaii.[61]

Richard was an energetic and effective minister of public instruction. While he could not agree with the strict separation of church and state insisted upon by his missionary colleagues, he firmly believed and taught his son, Samuel, that the only role of the state in education should be to fund it. He valiantly, but unsuccessfully, struggled to remove both the schools and himself from island politics. During his tenure in office, he created over five hundred schools in the Hawaiian Islands. Richard never ceased his missionary work, despite the criticism of his colleagues. He continued to preach at his old church and to the royal family, but his focus was on his schools, and he visited every one of them periodically.[62]

Two other aspects of Richard's vision for the schools are important for understanding his educational philosophy and its impact on Samuel Chapman Armstrong. First was Richard's growing belief in manual labor training. Second was his belief in the universal utility of such training for children of all races. The senior Armstrong oversaw Lahainaluna Seminary and Hilo Boarding School, which utilized the manual labor format. Along with their studies, students worked on the school farm, learning the principles of good agriculture, growing most of their own food, and raising a surplus which helped finance their education.[63]

Lahainaluna and Hilo were primarily for common Hawaiian youth. Armstrong also applied the manual labor principle at the Punahou School in Honolulu, attended by many missionary children, including Richard's own sons. Forty years later, Samuel Armstrong would recall those days: "Most distinct is my recollection of our manual labor drill. [We were] required to hoe our patches . . . of melons or corn or summer squash till we could count seven stars. We studied the heavens as I have never done since."[64]

Richard Armstrong's goals for Hawaiian education included more than rudimentary education for the masses. In his study at home in Honolulu, he and several colleagues from the island's elite planned to augment Punahou, a secondary school, with an advanced branch, Oahu College, which ultimately would offer the equivalent of the first two years of a college education at American institutions. Oahu opened in 1854, in time for Samuel Chapman Armstrong to become one of its earliest graduates six years later.[65]

2

SAMUEL CHAPMAN ARMSTRONG

Coming of Age in Hawaii

*His plumb "survigorness" gave him an eternal
effervescence.*

—*John Denison, 1894*

Samuel Armstrong was born in January 1839, at his father's missionary station,
Wailuku, on the eastern side of Maui. He was to be the fifth Armstrong child
to survive. Two brothers, William Nevins (1835) and Richard Baxter (1837), and
two sisters, Caroline (or "Carrie," 1832) and Mary Jane (1836) preceded him.[1]

The most striking contrast that may be made between Richard
Armstrong, the father, and Samuel Armstrong, the son, is the nature of their
boyhoods. Richard was born in Northumberland County in north central
Pennsylvania. It is a mountainous terrain, colored almost entirely in dark
shades of green, gray, and brown. For at least nine months of the year, the
sky itself is frequently gray, too; and for those months, there is usually a
distinct chill, or worse, in the air. Perhaps merely by coincidence, the land
reflected the somber character of the Scotch-Irish Calvinists who settled
there, including the Armstrongs. Richard was sickly as a youth and was
chosen as the family's scholar, while its other members carried on the work
of the farm.

The Hawaiian Islands where Samuel Armstrong was born were then,
even more than now, "island paradises," especially for a young boy. Bright
colors of red, yellow, mauve, and green flourished everywhere beneath a
brilliant azure sky. Balmy trade winds brought the islands a delightful climate. Even the rains usually were warm and refreshing. It was in this environment that Samuel grew up as a robust, healthy, high-spirited, and often mischievous youngster. He would acquire self-discipline and learning
as he grew, but never would he lose the energy and the sheer exuberance
that his first twenty-one years on Hawaii instilled in him.

Also striking are the similarities between Richard and Samuel. At first glance, it would seem that Richard was a reflective, self-doubting introvert and that Samuel was an energetic, self-confident extrovert; that Richard was a man of God and that Samuel was a man of "the world." Closer inspection refutes these notions. By the time Samuel was born in 1839, Richard had made his peace with his God and found his own voice in expressing his faith. Far from continuing to agonize over the adequacy of his faith, he was certain of it. He was ready to take on anyone—including the king of Hawaii—in his advocacy. Likewise, the Richard Armstrong with whom Samuel grew up was no longer the struggling missionary on remote outer islands of the kingdom. He was pastor of the largest congregation on the islands, a member of the king's Privy Council, and minister of public instruction.

This was the man after whom Samuel modeled himself. He internalized his father's energy and commitment, and he internalized much of his father's *faith* as well, especially as Richard manifested it in Samuel's youth. The younger Armstrong never was much given to the "rituals" of religion. Even as an adolescent, he had committed himself firmly to "Practical Christianity." His duty was to live a Christian life and to bring both spiritual *and* physical salvation to those less privileged than himself. Later in life he would argue, "Work is the best prayer!"[2] As one of his Williams College classmates would say years later, "General Armstrong never stopped viewing the world as it looked from the front door of the missionary house in which he was raised."[3]

It was well that Samuel Armstrong absorbed so much of his father's vision in his youth. When he set out on his own for America in 1860, he had only memories of his late father to sustain him.

Wailuku, Maui, is a most exquisite place, even for the beautiful Hawaiian Islands. It lies in a valley between two mountain peaks. At the head of the valley is Mount Haleakala, ten thousand feet high. Atop that mountain is the largest extinct volcanic crater in the world. But the infant Sam would come to know that place only later, as a teenager. When Sam was six months of age, his father, Richard, was transferred to the mission church in Honolulu; and it was there that the younger Armstrong shaped his vision "from the front door of that missionary home."

"Stone House," in which the Armstrongs resided throughout Sam's youth, was a splendid coral structure built originally for a British Admiral. By 1840, it was owned by the Kingdom of Hawaii, and it became Richard Armstrong's official residence when he became minister of public instruction. "Stone House," surrounded by two acres of grounds and gardens, was a perfect place for the energetic and adventuresome Armstrong clan to grow. It was located on "one of the best streets" of Honolulu, next to the home of the former Queen Liliuokalani.[4] There Clarissa Armstrong sought to raise and control her ever-increasing brood of youngsters, nurture the garden about which she cared deeply, be a helper to Richard, and give appropriate attention to the native Hawaiians who flocked to their residence.

Clarissa was a dedicated missionary wife, but she did not embrace the Hawaiians with the same enthusiasm as her husband. Her "serious manner . . . the result of not only a certain Puritan habit of repression, but of intense moral earnestness," meant that "Stone House" was not an entirely welcoming gathering place for either Hawaiians or missionary children full of fun. Of the former, she remarked, "When [Richard] is here, the room set apart for the natives is full from morning till night. Books, schools, medicine, must all be attended to. And the natives talk so loud that it is almost unendurable."[5] Like many another missionary wife, she was prepared to do her duty to "uplift the savages," but she was not about to let her offspring associate too closely with them. She conducted Bible and sewing classes, "gathered about her the lowest outcasts of Chinatown, urging the women to leave their lives of sin"; but at the same time she furiously, and unsuccessfully, resisted Richard's efforts to teach the young missionary boys the Hawaiian language. She feared they were already becoming too "native" as it was.[6]

Clarissa had legitimate cause for concern about her youngest son, Sam. On the one hand, the missionaries to Hawaii were prodigious breeders of children (the Armstrongs had ten children, and their fellow missionaries produced similar numbers), so that by 1840 there were enough missionary children to form a social group of their own, quite apart even from other Caucasian children on the islands.[7] Young Sam Armstrong seldom encountered the "less reputable" whites on the islands. He grew up among missionary children like himself and with the native Hawaiians. On the other hand, many of those white youngsters were as high-spirited as he, and equally prepared to engage in whatever adventures their Hawaiian friends might propose.

If photography had been available in Hawaii in the mid-1840s and the Armstrong clan had been a subject, in the middle of the photograph, between his father and taller, older brothers and sisters on one side, and his mother and his younger siblings on the other, would have been seven- or eight-year-old Sam. He would have been "clad in faded blue denim, . . . blond and slim, full of his father's fun, with long shaggy hair tossed back from dancing eyes." His denim bibbed coveralls would have had several concentric pale rings rising from the ankles, about an inch apart. Frugal missionary families bought clothes to last. Several tucks were sown into the legs of boys' pants, and a tuck was taken out as they grew inch by inch. If this were a "formal" family portrait, young Sam also undoubtedly would be wearing an apron—an adornment that loving missionary mothers put on all their children, and the first thing the young boys took off as soon as they were out of sight of their mothers.[8]

Denim overalls stayed on hardly longer; the boys would dive into the salt ponds or the ocean and frolic in the warm waves of the bay or sea. None

Samuel Chapman Armstrong (about eighteen years old), with sister Jennie and brother Richard Baxter, c. 1857. Courtesy of Hampton University Archives.

of this was met with approbation by missionary mothers. As Samuel recalled cryptically years later, "The rod was not spared" in missionary households.[9]

The greatest joy of Hawaiian boyhood, Samuel Armstrong would claim, was going barefoot year around. Only on Sundays at church were the young folks forced to wear shoes. This aversion to shoes stood in marked contrast to their native hosts' delight in wearing shoes and dressing up for church services. The squeakier the shoes, the better. Often the Hawaiian father would enter the church first, making an appropriate statement with his loud squeaks; he then would pass the shoes out the window so that his wife could make a similarly noisy entrance. The Hawaiians also were very protective of their Sunday finery. If a rainstorm arose at the end of services,

Birthplace of Samuel Chapman Armstrong, Wailuku, Maui, Hawaii. Courtesy of Hampton University Archives.

they simply took their clothing off, scandalizing the missionaries who wanted to believe that they had "finally made Christians of them." Western missionaries confused their own cultural norms with Christianity. In later years, even Samuel would reflect this arrogance, claiming, "The heathen saint is about up to your New England sinner."[10]

In his youth, however, Sam Armstrong could have been a match for any of the "heathen" in his mischief. He was known (and appropriately punished) for such antics as stealing the delicacies that the Chinese placed over their ancestors' graves, and for lowering the American flag over the nation's consulate upon the demise of the family's pet cat. Nor was he above hanging his sisters' dolls and giving the little girls pompous lectures on the sin of practicing "i-doll-try."[11]

Perhaps it was in response to the stern regimen at home that Sam became such a prankster. Typical of the Armstrong family's lifestyle at Stone House was their usual Sunday routine. It began with Clarissa and the children attending the "English" church, while Richard preached at the Hawaiian one. Sunday afternoon was a time for the children to play and study, while father Armstrong preached at another Hawaiian church and mother Armstrong did mission work among the Hawaiian women. Sam's sister Ellen would recall, "Sunday afternoons we studied our catechisms under the trees. Sam would stretch at full length on the soft . . . grass with his book before him, and Ponto, our noble mastiff, seated squarely over his book to attract attention. . . . In the corner of the garden was the cemetery for our cats, dogs, birds, and pet chickens, all given decent burials [by Sam]."[12]

After supper and Richard's return from services for the Hawaiian royal family, the clan gathered in his study. There Richard quizzed the children on the sermon they had heard that morning, usually gently chiding his boys for having less command of its meaning than their sisters. This was followed by a reading from the Bible, brief prayers, and spirited singing of favorite hymns.[13]

As he matured, Sam continued to delight in the wonders that his island home provided. There were moonlit horseback rides with other missionary children along the Oahu beaches. With siblings and friends, he explored the volcano Mauna Loa, on the "Big Island" of Hawaii. As a sixteen-year-old, Sam returned to his birth island of Maui and discovered many of its beauties. He and his companions explored the forests and valleys, naming newly found waterfalls after the female "cousins" of whom they were then enamored. He recorded in his journal:

> In the afternoon we came to a quiet lovely valley in which was a beautiful sheet of water which we called "Pauline's Mirror." Exploring the valley a little further, we found the finest falls we had yet seen. . . . [They] were at least 200 feet high and a large stream poured down. The basin was large and very deep. Here we had our finest bath. The water was cold and perfectly pure; we could drink it as we swam. . . . It was grand and terrible, and the beauty of the place made it all the more impressive. . . . A Kanaka [native Hawaiian] guided us across the stream to the native minister's house, where, after a supper of raw clams and . . . poi, we went to sleep on the nicest, widest bed we have had in our journey.[14]

Samuel was a diligent student. He mastered Latin, Greek, and the classics. He studied prodigiously even during school breaks, rising at dawn, reading until breakfast, returning to his studies after a swim in the ocean, and then spending the afternoon on one of his innumerable projects. He recorded typical days in his journal:

> Nov. 27, Friday. This A.M. I finished my review of the Greek grammar to Sec. 133; burrowed round among Dr. Coan's books to find some classical authors. It was very rainy all day and favorable to study. Delved into Telemague as yesterday and read two books. . . . Made a topmast and squaresail spar for the "Telemachus" preparatory to tomorrow's sailing. The evening closed early and I read aloud in "Peter Parley's Recollections of a Lifetime" most of the evening. Read Carrie [his ill older sister] to sleep from "Blair's Rhetoric."[15]

Monday, Nov. 30. This morning I studied my Latin grammar before breakfast . . . till Rufus Lyman came in and asked me to go to the Rainbow Falls and swim under them. . . . Our company number[ed] seven in all. We descended the bank first, then undressed and took our clothes to the other side and swam up, intending to get under the falls, if possible. We proceeded some distance battling huge waves which, with opposing current, were almost too much for us. Finally we came to the worst part, shivering with the piercing cold, and crawled up the sides into a cave, where we held a council of war and decided it impracticable to go further, on account of the high water. Accordingly we dashed into the rapid current and shot down stream in beautiful style, landed and dressed up. . . . My head felt bad from the over exertion and I had to sit still awhile. . . . We got home at 3 P.M. glad enough to be back and have something to eat. I loafed downstairs awhile, then ran over a few pages of the Latin grammar.[16]

Richard Armstrong firmly believed that his children should know how to do things as well as acquire book knowledge. He apprenticed Sam to a local carpenter. Practicing his new skill, the younger Armstrong built a house in back of the family's for their Chinese manservant, Akio. But such manual labor did not long distract him from his studies and other activities. He spent late afternoons studying and evenings singing in the church choir.[17]

Sam was an enterprising youngster. Even missionary children wanted spending cash. During school breaks he worked as a tax collector. His task was to extract the despised "dog tax" from recalcitrant native Hawaiians. "Six weeks of hard work would bring in fifty dollars," he recalled. The Hawaiians were fond of their dogs, both as pets and as an occasional main course for dinner. When the tax collector was due, the Hawaiians would go to any extreme to avoid discovery of their dogs, hiding them in calabashes (gourds) or underneath the skirts of their mistresses, or tying them to distant trees. One earnest Hawaiian legislator delighted Sam with his proposal that the tax be amended so that only "bad" dogs were taxed. The amended legislation failed only because the tax was a primary source of income for the Hawaiian royal family—one not to be sacrificed just because their subjects loved their pets.[18]

Samuel grew to love the gentle hospitality of the Hawaiian people. They were invariably kind to those who treated them in a caring manner, even if they were strangers. Sam recalled a visit his father made to an arid section of an island. The Hawaiians expected him and put out watermelons along his anticipated path, so that he might refresh himself as he approached.[19]

Even Sam, as the young "dog tax" collector, profited from the warmth that the Hawaiian people were prepared to extend to the son of a trusted friend. "For these kind Hawaiians, . . . it is their custom to transfer their loyalty to the children of their friends, and I prize more than I can tell my own heirloom of Hawaiian affection."[20] He recalled with pleasure "sleeping on their fragrant homemade mats, eating their nourishing 'poi,' to me the most satisfying food in the world, or their fish cooked on hot stones underground. . . . and [then] a good lomi-lomi all around."[21]

Though still an exuberant teenager, Sam was developing a more serious side of his character, becoming both a pedagogue and a leader. When the geometry teacher at Punahou became ill, Sam was picked as temporary replacement. He taught his pupils so well that they produced the finest exams in the history of the school.[22] During the same period, Sam became secretary and then head of the Children's Mission Society. While a first-year student at Oahu College, he edited *Hae Hawaii*, a Hawaiian-language newspaper read by most literate Hawaiians. He led the Children's Mission debating team on Oahu and helped to organize similar groups on the other islands. He was so busy that his family began to worry about his health. Indeed, he did fall ill occasionally and was troubled frequently by eye fatigue.[23]

It is, perhaps, characteristic of a youngster of his age, period, and background that Sam conscientiously kept track of what he read and did but seldom recorded what he thought or felt. He wrote of caring for his older sister, Carrie, who was ill, but never of his concern for her. He talked of his father frequently in terms of their work together, but almost never of his mother, to whom he was very close in adult life. He truly loved his father but as a youth expressed it primarily through his enthusiasm for his company. In 1857, Richard traveled to the United States to raise money for Oahu College. Upon his return from America in January 1858, young Sam rushed to the harbor. Unable to wait for the *Fannie Mae* to dock, Sam commandeered a boat and rowed out. In his journal he wrote, "Soon I was aboard and first met Father. . . . Father looked well and I guess his face had been perhaps slightly smoothed by his trip."[24]

From those teenager's journals and later recollections, three crucial experiences particularly seem to have shaped young Sam. The first was his personal conversion to Christ while a student at Punahou. Second was his work as his father's "chief clerk" in the Ministry of Education. Third was a dramatic alteration in the role of the American missionary enterprise in Hawaii in the 1850s.

As with anything that had to do with his personal faith, Samuel Armstrong was reticent concerning his conversion experience. Although he claimed to have been "born again at Punahou" in 1854, his only reference to that experience was in a speech many years later.[25] The nature of the young Armstrong's faith, however, is not difficult to discern. His commitment always was to "Practical Christianity," a notion instilled in him by his father. "The shorter one's creed, the better," he would argue, adding, "Simply 'to Thy Cross I cling,' is good enough for me."[26]

Richard's duties as Minister of Public Instruction necessitated that he hire assistants. For these posts he chose two of his adolescent sons, Richard Baxter and Samuel. The latter proved more interested in Richard's educational work. In fact, while Richard traveled to the mainland in 1857, Samuel served as his "chief clerk," and in truth was de facto Minister of Public Instruction. Years later, Sam would recall those experiences: "I accompanied my father . . . on . . . his inspecting tours around the islands, and found [the Hawaiians] living in pretty much the old way. . . . All were happy and careless of the future. . . . The power to think clear and straight comes from proper training, but is most successful when that training is obtained from self-help, which underlies the best work of all men."[27]

Richard Armstrong was absolutely intent upon his belief in manual labor as a part of each school he founded. Gradually young Sam developed a philosophy very similar to his father's about how "backward people" should be educated. When Sam, at the age of sixteen, was called upon to speak to Hawaiian students, he "exhorted them to apply their instruction and mental improvement to practical life."[28]

Full of youthful self-assurance, Sam never questioned the motives or consequences of what his white peers were doing. In his address to the Mission Children's Society in 1858, he said:

> The most interesting feature of the times is, perhaps, the wonderful spread of truth. . . . This progress is principally influenced by two agencies; these are commercial intercourse and the missionary cause. The spirit of enterprise and the spirit of philanthropy seem to be means peculiarly adapted to spread the blessings of Christianity and civilization, and if they were united in this cause, the remotest abodes of ignorance and deepest human nature would soon be cheered by the dawn of better days. It would not then be long before superstition, the arch despot of heathen countries, would be driven from its last hiding place.[29]

There were understandable reasons why maturing missionary children in Hawaii could discover worthiness in the alliance between the church and "enterprise." A decade earlier, the American Board of Commissioners for Foreign Missions, in Boston, had decided that the Hawaiian Islands "had been virtually Christianized, that the nature of the work had therefore changed, . . . and . . . what was needed was pastors rather than missionaries." The missionaries on site in Hawaii vigorously dissented, but to no avail. The board believed that "proper materials for pastors could be found among the many thousands who had been called by the Holy Spirit."[30]

"In reply," as Samuel Armstrong wrote in 1891, "the Hawaiian missionaries urged the instability and moral weakness of even their best converts; but they were finally overruled. . . . [N]ative pastors were appointed as the equals of the missionaries in rank and councils. The missionaries accepted the change with deep misgivings, and in 1880 told me that they regard it as a serious mistake."[31]

The heart of the difficulty for the adult Samuel Armstrong in the 1890s, as for his elders four decades earlier, was that they saw "the work" as *parental.* "Of true morality," the adult Sam would argue, ". . . the childish Polynesian, Africans, and Indians . . . have little or none, because they do not possess its conditions, which require self-control rather than pure devotional life. Their language is rich in words of reverence and adoration; it makes prayer easy; and, on the spiritual side, their lives flower without effort and with a grace and beauty wholly their own. In our own highest civilization, morality is common, but spirituality is rare."[32]

As was typical of men and women of his generation, Samuel took his Euro-American culture and religion as givens and as inseparable. It was impossible for him to understand that his "civilization" quite literally was *killing* the Hawaiians. The efforts of his father, no matter how well intended, were not so much training the indigenous population for self-sufficiency as preparing them for labor on the developing cattle ranches and sugar cane and pineapple plantations. Many of these establishments were owned by those very missionary "cousins" among whom Sam Armstrong proudly counted himself. When the remaining native population proved too small to supply the labor demanded, additional workers—first Chinese and then Japanese—were imported.[33]

In 1860, these issues were of little concern to Sam Armstrong, the boy about to become a man. His father, Richard, had become a close friend of Mark Hopkins, president of Williams College and a member of the American Board for Foreign Missions. Through Hopkins, Richard arranged for Sam to enter Williams College, in Williamstown, Massachusetts, upon completion of his sophomore year at the new Oahu College. The spirited Samuel had only vague thoughts about his future. Writing to his sister Jennie, he said, "Next Monday I'm 21 ys. old. I wonder if Father plans to lecture me on the occasion . . . By some curious process contradictory to nature I feel more *impish* as I grow old. I don't get sober at all and laugh more than ever and even play tricks occasionally and have danced a little for instance."

Of his homeland, from which he knew he would soon depart for the first time, Sam continued, "I'm in love with the country more than ever; these islands will always be the Garden of the Hespenies to me. . . . I've seen so much beauty and sublimity on these shores, and the keenest pleasure has always attended my rambles, that I know nowhere on earth could I ever feel so contented and so much at home as here.—Not that I intend to live here—it is my purpose *not to.*"[34]

Tragedy forced that exuberant boy suddenly to become a man. In September 1860, Richard Armstrong was thrown from his horse and trampled. At first it seemed that he might recover, but a bone splinter entered an artery, and he died unexpectedly. He was buried in the cemetery of Kawaiahao Church, at which he had preached for so long. His gravestone read simply, "For he loved our nation."[35]

The Armstrong family faced its most serious crisis. Sam's oldest brother, William, was already in the United States. His older brother, Richard Baxter, had a cattle ranch on the "Big Island" (Hawaii). Sam felt it his duty to stay in Honolulu and care for his family. Clarissa, his mother, would have none of that. Attending Williams and studying with Mark Hopkins had been Richard's fondest wish for Samuel. So a subdued, sad Sam Armstrong boarded a whaler and went off to an America he had never seen—an America about to be transformed in unimaginable ways through fratricidal war.

But in his first years at Williams, America's tragedy would take second place to his own. In an early letter from Williamstown, Samuel shared his sense of both loss and filial pride with his younger sister, Ellen: "I am glad that I was permitted to see so much of his unselfish, consecrated life; it shall ever be a beacon to me, as I go down the stream of life, guiding me onward to a noble end. He did not cease to live when he ceased to breathe but while his mortal part was buried and his faults forgotten, the true essence of his being must ever remain."[36]

Many sons may have penned such words upon the demise of a beloved father. Few have lived up to them in quite the way Sam Armstrong did. Richard's strengths and faults both would be apparent in the ways Sam acted out his life. But at the core of his personality was always the impish, white-skinned Hawaiian missionary boy, with all the consequences that such a racial, religious, and cultural upbringing imply. For better or worse, Samuel Chapman Armstrong was to reshape the way black, red, and white Americans thought about education well into the twentieth century. And he did it always from a view "out the front door of that missionary home," with his father, Richard, always there, encouraging and cajoling him.

3

ACCULTURATION AND MATURATION

A Hawaiian in America

After the contest, the victory. After the cross, the crown.
—*Motto of the Class of 1862, Williams College*

A few weeks after Richard Armstrong's death, Sam followed his father's wishes and embarked for the United States. In some ways, departing for new experiences in America was exactly the right "therapy" for Sam. It was one more "grand adventure," and he was ready. But, just a few miles off shore from Oahu, Sam had his first bout of homesickness. "I glanced along the Huaanu road,[1] where memory could play for hours, calling up the good times to which it has borne us and whence it has brought us. . . . Those familiar slopes and summits were clothed with a charm that is only seen by him who wanders for the first time from the 'old house at home,' and his Fatherland."[2]

Depression in the wake of his father's death weighed heavily as well. "My . . . train of recollections recalled a lonely traveler on that road, a sudden plunge, a fall and a death-blow; and how the aged traveler lay groaning in the dust and shivering in the chilly air. How Hope had never smiled more brightly and never fled more quickly."[3]

Like his father, Richard, the younger Armstrong documented his first transoceanic journey—in Sam's case, through a multitude of letters. He delighted in his voyage. Even being becalmed for five days within a twenty-four hour sail to San Francisco did not dampen his spirits. On his last morning at sea, he could see the western coastline of America. "I walked the deck and whistled 'Hail Columbia' and longed to plant my feet on the shore."[4]

Then he arrived. "I stood at last on the shores of the New World. An utter stranger." Actually, his sister Janie, along with her husband and former teacher, Edward Beckwith, welcomed him and his two younger sisters, who had accompanied him. The trio toured San Francisco with the Beckwiths.

They took a river trip to Sacramento and stayed a week. Sam said of the experience: "[W]as introduced to about six ladies per hour, bowed six times . . . , forgot all their names and felt considerably more dignified and important than I had any right to." Already one of California's most distinctive traits was evident. "This is the land of perpetual youth," young Armstrong observed.[5]

Sam's journey to New England would not be as arduous as his parents' voyage to Hawaii had been. He sailed south from San Francisco to the Isthmus of Panama; traveled by boat, cart, and train across it; and on the Atlantic side boarded another steamer for New York.

Along the way, Sam gave some indications of the snobbish (and, perhaps, frightened) manchild he truly was. His Pacific ship stopped in Acapulco en route to Panama. "A couple of Mexicans rowed us ashore." He wrote home: ". . . The people had all got up and lit torches and brought out their oranges, cocoanuts [sic], limes, coral, bananas, etc. for sale. They assailed us on every side with their nasty jargon. . . . They are a dirty, nasty-looking set and smell worse than brimstone."[6]

Sam was a bit fonder of Panama, though not of its inhabitants. "The scenery was quite Hawaiian-like and the luxuriant foliage was good for the eyes. . . . I managed to procure a lot of excellent sugar cane, which was a delightful luxury to the girls and myself."[7] Still, he was not entirely pleased with what he saw. "It is now night.," he wrote, " . . . the train thundered along, rousing the dogs in the little dirty hamlets we passed through, and the dark, oily-skinned savages would come with lights to their doors to see us and give us a salutary yell as we passed along; while naked little imps would throw sticks at the cars."[8]

After an eight-day voyage up the Atlantic coast from the Isthmus, Sam arrived in New York. He was greeted by his eldest brother, Will, a commodities broker in the city. This mercantile capital of the United States he found more to his liking, but not completely. His first reaction that November was much like that of the African ancestors of the students he would be teaching in a few years: "It became horribly cold!" After the climate, the female half of the race was the next item he judged: "The girls here make little or no impression on me. Few are well educated. I haven't discovered one whom I thought beautiful. Beauty is scarce the world over I believe; moreover half of the real beauty is spoiled by the consciousness of possessing it."[9]

New York underwhelmed Sam: "It seems sure enough a great city. . . . It gratifies my curiosity to see the marble palaces and majestic buildings, but excites no feeling, no emotion. . . . I only think, how much these houses cost. Things are generally exaggerated; the crowds on the sidewalks are not so great after all. . . . In these crowds a fellow feels as he does in a wilderness, except that in the latter there is a certain solemnity and sacredness. In both, one feels that no one is noticing him and he can do just as he likes."[10]

With the help of brother Will, Sam did discover many of the amenities of America's largest city. Will took him to the opera and Sam, with boyish exuberance, wrote, "I was, and am, a convert to the opera! Such sylph-like grace in acting, such queenly beauty, rich melodious voices, gorgeous robes, magnificent scenery . . . were enough to inspire me with a flow of delightful sensations such as I never have known."[11]

After the opera, Will took Sam to Laura Keene's theater. The play included a "representation of Paradise." Sam wrote, "[It] was exquisitely superb. . . . I did not know that the human fancy had such power."[12] They went ice-skating in Central Park. There Sam helped his sisters and any other nearby female on with their skates. But the boy becoming a man had other matters to which he had to attend.

First came visits to the homes of his father's relatives. From Philadelphia he wrote, "I'm here in Aunt M's parlor; Cousin M is right by my side—I've just been holding her hand. Cousin Jane is on the other side of the room, and little cousin May (eleven years old) whom I hold on my knee sometimes . . . is near the stove. Aunt M is reading by my lamp, and Cousin Will is walking the room."[13] In that household lifelong friendships were initiated. But another trip remained.

Sam visited the Armstrong homestead in Lockhaven, Pennsylvania. He learned of his father's childhood from his Uncle Jim (Richard's brother). With his Aunt Mollie, he visited the cemetery in which his paternal grandparents were buried. Armstrong gave in to the maudlin sentimentality that plagued him during his first months in America: "I felt very strangely as I stood over the remains of my grandfather—very strangely indeed . . . I thought how, in his plain homespun suit and rough shoes, that weeping boy [Richard] stood on the very spot where I was standing and saw the coffin which contained his father's corpse sink into the cold arms of the grave; and few there were to comfort the boy; no nation's grief was mingled with his own . . . Little did that boy think at the time that one day his son, just about as old as he was then, would stand on the very place where he was."

Later, recalling that experience, Sam wrote to his sister Clara: "Father's death was very deeply felt [t]here. . . . It is wonderful how strong the attachment to him was. . . . I never knew how I loved the living and the lost at home till I buried myself in the retirement of Williamstown. I never spent such hours before and cannot describe them."[14]

Young Armstrong was still deeply depressed in the wake of his father's death. Writing with his father's gold pen that he always kept with him, he confessed: "I've wept much in Williamstown. . . . Before I left home, I was really too bewildered to feel. I felt as though there was something wrong, something gone, but the habit of only thinking of Father as alive stopped my thoughts [t]here and deadened every emotion. . . . My deep feelings never play except when I'm alone for some days."[15]

Williamstown, Massachusetts, and Williams College were new worlds for
Sam Armstrong. Neither he nor they would ever be quite the same after
his passage through them. Williamstown lies in a valley of the Berkshire
Mountains of northwestern Massachusetts, close by the Vermont and New
York borders. It is a region of great beauty, though of a splendor starkly
different from the sort Sam had known in Hawaii. At first, the homesick
Sam was less than thrilled with his new environment. He described it as
"this remote and wild region, the Northern wilderness." On the difficulties of travel, he added, "When an Hawaiian calls a road bad, you may
suspect that something is the matter with it."[16] "The mountains here," he
told his sister, "are nothing more than Nature's warts, little stuck-up hills
that you could cross in an hour on a donkey, going backwards faster than
forwards."[17]

What did intrigue the young Hawaiian was that the locale had four
distinct seasons. The fall is always the most colorful. The trees in the valley
and on the surrounding mountains delight the eye with a kaleidoscope of
colors. The winter, during which Sam arrived, and which—to the young
college man—never seemed to end, has its own austere beauty. The ground,
from mountain peaks to campus lawns, usually is covered with snow to a
considerable depth. The winter sun, reflecting off this brilliant white, often makes the lovely terrain painful to the eye. Still, there are enough ever-
green forests to lend balance to the scenery. None of this was appreciated
by the homesick Sam Armstrong in the winter of 1861–62. He said,
"Williamstown is shockingly lonely. . . . I suspect that they keep the girls
tied up or that they stay abed all the while, it's so cold!" To his sister he wrote,
"This morning and all day it has blown a perfect hurricane, driving sleet
like shot into our faces, so that [I] had to walk to breakfast backwards. I
have never heard of such slippery walking. . . . One day I tumbled six times
in the street in spite of myself. . . . walking has been actually dangerous."[18]

The spring was more to Sam's liking. It brought the thaw, the wild
flowers, and green grass made all the greener by having been covered under a blanket of snow for so many months. Understandably, the favorite
season for Sam, the Hawaiian, was the summer. While the delightful trade
winds and warm streams of his native land were absent, he did not experience the oppressive heat and humidity of the South that would assail him
in later years. Instead, summer in New England is a time to enjoy the great
variety of trees in full foliage and to explore the mountains and lakes that
this area of Massachusetts, Vermont, and Upstate New York feature in such
abundance. During his two summers in Williamstown, Armstrong took full
advantage of these opportunities.

From the very beginning, young Sam Armstrong was more fond of
Williams College than of the environment in which it was located. In some
ways, the college and Armstrong were ideally suited to each other. Williams

had been founded in 1793 through a bequest by Col. Ephraim Williams of the Massachusetts Militia, who had been killed in 1755 at the Battle of Lake George in the French and Indian War. Williams left his endowment with the proviso that West Township be renamed Williamstown. The township fathers happily complied.[19]

Ephraim Williams had chosen his site very carefully. He wanted his college isolated from what he viewed as the excessive religiosity of colleges further to the east.[20] Williams College was intended primarily as a secular school, to provide education for the offspring of working-class men like Williams himself. Unique among colleges of that time, for example, the Williams charter did not mandate the inclusion of ministers on its Trustee Board. Williams was explicitly unrelated to any specific denomination; it was under the control of no "church board" or group of ministers. Its purpose was to train men for the "real world" rather than for the ministry. That did not mean, however, that Williams was hostile toward religion. Its emphasis simply was more on the practice of "practical" Christianity than the inculcation of doctrine.[21]

Williams College in Armstrong's day did not, and was not designed to, offer a particularly rigorous intellectual environment, compared with some of its fellow schools to the east. Its mission was to build character, to make Christian men, not to turn out scholars. Students in the first two years usually were taught by inexperienced recent college graduates. Even upper-class courses were taught by faculty whose caliber "was never very high." Recitation and memorization, rather than creative thinking, characterized the curriculum.[22] Indicative of the almost anti-intellectual climate of Williams in the 1860s is the fact that the college library owned only ten thousand volumes and was described as "a full century behind the wants of the present age." In fact, the library opened only two afternoons a week, one afternoon for freshmen and sophomores, and one for juniors and seniors. Even then it was opened solely for the purpose of checking out or returning of books; students could neither browse nor study there.[23] Samuel Armstrong conceded that his college was wanting in some areas. "Comparing what I know of Williams with what I hear of Yale, I admit that the first two years here are not much," he told his sister, Ellen, "but that as to the last two and especially the last there is no comparison—I never shall regret my choice."[24]

What made that last year so special was the course in moral philosophy taught by the college president, the renowned Mark Hopkins. Hopkins, who served as president from 1836 to 1872, had made Williams into a reflection of his own personal and educational beliefs. "Hopkins," his biographer Frederick Rudolph wrote, "combined with his Puritanism an almost inbred distrust of the world beyond the narrow confines of Berkshire County, where Puritan ways remained almost untarnished by new and foreign ideas. . . . At the basis of his provincialism . . . was his own certain conviction that he had already found all the truth that was necessary, both for himself and for the Williams students who, in so many instances, became his agents."[25]

Whatever the limitations of the intellectual atmosphere at Williams, it is clear that Hopkins was devoted to his students and they to him. Both took their educational mission, as Hopkins defined it, very seriously. The capstone of a Williams education was Hopkins' course in moral philosophy, required of all seniors. Years later, John Denison, a roommate of Armstrong's, would wax eloquent about Hopkins and the course: "He was a man of undoubted genius, and, happily for his students, that genius had specialized itself in teaching. Furthermore, his genius was fed by a great overshadowing personality. He was a philosopher from sheer love of nature: therefore his philosophy was not of the dryly intellectual kind; it was filled with life, and was deep rooted in the man's heart. He drew out each student in turn, and generally compelled each member to wrestle with him. . . . The whole process was exciting, amusing, and stimulating to the last degree."[26]

As Sam Armstrong wrote home to the Cousins' Society, "[Had] recitation in catechism to Pres. Hopkins, and a glorious one; 'Prez' makes a man think and think quickly too."[27] Moreover, "his very looks show he is a great man and he is as plain in his meaning as a little child. There are few such men."[28]

Hopkins shaped the entire Williams College environment to reflect the vision he expounded upon in the moral philosophy course. He used "a devout faculty, friendly relations between faculty and students, love and influence as a substitute for stringent discipline."[29] When a student achieved the goals Hopkins set for him, the president was generous in his praise. Of Armstrong's schoolmate and the future president of the United States, James Garfield, Hopkins said, "He . . . did for himself what is the object of a college to enable every young man to do—he made himself a man."[30] Garfield returned the compliment, saying, "The ideal college is Mark Hopkins on one end of a log and a student on the other."[31]

Perhaps Garfield's praise was a bit hyperbolic, but for Samuel Armstrong, surely there were few opportunities for more personalized education than to live on the upstairs floor of President Hopkins' house. During his first month at Williams, Sam roomed with Denison in East College, but in February, President Hopkins invited him into his own home. He shared a room with Hopkins' son "Archie," who became Sam's lifelong friend, and had breakfast with the president many mornings.[32]

Mark Hopkins became Sam's mentor and substitute father during a time when Sam needed both. He was suffering from the tragic and sudden loss of his natural father, who had filled both those roles. Perhaps Hopkins, long a friend of Richard Armstrong, understood the younger Armstrong's need. First he guaranteed Sam's financial security, arranging a full scholarship for tuition during his years at Williams. Then Hopkins went further. He did not merely allow Sam into his home as a boarder; rather, he incorporated him into his family. Sam sang and played with the Hopkins daughters; he shared his letters from Hawaii with the president and his wife. On occasion, the president even climbed the steps to Sam and Archie's room. "I have had many pleasant chats with the Doctor. He comes up to my room and 'loafs' sometimes; a grand old man he is."[33] When special events were held for the senior class, Sam was always included, even though he was still a junior. And when Mrs. Hopkins died in January 1862, her husband asked Sam to be one of the mourners who sat with his son watching over her body.[34]

If Mark Hopkins meant to shape Sam Armstrong in his own mold, certainly, from Sam's point of view, he fulfilled his purpose. Armstrong later would claim, "Whatever good teaching I may have done has been Mark Hopkins teaching through me."[35] Hopkins' speech to the graduating class in 1862 reads almost as if it had been written specifically for one particular member, Samuel Chapman Armstrong: "Go to the ignorant, the vicious, the proud, the sensual, the selfish in every form, and teach them that wisdom of God which consists, not in getting any thing, or in achieving any thing, but in becoming as little children before him. . . . Your usefulness will not be as your talents, but as you may communicate vitality. . . . Apply it in your lives, unmoved by the sneers of skepticism, or by the success and self-complacency of the worldly wise."[36]

Sam Armstrong arrived at Williams during its winter break in 1861. With the embrace of the Hopkins family and the return of the other students, Armstrong's innate exuberance for life could not long be restrained by depression. Soon all about him were making note of the arrival of this new "Hawaiian boy" on campus. He was not the first son of Hawaiian missionaries to attend Williams College, but none had been quite like Sam Armstrong. John Denison, Armstrong's first roommate, recalled him vividly many years later:

> [I]nto my introspective life nature flung a sort of cataclysm of health named Sam Armstrong. . . . He was a striking illustration of that Robinson Crusoe like multiformity of function that grows up perforce under the necessities of a missionary station. New England energy, oceanic breeziness, missionary environment, disclosed themselves in him. . . . He was a trifle above middle height, broad-shouldered, with large well-poised head, forehead high and wide, deep-set flashing eyes, a long mane of light brown hair, his face very brown and sailor like. He bore his head high, and carried about an air of insolent good health.[37]

Denison found himself a bit overwhelmed by young Armstrong; he continued his description saying, "His 'plumb survigorness' gave him an eternal effervescence; in fact, his body was a kind of catapult for his mind; it was forever projecting his mental force in some direction, so that he was continually carrying on intellectual 'high jinks,' going off into extravaganzas, throwing every subject into a grotesque light; as a result, he was never serious, though always earnest."[38]

Samuel liked his roommate in return, but in a patronizing way. He wrote to his mother, "He is a good-humored, talented fellow and a very pleasant chum; he is a fine scholar and writer and aims, I think, at the ministry. His eyes are very weak, however, and I pity him. . . . I read him the lesson at night."[39] Sam delighted in contrasting his physical strength with that of the New Englanders he was meeting. He said of Denison, "[We] fence every day for exercise, but he is not very skillful. . . . I'll say that I am feeling finely. I weigh 164 lbs."[40]

John Denison went on to become a successful minister, but even as a student, he had remarkable insight into a classmate whom he would know for the rest of his life. Of Sam, Denison said, "He lifted his . . . voice and made intellectual pandemonium at the dinner table. . . . He had a profound faith in God, and a deep reverence for his father's life and work. . . . Yet everybody felt he was under tremendous terrestrial headway. Sometimes he seemed to have little respect for the spiritual. He shocked people by his levity; he was irreverent in speech. . . . Other men were original in thought; he was original in character; but above all, there was an immediacy of nature." Even in 1861, Denison claimed that he could sense the centrality of Armstrong's missionary upbringing for his future pursuits. He continued, "Like other missionaries' sons, he poked fun at natives, and entertained with the ridiculous phases of missionary life; yet he was a kind of missionary in disguise, always ready to go out of his way for the purpose of slyly helping somebody up to a better moral or physical plane."[41]

Another classmate, Henry Pitt Warren, remembered Samuel Armstrong in a similar vein. He wrote years later: "He was but a boy of twenty—a glorious rollicking boy, a magnificent animal with the grace of a Mohawk Indian and the unconsciousness as well. His smile was winning, his intellect was keen, he had a fine contempt for the commonplace, and if he had the imperiousness of manner like[ly] to come to those who have to do with inferiors in age or capacity . . . it, too, was unconscious."[42]

Some of his classmates were actually frightened by Armstrong's physical vigor and the abandon with which he used it. Frank Carter recalled that "when . . . fencing with him . . . his chum told me that the intense keenness of his eye and the swift lunge of the foil sometimes terrified him." Armstrong's opponent feared that he "would actually run him through!"[43] Sam relished his reputation. In a heated debate over the impending war, Sam wrote, "Our whole class almost got into a fight at one time." Sam took the Union side and defended the "weak slim fellow beside me." He bragged,

"I anticipated hard work for awhile, but the fellows didn't venture to interfere. I find (*inter nos*) that I am somewhat notorious for striking hard blows in boxing."[44]

Sam Armstrong launched into his studies at Williams with the same energy that his classmates imputed to him in athletics. He spent eight to ten hours a day studying the classics, "Mechanics," "Evidences of Christianity," and the required courses in the junior curriculum. He found the instruction less than inspiring. Of his Latin professor and the Civil War that had just begun, he quipped, "The only way I can see to avert war is to get Prof. Sinc. to go South and deliver his lectures on the conjunctives to the excited rebels—it w'd calm them down in ten minutes and might lead them to consider their ways."[45] Armstrong concluded that his education at Oahu had prepared him well for Williams and that the instruction there had been superior. "Study, and not thought, seem to be the aim of the College experience [here]," he mused.[46]

Young Armstrong may have found his studies at Williams uninspiring, but he delighted in the social environment. He claimed to his brother, back in Hawaii, "I can never be Yankeefied."[47] In fact, Sam rapidly was becoming acculturated to American ways and enjoying the process tremendously. He joined with seventeen others of his class in an eating club at which he took his evening meals. He was the only Hawaiian in the group. "The resultant has been many a pleasant hour, and pleasant song together. . . . Some warm friendships have been formed by this alliance of knives and forks, and we will all part with the best feelings for each other."[48] In his senior year, Armstrong was selected as an editor of the *Williams Quarterly,* a distinction that caused him to exult. It was "given to five fellows in the Senior class for the whole year, and about the highest honor in the gift of the class."[49]

Most of all, Sam very much wanted to fit in, and he became increasingly aware of his "provincial" background and relative poverty compared to some of his classmates. Writing home, he lamented about the need to stitch his well-worn trousers, and asked his brother Baxter (who handled Sam's savings in Hawaii) to send him money for some new suits. "The fellows, many of them from New York City, are genteel, dress well and exhibit polite manners; their society I value a great deal for its reforming influence; and I need it because my manners at the islands became very poor and rough by my never mingling at all in good society."[50]

Sam was developing a need to be accepted by the upper echelons of northern society. This need would remain with him all his life, sometimes hindering his understanding of the motives of his elite friends in their support of his work for "backward races." But in his college days, Sam—like all young men his age—merely wanted to be part of the group. He explained, "I find it pleasanter to be received as an equal than to be looked upon as out of my place when I meet with the well-dressed of New York or even of Williamstown. I . . . must rely on my own merit for getting friends. . . . When a man's history isn't known, dress has a great deal to do with his position."[51]

One reason for Sam's concern about his appearance was his intense interest in members of the opposite sex. Now five thousand miles from Honolulu, he was free to meet young women who were neither literal nor honorary "cousins," and he tried to make full use of his opportunities. He seized every chance to attend occasional soirees sponsored by President Hopkins or families of Williamstown, even though the men there usually outnumbered the ladies by five to one. He also took advantage of his periodic trips to visit his brother Will in New York City to meet young women.[52] After one such visit, he wrote home, "I almost fell in love with a girl I met, . . . a radiant being of rather stout proportions, but fair as the moon, somewhat given to singing and playing, blessed with beauty and elegantly attired." Sam was smitten. "For nearly a week, images of her would dance before my eyes as I sat reading Hamilton, and several times I examined myself and finally I said to myself, 'Samuel, you are in love.'" But Sam was also fickle. "The last time I called on her, my feelings were 'played out.' She is a capital girl, nevertheless, and I like her. With most of the young ladies I have had pleasant times." And, knowing no shame or modesty, Sam concluded his letter with a list of the young women he had called upon on New Year's Day.[53]

Despite Sam's preoccupation with those things that eternally have been foremost in the minds of young men—their own physical development and their attractiveness to women—he also possessed a more reflective side. It did not surface as readily or frequently, but it was there. Young Armstrong never tried to deny his missionary roots. During his trips to New York, he frequently visited Sunday Schools and was asked to speak of his Hawaiian missionary background, which he did happily. He joined other Williams students in a group called the "Missionary Band" which discussed the notion of "going on foreign missions." He wrote to his mother asking for a candid description of missionary life, with instructions for "how we might fit ourselves" and for any warnings she might offer about the pitfalls of such a career.[54]

In March 1861, there had been a religious revival on the campus and Sam felt himself much influenced by it. "I think I have become a better Christian than I used to be. I look forward to a life of doing good with joy," he wrote, ". . . My aim is to study for the ministry, but yet I hesitate to take the solemn vows—the responsibility is so awful."[55] A year later, however, his choice of vocations had changed. He explained to his sister, "You and mother talk of helping me through the Seminary if you possibly can. I shall give you no chance to do that; your expectations in that line are doomed to disappointment." He added: "I have about made up my mind to go into business after I get through college to repair my fortunes and help the rest of the family along."[56]

As graduation approached in the spring of 1862, Samuel Armstrong pondered his future and found no obvious career path. Earlier he had written: "God has not done all this to me for nothing. I wonder what He would teach me by this."[57] His environment and his mentors had shaped Armstrong's character and his values. He always would remain the "rollicking young boy," full of fun, full of energy. Sam also would ever be that "missionary on the sly," out to do good. And he would be the young man who identified himself with America's elite, a man anxious to be welcomed in elevated social circles. Armstrong's belief in God was genuine, but his Christianity was of an "active," rather than a "meditative," variety. He was, as his friend Denison said, "under tremendous terrestrial headway."

What Samuel Chapman Armstrong lacked in the summer of 1862, as he watched most of his class enlist in the Union army, was a sense of purpose. As he was to do many other times in the future—often to the disadvantage of himself and those he sought to help—Armstrong allowed events and circumstances to shape his decision. Having no clear purpose of his own, he chose that of the North. As his class motto dictated, he went in search of the "contest" and the "victory." He went to war.

4.

"To Save the Union"

Samuel Chapman Armstrong and America's Civil War

I am glad I entered the army[.] . . . we soldiers are more candid, honest, and natural for being soldiers.—Here it is that the man comes out.

—*Samuel C. Armstrong, 1863*

In December 1862, Samuel Chapman Armstrong visited the charnel fields that remained after the Second Battle of Bull Run. "[The field] was studded with little earth heaps which lay in clusters telling where the fight was the hottest. The graves consisted of little heaps of earth dug out on either side [of] the corpse and then thrown over it; the body was simply covered with a few inches of dirt, and often an elbow or knee, a hand or head would stick out. I saw one pit where 100 men were buried. . . . There the carnage had been awful."[1] Armstrong had chosen to become a Union soldier. He discovered the horror that *is* war. Yet he also found purpose for his own life: "We are fighting for humanity and freedom; the South for barbarism and slavery."[2]

As an officer, first in 125th New York Regiment and then in the 8th and 9th regiments of the United States Colored Troops, Samuel Armstrong learned how to lead men through a proper mixture of orders, inspiration, and nurture. He found he quite enjoyed having control over the lives of men he considered below him socially or racially. At the same time, he felt obligated to nurture those who were dependent upon him. Throughout his life, he would retain and employ the abilities and attitudes he acquired through these wartime experiences.

Participation in the American Civil War was the final ingredient in shaping the adult persona, "Samuel Chapman Armstrong." From the day Secretary of War Stanton certified his battlefield promotion to the day of his death, Armstrong would be addressed and referred to as "General." Only his family and intimate friends still called him "Sam." Armstrong clearly relished the title and the status that it conveyed.

As the secession crisis mounted in the winter of 1860, Armstrong's feelings about the impending conflict wavered between cool and warm. "Political excitement runs very high here, but I wonder at my own indifference to it," he wrote home from Pennsylvania, ". . . I take less interest in American politics here than I did at the Islands." He added, "The people of Lancaster County of this state, where Buchanan's home is, will likely burn up or tear down his house. They've warned him of it and are in earnest. . . . There is no end to political talk and that is why I care so little about it."[3]

Once the war began, Samuel became somewhat cynical about the whole business. To his brother, Baxter, he quipped, "The longer the war lasts, the better for our 'Haiku' [sugar plantations], so don't pray for it to stop."[4] In fact, Samuel's primary concern at the beginning of the war was that the regular receipt of money from his savings in Hawaii could be disrupted. He asked Baxter to send all his savings so that he might deposit them in a New York bank.[5] He speculated that his oldest brother, Will, would enlist. "People take him for an American and think he must do an American's duty." Of himself, Samuel said, "I shall go to the war if I am needed, but not till then—were I an American, as I am a Hawaiian, I should be off in a hurry."[6] That said, Samuel Armstrong returned to Williamstown to complete his final months of college, giving considerably more thought to his studies than to the war. "You may be surprised that I say nothing of the war," he wrote to sister Clara, "[but] we here make nothing of it; things poke along very much as they do at the Islands."[7]

Sam's final days at Williams were arduous yet idyllic. He delighted in the time-honored occupations of American college seniors—hard work interspersed with much celebration. "We had to work like beavers for senior examinations. . . . Almost every night Carrie H[opkins]. would put her head in through the door and sing out 'Another party.'. . . So at ten o'clock, Archie and I would close our books and run down the street and pitch in for a good time."[8]

For Sam and most of his classmates, things went well. He graduated fifth in his class, noting with pride, "There are only four above me and they are all valedictorians from the finest preparatory schools in Massachusetts." Characteristically, Sam claimed his experience to be superior to all others. He boasted: "I ignore Yale—what is its senior year? Ours is a perfect festival, a time when we grow more than in any other three years. . . . Besides, we have the consolation of having lived at very much less expense with no less enjoyment."[9]

"Class Day" was the culmination of Armstrong's Williams experience. "[It] passed off gloriously and was a perfect success," he wrote, ". . . Every man spoke . . . a few parting words; this we did as the sunlight streamed in at the windows and found many a tear in eyes that were not wont to weep. . . . I shall never forget the scene. We then marched up to the green lawn of East College and shook hands all round and then there was a fresh flood of tears—it was the last parting: how the fellows hung on each other's necks! There is an immense amount of true, manly affection among our fellows. College life is ended—the pleasantest chapter is closed, and the future is dark."[10]

Most of his friends, after graduation, left immediately for the Northern army; Sam soon joined them. It was neither patriotism for America nor dedication to the ending of slavery that led him to put on the Union blue. Now a college graduate, five thousand miles from home, he found himself with no defined course. Defense of the Union offered a direction. "I hear the roar of drums and the din of battle. We must to arms! We must fight! The next breeze from the South will bring to our ears an urgent request for more men."[11] Like thousands of his American-born cousins, Sam saw the war as a "Grand Adventure." For him, unlike hundreds of thousands of others who did not return or who came home crippled or maimed, it fulfilled its promise.

Sam graduated from Williams on 8 August 1862, and by the next day he was in New York City seeking an army commission. The best opportunity proved to be in Upstate New York, so he departed for Troy. There he, a classmate, Patrick Carden, and a local resident, Thomas F. Sheldon, arranged to organize a company of which Armstrong would be captain.[12] To be confirmed in that post, Armstrong had to raise a full complement of men. He traveled the countryside, speaking at churches and Sunday schools. The young captain's reputation as a Williams graduate and son of missionaries preceded him. His brother Will recalled one such meeting in which "several plain hardworking women came forward and said to [Armstrong] that their boys wanted to enlist, but that they had held them back for fear they would get with bad associates; but that now, after hearing the 'Captain' talk, they were quite willing to let the boys go."[13] Armstrong and his officers took advantage of the social possibilities their new positions and duties created. Many an hour that could have been devoted to the study of tactics instead was spent pursuing the patriotic young ladies of Troy.[14]

Samuel Armstrong found the recruitment process fascinating. "Such a life I never led before—how this recruiting business lets one into human nature—it is the best school I ever had. . . . We have met the very meanest and the very best of men; some enlist for money, and some for love of country."[15] With characteristic braggadocio, Armstrong claimed, "I have the most respectable company by far." Not all were "saints," especially by missionary standards. As Sam penned the above, one of his men had just been returned to camp drunk and was in the guardhouse, singing "in the most comical manner."[16]

In a few weeks, Armstrong's Company D of the 125th New York Volunteer Regiment was fully manned, and it marched off to the hurrahs of thousands. At each stop along the route to Philadelphia, the men were greeted with similar outpourings. Samuel Armstrong, ever the ladies' man, took full advantage of the situation. "I made out to kiss several pretty girls—they didn't object at all," he wrote. "Brass buttons and shoulder straps will take a man through."[17] It was an auspicious beginning for an enterprise that soon would come to a most ignominious end. Within a month, Samuel Chapman Armstrong was a prisoner of war "on parole."

After a train journey in closed boxcars through Maryland, the raw recruits of the 125th were sent to Martinsburg, at the very front of the Union lines in Virginia. During the journey, as Armstrong looked out upon the ravished landscape of northern Virginia, he began to sense what total war meant. "The whole country is so desolate—the curse of war in its reality is a disheartening, dreadful thing—the ground itself seems cursed under it."[18]

In the following weeks at Martinsburg, Armstrong also learned much about the nature of command. When the first volunteer regiments were raised in the North, it was far from clear that men like Sam—middle-class white college graduates one day, commanders of often unruly but enthusiastic volunteers the next—were up to the task. These farm boys and workers in the nascent factory system of the North were very different from the college men who proposed to lead them. Would, could, the latter gain the respect of the former?

Sam Armstrong succeeded in the undertaking because he seemed instinctively to know that military leadership required a combination of nurture and insistence upon obedience. When one of his soldiers asked for water during the grand send-off of the 125th in New York City, Sam set out to find some. His brother Will reprimanded him, saying, "It seems to me that it is not very good military discipline for the Captain to be running around for water for his men." Sam responded, "The men must have water. I'm bound to see that they get it."[19]

During one of his unit's forced marches, other officers feasted on the provisions to be had in the larders of occupied mansions, while issuing spoiled bacon and hardtack for their troops. Armstrong prided himself on raiding those same kitchens, returning to camp with whatever he could carry, and sharing it with his men. Such actions, Sam believed, were what inspired his troops' loyalty, devotion, and low desertion rate.[20] He argued, "[A] Captain . . . is practically the father of ninety children. Men in camp, sensible men, lose all their good judgment and almost their good sense; they become puerile, and come to the Captain on a multitude of silly, childish matters. A Captain does not only his own but all the thinking of the company."[21] Here Sam, at only twenty-three, already was articulating his version of the paternalistic missionary vision. He was able to lead because he nurtured and guided those less able than himself.

On 11 September 1862, Armstrong's regiment was ordered north to help defend Harpers Ferry. None realized it, of course, but they were about to become a part of the greatest battle of the early war, and the bloodiest single day of combat in American history, Antietam. The march to Harpers Ferry was chaotic. Many of the men, unused to long marches, threw away their knapsacks; others left the ranks in search of food and water; and some simply deserted. In Harpers Ferry, the position of the 125th became desperate. They were positioned below the Maryland Heights, from which they were easy targets for Confederate artillery. "You can't imagine the infernal hissing of these shells," Armstrong wrote, "it is devilish, and very appropriate to such fiendish work." He continued:

> My Company was, I think, the most exposed of any. . . . With my men around me and being conscious of their gaze, I felt calm, and when the shot struck near me, I didn't move a muscle, but when we moved to a place of much greater safety and I was sitting before the bushes, I felt much more fear of the shells than before. I tell you, it is dreadful to be a mark for artillery; bad enough for any but especially for raw troops; it demoralizes them—it rouses one's courage to be able to fight in return, but to sit still and calmly be cut in two is too much to ask. . . . The firing ceased—Our Colonel cried bitterly at the sight of the white flag. Harpers Ferry had surrendered.[22]

The fall of Harpers Ferry was an important victory for the Confederates, but General "Stonewall" Jackson, in command of the Southern forces, had a more important task ahead. He needed to rush to Antietam to reinforce Robert E. Lee against George McClellan's much larger Union army. He had no use for thousands of Northern prisoners. After arranging the most perfunctory agreement of parole for the captured Yankee units, Jackson "galloped off," and the defeated Union forces began their march North to internment camps.[23]

This first encounter with rebel troops and first defeat caused Armstrong to reflect upon his enemy, and the meaning of the war. "We were most civilly treated by the rebels, whom we found to be in truth 'bone of our bone, and flesh of our flesh,'" he observed. "They shamed us; they fought, they said, not for money but for their homes, and wanted the war to cease." "Comparing the rebels to Northern troops," he continued, "our system of munificent bounties and fine clothing diverts us from the principle for which we are contending, and few of us really know what we are fighting for. I felt the want of a clear apprehension of it in the hour of danger."[24]

Armstrong's paroled regiment marched the 123 miles back to Annapolis, where they once again boarded closed boxcars for their journey to internment at Camp Douglas in Chicago. Along the way, especially in Ohio and Indiana, they were greeted not as defeated troops but as heroes. At first, such accolades cheered the soldiers, and all went well in the parole camp. The men kept up their spirits with nightly songfests. Samuel wrote to his sister: "On the right wing, a crowd of fellows are singing boisterously the 'Star-Spangled Banner'; on the centre of the battalion, there is a prayer meeting, just to the left of my tent—they are now singing 'Marching Along'; they have just sung, 'There is rest for the Weary.' It is wonderful how these simple Sabbath school airs have such popularity and such a control over the feelings of strong men; there is nothing that the soldier likes so well as these simple, sweet melodies."[25]

Inaction soon led to boredom, however. There were several thousand paroled troops at Camp Douglas. Within a few weeks, that army began to melt away. These "civilians-in-uniform" quite logically felt that, if they could not fight, they might as well go home and help their families. Desertion became common.[26] Those who remained at camp sometimes became mutinous and refused to drill. On one occasion, the unhappy soldiers even set fire to the camp. Armstrong spent much of his time at Camp Douglas on court-martial duty, in a vain effort to maintain discipline among the disaffected troops.[27]

Young Captain Armstrong shared the frustration of his men: "I am sick of the parole. I wish to be in the field. It galls me to think of my chum, Arch Hopkins, in the advancing army and I here."[28] Still, Samuel tried to make the best of his forced inactivity. As he did throughout his life in any place where he lived or visited, Armstrong sought to explore the natural wonders of his environment. He became enamored of Lake Michigan, six miles from the camp. "How grand the Lake looked when we first saw it! I was astonished that fresh water could seem so magnificent." He visited the grave of Stephen Douglas, for whom the parole camp was named. Armstrong described the scene as "surpassing in its loveliness; the grave, the green lawn, . . the dark, lowering forest around the lawn; the lake, ocean-like, stretching away in the distance;—all combined to impress the feelings deeply. I really feel satisfied and at home when I see the lake." Young Samuel became equally, though only temporarily, enamored with the "gentler sex" of Chicago. He found time from camp duties to socialize, calling upon families and young ladies to whom friends and classmates back east had sent letters of introduction.[29]

Nothing better underscored the unpreparedness of those enthusiastic volunteers of the 125th New York Regiment than the fact that the unit nearly fell apart after an internment of little more than six weeks. By 21 November 1862, the regiment had been reactivated and transferred to Centreville, Virginia, a few miles southwest of Fairfax, the winter encampment of the Army of the Potomac.[30]

The Union command had begun to learn the lessons of the early months of war. The Confederacy would not be defeated by ill-trained, undisciplined troops. In the winter of 1862–63, the 125th, along with dozens of others, was shaped into an excellent, finely tuned fighting unit. It proved to be time well spent, for, within six months, the 125th would take part in the great, climactic battle of the Civil War.

Samuel Chapman Armstrong relished the training and camp life. He wrote to his mother: "Once I was a careless college boy, living the easiest kind of life at home; with friends, lots of horses to ride and everything to enjoy. Now I am a commander of a Company in the American Army, stationed on sacred soil to repel the advances of Southern rebels. My responsibilities are great, my duties arduous. . . . I have not found [the army] demoralizing. I have gained rather than lost spiritually since I entered it."[31]

In a similar vein, Sam wrote to the Cousins' Society back in Hawaii: "I am glad I entered the army[.] [T]here is no schooling like it—I think that we soldiers are more candid, honest, and natural for being soldiers. No one here ever praises a man because he is tall and handsome; we care not for and envy not such; we praise the man who does his duty. . . . Oh how the handsome fellows fizzle out! How they are cursed and laughed at—here it is that the man comes out."[32] Armstrong did not mean to suggest that all was idyllic. He added, "We live in tents, our fare [is] poor, we face any storm, we endure any hardship, we shrink from nothing in order to serve our country and do our duty."[33]

The young captain omitted at least one consequence of a soldier's life that he, himself, began to reflect—a self-protective callousness. Although he was appalled by what he saw on the Bull Run battlefield, he behaved like thousands of others: "I cut from the body of a Union soldier a belt-plate with a part of his belt which was still clasped around him. . . . took a few cartridges from the box of a rebel soldier who was lying just as he fell; I have also a bayonet which I picked up from the field; all these I shall try to send home."[34]

By the end of January 1863, the inactivity of the 125th had begun to wear on Samuel Armstrong. "I'm tired of this puttering around in Virginia; it isn't manly or soldierly. . . . I am sick of it all, and wish to be engaged in something earnest," he wrote to Archibald Hopkins. From Archie he learned that their fellow Williams alumnus, James Garfield, now a Union general, was organizing his staff. Armstrong journeyed to Washington in the hope of getting an assignment with the general, but to no avail.[35]

Armstrong's discontent with his inaction was counterbalanced by his enthusiasm for the new Emancipation Proclamation. At first, his commitment was more to the principle of freedom rather than to the slave. To his brother Baxter, Armstrong wrote, "These negroes—as far as I've seen yet—are worse than the Kanahas [native Hawaiians], and are hardly worth fighting for."[36] But on the very same day, he wrote to Archie Hopkins, "Chum,

I am sort of abolitionist, but haven't learned to love the negro. I believe in universal freedom; I believe the whole world cannot buy a single soul. . . . I go in, then, for freeing them, more on account of their souls than their bodies I assure you."[37] Clearly Armstrong's attitudes were in a state of rapid evolution, for on 20 December he enthused to his mother, "[T]he first day of January is at hand—possibly the greatest day in American history—the sons of Africa shall be free. To wait until that day I am content, and then I shall know for what I am contending, for freedom and the oppressed. I shall then be willing to go into the fight, and you will feel the less grieved if I fall for such a cause. You and I will then have occasion to congratulate ourselves that our family is represented in the greatest struggle of modern times for the most sacred principles."[38]

In fact, Armstrong made the Emancipation Proclamation the litmus test for his continued participation in the war. As debate mounted about the legality and enforceability of the order, he advised his mother, "If his [Lincoln's] proclamation shall be canceled in any way, I think I shall resign."[39]

The commitment of the North to a War for Emancipation and the coming of spring cheered the troops encamped at Centreville, but good weather also brought increased discipline problems. Even the veteran troops had seen no real combat for some months, and many were becoming lax in their duties. Samuel Armstrong once again found himself on the dreaded court-martial duty. He hated the assignment. Sam sounded almost Lincolnesque when he wrote, "I have more than once voted 'Death' and other punishments almost as terrible, and I am tired of it. It is too dreadful, too sickening for me, especially when the criminals are often harmless, willing boys who were too eager to go to the war—some under eighteen years of age."[40]

In an ironic twist of fate, Samuel Armstrong briefly found himself on the other side of the court-martial bench, accused of mutiny. According to Armstrong, a major in the 125th had made a "monkey and fool of himself." Some of his subordinate officers, including Armstrong, called upon him and asked him to resign. In response, the major had Armstrong, who had led the delegation, arrested and charged with mutiny. Fortunately for Armstrong (as he was at least technically guilty of the charge), the major was dismissed from the service for incompetence before the trial. Armstrong was fully exonerated and commended by Maj. Gen. Silas Casey.[41]

Except for that incident, all went very well for young Armstrong in the spring of 1863. He proudly wrote home, "Ours is now a splendid regiment. We have been mutinous, demoralized, good for nothing. Now we are perfectly obedient, in splendid trim and spirits, and spoiling for a fight."[42] The lull of early summer also allowed Armstrong to pursue his social inclinations, dining with young "rebel" ladies who apparently had

reconciled themselves to the Yankee occupation, and picnicking with female visitors to the camp who came out from Washington.[43]

A week after one of Armstrong's gala picnics, on 15 June 1863, wagon
trains began to assemble at Centreville. On 27 June, the 125th, now attached
to the Second Corps of the Army of the Potomac, began a forced march
north to the environs of Gettysburg, Pennsylvania. Rumors were rampant
among the troops that a major battle was brewing. Given their surrender
at Harpers Ferry, the 125th was largely unbloodied. Enthusiasm was high,
and none felt it more than Capt. Samuel Chapman Armstrong. Once again,
neither Armstrong nor the men of his company were cognizant of the grand
scheme in which they were involved.

The Second Corps arrived on the second day of the Battle of Gettysburg
(2 July 1863) and was positioned atop a hill overlooking the battlefield from
the east. Armstrong recorded, "About 5 P.M. our Brigade was marched off to
the left centre, formed into a line, and charged into a valley full of rebs who
were sheltered in a dense growth of underbrush. . . . the bullets whistled by
me by scores, but I didn't mind them; though all the while perfectly conscious
what might happen. . . . We peppered away at them and charged furiously and
drove them like sheep. But we were ordered to fall back, amid an enfilading
fire from a rebel battery. We fell back and returned in order to our old ground,
losing many men from rebel canister and grape. This was our first fight—
my first—a long and great curiosity was satisfied. Men fell dead all around
me . . . I did not allow a man to get ahead of me."[44]

On the morning of the third day (3 July), Armstrong and the brigade
to which he was attached once again were positioned on the hill at the
northern end of the Union line. They were ordered to attack rebel skirmish-
ers situated below them to the north and west. He continued his narrative:
"It was a foolish order, a fatal one. I led that charge, if any one did, jump-
ing to my feet and waving my sword for the men to follow and rushing
toward the sharpshooters. . . . There were four captains in that charge; two
were killed near me and one wounded—I escaped though I was within fifty
yards of the rebs. We drove them and took their line, but they rallied in
great force and deliberately advanced—then it was hot. . . . The charge was
unnecessary, but it was ordered."[45]

After that encounter, Armstrong and his men were ordered into reserve units to rest. An enormous cannonade ensued from both sides, with
some shells actually falling among his troops. Then came the climactic
action of the battle, and of Armstrong's wartime career. He wrote:

> Finally the rebels came out of the woods in three long lines several
> hundred yards apart; with glittering bayonets and battle flags flying. . . .
> I rushed to the skirmish line—saw our opportunity, . . . returned and

assembled the reserves, and with the men and officers of the 8th Ohio
Vols. hurried toward the flank of the rebel lines of battle and gave them
fits—then it was grand. . . . I felt no fear, though I never forgot that any
moment I might fall—the responsibility and the high duty assigned me
sustained me; and it was wonderful that my own men didn't shoot me,
they were so excited and were behind me . . . Well, we turned the rebel
flank; and no wonder, for we did terrible execution; besides our batteries
and line of battle in front were mowing them down. This was too much
for them. . . . Thus the rebs were served all along our line, and on the
whole it was one of the severest fights of the war and a glorious success
for us.[46]

Such was Armstrong's description of his participation in three crucial encounters of the Battle of Gettysburg: the Union charge and retreat
at Devil's Den below Little Round Top on the second day, the defense of
Culp's Hill and Cemetery Hill on the morning of the third day, and turn-
ing back Pickett's famous but futile charge on the afternoon of the third
day. Like all ordinary soldiers in battle, he would learn the significance of
those encounters later. Except for a letter to his sister twelve days later,
Armstrong never again spoke in detail about that experience. It had sobered,
perhaps even terrified, him as to the nature and consequences of war. He
concluded his 5 July letter to his mother with the following observation: "I
cannot describe the battlefield—the dead—the wounded—the piteous
groans and the prayers of agony that went up to heaven all night and day.
The usual expression is "Oh, Lord!"—it can be heard on every side—and
when one approaches they cry for water most piteously. . . . I have made
what inward preparation I can for death. I keep a little volume of Psalms
with me and strive to act the soldier of Christ. . . . My sensations in battle
are not strange—I feel simply resolved to do my best, to lead my men, and
to accept my fate like a man."[47]

Seventeen years later, Armstrong visited his native Hawaii and observed Mauna Loa erupting at night. He wrote, "This and the battle of
Gettysburg are the chief pictures in my mental gallery, and have been most
educating and inspiring—a help to faith, a proof and sign of God."[48]

Although Samuel Chapman Armstrong may have been shaken by his
experiences at Gettysburg, his heroism did not go unnoticed. He was promoted to the rank of major and, perhaps as an intended additional reward
for valor, given "detached duty" to recruit replacements for the 125th New
York Volunteers (the regiment had lost 136 killed or wounded out of the
302 men who went into the battle).[49]

Major Armstrong's assignment to the Riker's Island recruiting depot
proved to be the duty he liked least up to that time in his military career.
He described it as "a hell on earth." His circumstances were made all the

more unpleasant because he was also charged with rounding up and trans-
porting deserters and draftees, as well as volunteers.[50] In the summer of 1863,
New Yorkers, especially those in the city, were extremely war-weary. The
anti-draft, anti-black riots in the city, which had coincided with the Battle
at Gettysburg, were indicative of the daunting challenge given the newly
minted major.[51]

Nevertheless, relief from command and the heat of battle also gave
Samuel Armstrong time for reflection. It was during those weeks of waning
summer and early fall in New York City that Armstrong came to the most
momentous decision of his life. He would volunteer to serve with one of the
new black military units being organized by the North. This choice would
determine the path of his future career and greatly influence the nature of education for African Americans well into the next century.

5

"To Make Men Free"

Commander of Black Troops

We want no cowards in our band,
That will their colors fly;
We call for valiant-hearted men,
Who're not afraid to die.

—*"The Negro Battle Hymn"*

In the summer of 1863, while Samuel Armstrong ruminated on Riker's Island in New York, the Union for which he was fighting faced a problem that seemed paradoxical. At Vicksburg in the west and Gettysburg in the east, the North had achieved conclusive victories. The North, it appeared, had merely to persevere to win. In fact, however, the Northern public had become war-weary. Parents no longer were so naïve about the nature of fratricidal war. As too many of their sons came home in coffins or horribly maimed, they became increasingly unwilling to send their remaining boys into the ongoing carnage.[1]

In that summer of 1863, the new draft and the United States president and his administration, who oversaw it, grew increasingly unpopular. There were too few volunteers, and the Union draft law was biased in favor of the wealthy. Draftees could either hire a substitute or pay three hundred dollars to be exempt from service. The Northern strategy, after the Gettysburg victory and Grant's rise to overall command of Union forces, was to conduct a war of attrition. More and more Northern men would be required. Fewer and fewer volunteers or draftees, however, willingly came forward.[2]

At this juncture, one implication of Lincoln's Emancipation Proclamation became dramatically apparent. Why not employ the freed slave men in the struggle for Union victory? The idea had not originated with Lincoln. Indeed, he had resisted the notion during most of the first two years of the war. His stance had been that the war was over union, not slavery. But now that the conflict also was about emancipation, the inclusion of slaves in the struggle as soldiers became both logical and politically expedient.[3]

Many northerners opposed the use of black troops or feared that they would flee rather than fight. Thus the first black regiments, organized in 1862, were confined to labor duties. The blacks' willingness and capacity to fight were demonstrated through the combat successes of early black regiments, most notably the First South Carolina Volunteers, made up entirely of escaped slaves; and the 54th Massachusetts Infantry, composed largely of black freedmen from the North. By the summer of 1863, enlistment of black regiments in the Union army was in full swing.[4]

There remained widespread fear that black soldiers, once armed, would be uncontrollable. The decision was made, therefore, that all officers and most NCOs in black regiments would be white. This decision also represented a ploy to make the black units more acceptable to whites, both civilian and military. White soldiers could win promotion by volunteering to serve in black regiments.[5] Some white troops risked their parents' wrath when they volunteered to serve in the United States Colored Troops (USCT). The father of Samuel Evans from Ripley, Ohio, for example, nearly disowned his son upon discovering that he had made such a choice. "We hear that you have enlisted in the Nigger service. . . . If such is the fact, your Stomach has become quite strong compared with its condition whilst you were at home," raged Andrew Evans. Sam Evans tried to placate his father, explaining that he would receive higher pay and a horse as a result of his new assignment; but to no avail. Andrew responded, "I would rather clean out sh—thouses at ten cents per day than to take your position with its pay. Alas what a step! . . . Never mind us, we will soon be out of the way."[6]

Samuel Chapman Armstrong's decision to join a black regiment was more firmly rooted than that of Sam Evans. His was as much the choice of a missionary as that of a soldier. Armstrong wrote on 29 September 1863, "I feel a little of the 'departing missionary's' spirit. . . . Here's to the heathen, rather, here's to the Negro!!"[7] Armstrong offered himself for examination by the military board considering officers for the new United States Colored Troops. He was accepted and promoted to lieutenant colonel of the 9th Regiment, USCT.

Armstrong's most cogent explanation of his decision was to his mother, who was distressed by his move, fearing that it would put him in greater danger. He wrote to her, "The Negro troops have not yet entirely proved themselves good soldiers; and if the negroes can be made to fight well, then is the question of their freedom settled. . . . The African race is before the world, unexpectedly to all; and all mankind are looking to see whether the African will show himself equal to the opportunity before him. And what is this opportunity? It is, to demonstrate to the world that he is a man."[8] For Armstrong, the good soldier—who was "candid," "honest," and "self-controlled"; who "did his duty"—was the embodiment of manhood. These were the characteristics he wanted to instill in his black troops and, later, in his Hampton students.[9]

Once again indulging his propensity for hyperbole and grandiose visions in which he would play a starring role, Armstrong continued: "The star of Africa is rising, . . . their future, in my opinion, rests largely upon the success of the Negro troops in this war. Their honor and their glory will insure the freedom of their race; their dishonor will result in the disbanding of the troops and in universal contempt for the race. I gladly lend myself to the experiment—to this issue. It will yet be a grand thing to have been identified with this negro movement."[10]

With the decision made, in November 1863 Sam Armstrong took leave of his comrades in the 125th New York Volunteers. "It was harder," he wrote, "than leaving my classmates when I left College. . . . I think many of my old Company love me. I know it, and I love them. They have said they would 'go to the Devil' for me, and I know that they would never desert me in the hour of trial."[11] Ironically, it was not the Devil, but mosquitoes, malaria, and boredom that plagued Armstrong during much of his eighteen months as lieutenant colonel and then colonel of black regiments.

The 9th USCT, made up largely of former Maryland slaves, was organized in Benedict, Maryland. Colonel Armstrong described the location as "a horrible hole, a rendezvous for blockade runners, deserters and such trash. . . . The place is unhealthy and many are dying of measles and small pox, etc." Nevertheless, Armstrong embarked upon his new command with all the exuberance that he had brought to his earlier adventures. Despite the surrounding countryside, he claimed, "our Camp is really beautiful, dressed in evergreens, with handsome stockades and well graded streets, and nobody says 'boo' to us."[12]

Armstrong finally had found his true purpose for fighting: "The Union is to me little or nothing; I see no great principle necessarily involved in it. I see only the 4,000,000 slaves, and for and with them I fight."[13] He considered his fellow officers in the USCT as far superior to those in the volunteer regiments in which he had served. One, who had given up a lieutenant colonelcy in the volunteers to accept a captaincy with black troops, was dedicated especially to Armstrong. He is reported to have said, "Tell Lt. Col. Armstrong that my heart, my hand, my head, my body, my boots are his to use for the Regiment."[14]

Samuel was pleased with his new troops as well. "I tell you, this service will get to be *the* thing—all are satisfied—the nigs are willing, learn very quick, and the regiment runs twice as smoothly as a Volunteer regiment," he told his friend Archie.[15] To his missionary "cousins" in Hawaii, he explained, "On the success of these regiments . . . depends largely the progress of freedom both for the African and for mankind. . . . The arming [of] the slaves is a magnificent scheme—and with those who lead them there is a great responsibility. . . . The task is holy, sublime. . . . We may fail, but that possibility will only make our triumph greater."[16]

Samuel Armstrong never considered his black soldiers to be his equals, nor had he viewed the white troops he commanded in the 125th New York Volunteers as equals. Class, rank, and mindset, as well as color, were involved. It is, perhaps, an intrinsic feature of the missionary character to presume a certain superiority over those whom one chooses to serve. The missionary, after all, has sure knowledge of a superior God. Too often, the missionary is persuaded, moreover, that his culture, in which he learned of that God, also is superior. Perhaps the test of a missionary should not be these notions of greater spiritual and practical wisdom. Rather, it should be the degree to which the missionary actually tries to assist those whom he would serve in the achievement of *their* goals. At least during the war years, Samuel Armstrong appears to have passed that test.

In Hawaii, Richard Armstrong had come to the conclusion that saving the souls of natives was futile if those same natives did not live long enough to realize they had souls. He had largely abandoned preaching to teach the skills required to survive in a world controlled by white men. His son, Samuel, took that vision one step farther. Men who wanted to be free, who would fight for their freedom, never again could be made slaves. That was the agenda of the black soldier and of the black women and children who supported his effort. Samuel Chapman Armstrong made that his agenda as well.

In this instance, the intent was there, but the opportunity was hard to gain. President Lincoln and many of his generals, especially Ulysses Grant, were fearful that, should black troops falter in battle or suffer a disastrous defeat, the North would be accused of sacrificing black men to spare white ones. Moreover, the wisdom of the Emancipation itself might be called into question. As a consequence, some black regiments—Armstrong's among them—saw very little action in their first months of service. After drilling throughout the winter in Benedict, Maryland, the 9th USCT and its companion regiments were transferred in March 1864 to Port Royal, on the Sea Islands of South Carolina.[17]

The environment was most pleasing to Armstrong; indeed, it made him homesick for Hawaii. "A strangely pleasant sound reaches my ears tonight," he wrote, " . . . It is the long, unwearied moan of the sad sea that seems to be eternally repeating its mysterious story—that has a voice for the human soul which fascinates us while we cannot understand it, yet leads us to think of the sublime eternity before us."[18] Nevertheless, Armstrong felt himself "exiled" to rear-guard duties off the South Carolina coast. Once again he became bored and eager for reassignment. His greatest joy while in South Carolina was firing a shell into the heart of Charleston, just a few miles away. That action did little to harm the Confederacy, but Armstrong's duty on the Sea Islands burdened him with an illness for which there was no cure. White slave owners on the islands had learned long before to flee their plantations during the summer for the healthier climates of Charleston, the South Carolina Piedmont, or even Rhode Island. The Union army of occupation was not so sagacious. Like many others, Samuel contracted malaria and suffered a periodic recurrence of it for the rest of his life.[19]

Since he and his soldiers had no real fighting to do, Armstrong involved himself with the emerging free black community on the Sea Islands and with the northern missionaries who had come to aid it. The South Carolina Sea Islands were the first area of the Lower South occupied by Union forces. In the spring of 1862, white plantation owners had abandoned their lands and their slaves for the safety of the mainland. The Union occupiers discovered upon arrival that they had several thousand former slaves for whom they must care. Moreover, these were the least acculturated of all African American slaves. These people, the "Gullahs," who had been isolated from other black and white Americans for more than a century, retained far more of their African heritage and language than slaves anywhere else in the American South. In response to Army pleas, the American Missionary Association (AMA) sent northern missionaries to work with the Sea Island "contraband," while the Treasury Department sent plantation managers to get the highly profitable plantations back into production. In their treatment of the ex-slaves, these Yankee managers often were as bad as, and sometimes were worse than, their southern white predecessors.[20]

Colonel Armstrong took an immediate dislike to some of the "Yankee entrepreneurs" who had been assigned to manage the cotton plantations. "The poor freedmen of these Islands," he complained, "have been much abused by Northern speculators and have found that Liberty is no dream—many of them are no better off than before. . . . I am doing my best to throw light upon the evil deeds of speculators and to help the people. I am in a position to do so."[21]

Ever the ladies' man, Armstrong's reaction to the lady missionary teachers was quite different from his impressions of their male colleagues. Some he termed "principally old maids and all destined to be." But he delighted in the company of some of the younger ladies, most of whom were from New England and New York and resembled the young women he had known while in college. He called upon them and enjoyed moonlit horseback rides along the beaches, reminiscent of his boyhood in Hawaii. He assured his family that he was still unattached, but "my eyes have been open."[22]

Sam's flirtatiousness was characteristic; but he also found himself fascinated by the task these teachers had set for themselves. They were attempting to educate both the civilian freedmen and those in the Union army. Armstrong took on the direction of one school he called "The College." It was held in an old tobacco barn, which could hold up to 500 men. "It is a sight to see the soldiers groping after the very least knowledge," he wrote. "Their eagerness is wonderful."[23] Two months later he would add: "The men are wonderfully persevering in learning to read—they carry their books with them constantly—many a time have I seen a sentinel with a spelling book under his cartridge-box belt. These men have wonderfully redeemed their claim to be counted in as human beings."[24] Armstrong already was reflecting upon the importance of education for the ex-slaves if they were truly to realize what freedom meant. Given the work he had done for his father in Hawaii, it undoubtedly was a notion that came easily to him.

Despite these educational endeavors, Sam Armstrong's primary concern in the spring of 1864 was *to fight.* "You cannot imagine a more violent contrast than military life in the 'Dept. of the South' and the 'Dept. of Virginia,'" he told his mother. "One is all ease and comfort and relaxation and rides and calls and flirtations and correspondence and safety—the other is the severest and sternest phase of a soldier's life—life imperiled every day."[25] It was the latter which Armstrong desired; and, in August 1864, that was what he received. His regiment, along with several others of the USCT, was transferred to southeastern Virginia. There it was to participate in Grant's final campaign against Richmond and Lee's Army of Northern Virginia.[26]

Armstrong first served under Gen. Benjamin Butler in an ill-conceived and ill-fated occupation of Bermuda's Hundred, a peninsula in the James River several miles south of Richmond. After two nights of forced marches from that site, the 9th USCT arrived at Malvern Hill, just eight miles from the Confederate capitol. Along the way, the men had their most significant combat experience to date. Ironically, it was with troops on their own side. The black soldiers were ordered to attack an emplacement presumed to be held by Confederate troops. They succeeded in routing a unit twice their size, only to discover that they had been attacking portions of the 4th New Hampshire Volunteers. "The affair," Armstrong lamented, was "a very sad one." But he could not resist adding, "[It was] a very fine thing in one respect, for we whipped five companies of the 4th NH with two and one-half of our own and threw the whole regiment into a panic. I tell you there were some sudden conversions that day to faith in the negroes."[27]

The only major engagement in which the 9th USCT participated actually occurred during Armstrong's absence. In a confrontation with Rebel troops at Fort Gilmer, southwest of Petersburg, on 29 September 1864, the regiment lost over a hundred men in a futile assault on the southerners. Armstrong was in the hospital during the battle. He had experienced his first major malaria attack and was suffering from "a slow, intermittent fever." He was "well nigh exhausted, and with a severe cold besides." Not knowing the true cause of his illness, he blamed his condition on fatigue and the rigors of duty.[28] The hospital in which he recuperated was located on the grounds of the Chesapeake Female Seminary in Hampton, Virginia. Only four years later, the building would become part of Armstrong's new Hampton Normal and Agricultural Institute.

Armstrong's malaria attack resulted in two experiences significant for his future. First, he was reunited with his sister Jennie, who had volunteered to serve with the American Missionary Association as a freedmen's teacher in Norfolk, just across Hampton Roads from the hospital. "She is doing a noble work," Samuel wrote his mother, and he speculated that he, too, might pursue education of the freedmen as a vocation after his army service.[29] Second, while still in the military hospital at Hampton, Armstrong was promoted to colonel and given command of the 8th Regiment, USCT.[30]

Although the troops of his new command participated in several skirmishes during the winter of 1864–65, they engaged in no major confrontations. This winter hiatus gave the still-convalescing Colonel Armstrong an opportunity to take his first leave in more than two years of service. He spent twenty-five days visiting friends and relatives in New York, Boston, and Williamstown. He greatly enjoyed his reunion with his mentor, Mark Hopkins, and his family. Through his uncle, Reuben Chapman, chief justice of the Massachusetts Supreme Court, he met some of the most powerful and prestigious men in Boston, including Massachusetts Governor John Andrew and the Higginson and Dana families. He was delighted (and perhaps relieved) to discover that his service with black troops enhanced, rather than diminished, his status among these upper-class New Englanders.[31]

During his leave, Armstrong also met George Stuart, president of the Christian Commission, and a Mr. Leigh, executive agent of the New York Freedmen's Aid Society. These were associations which would prove invaluable to Armstrong in the future, but at the time Sam thought primarily of return to his troops. "I had seen much of peace and splendor and wealth, and had received a vast amount of kindness on every hand;—but it all failed to satisfy, " he explained to his mother once he was back in Virginia. "This life is so essentially noble and just that civil life is insipid, meaningless, insignificant. . . . I find an abundant pleasure in looking after my own men, in the society of the many noble fellows around me, and in the inner sense of happiness that always attends one who does his duty."[32]

When Samuel Armstrong rejoined his regiment on 14 March 1865, he found it to be only seven miles from Richmond, within sight of the city's church spires. "I do not see how the Rebels can hold out much longer," he observed.[33] He was correct. Twenty days later, Richmond fell. Armstrong and his soldiers of the 8th USCT, however, were not among the triumphant Union forces who entered the conquered southern capital. They went with Grant's army in pursuit of the remnants of Lee's Army of Virginia. Through a quirk of fate, Armstrong again became a participant in one of the seminal events of the American Civil War. On 9 April 1865, writing from Appomattox Court House, Virginia, he exulted: "God is great! Today by His help, the great Confederate General and his army have surrendered unconditionally. I have just been viewing from an eminence the captive host, the artillery and wagon trains. . . . The first inkling I had of it was the continuous cheering of troops on our right—soon staff officers galloped up with the news that Lee was making terms of surrender—the firing ceased. . . . [I]t was impossible to realize that the terrible army of Lee was in existence no longer; the truth was stunning."[34] But Armstrong was mindful of his personal reasons for having given himself to the cause. He concluded, "As for myself, I felt a sadness—a feeling that the colored soldiers had not done enough, been sufficiently proved."[35]

The weeks and months after a great victory are, perhaps inevitably, anticlimactic. This certainly was the case with Samuel Chapman Armstrong. War's end brought him a promotion to brevet brigadier general of volunteers. During this time, however, Armstrong was thrown from his horse, which fell on him, breaking his right arm. Thus, after the war was over, Samuel suffered his only serious injury during military service. He never fully recovered the use of his right hand and unsuccessfully attempted to learn to write with his left.[36]

The end of the rebellion left Sam once again without a clear goal in life. "Now Peace is come I don't know what I shall do—I have no plans whatever," he told his mother.[37] His personal dilemma mirrored that of the nation, as it tried to accommodate itself to the relief of peace and the tragedy of Lincoln's assassination. Foremost among the problems facing the northern victors was what to do with the black soldiers who had played so crucial a role in the Union's triumph. In the South, they were one element in a volatile mix that included unrepentant former Rebels, newly assertive former slaves, and a Union army of occupation. Part of the government's solution, as it rapidly mustered out white troops, was to employ the USCT as that occupying army.[38]

For black troops in southeastern Virginia, however, a different strategy was employed. Gen. Henry Halleck, military commander of the Department of Virginia, deemed the 25th Corps of the USCT to be "poorly officered and in bad discipline, and altogether unfitted for the military occupation of Virginia."[39] Halleck decided to give those black troops a new enemy to fight—or at least to guarantee that those whom they fought were not their former masters. At the end of May 1865, the entire 25th Corps, including Armstrong's 8th USCT, was transferred to East Texas, purportedly to protect American borders against the soldiers of Mexican Emperor Maximillian and to assist the Mexican "liberal" troops who were seeking to overthrow him. Having no other specific purpose toward which he aspired, Samuel Armstrong stayed with his troops and led them into what proved to be a Texas quagmire. It was the nadir of his military career.

Even getting to Texas proved nearly disastrous. The voyage aboard the *U.S.S. Illinois* was pleasant enough, but the troops' arrival and first encampment hardly could have been worse. Off the Texas shore, north of Brownsville, the *Illinois* foundered on a sandbank. The troops were rescued by smaller boats;

and Colonel Armstrong, ever anxious to demonstrate his own manliness, took the rudder on one such boat, even though his broken right arm was still nearly useless. The troops who made it to shore must have wondered whether their survival had been worth the effort. Their new bivouac was on the floodplain of the Rio Grande, nine miles from the closest source of fresh water. They and their officers had only "hard-tack" and spoiled beef to eat. As Armstrong said, "When the Lord pronounced Creation 'very good,' this place must have been under a cloud where it could not be seen."[40]

Although conditions improved when the troops were moved inland, morale did not. The black soldiers were in a high state of anxiety concerning the reasons for their transfer to Texas. In most cases, what family and friends they had were all in the Upper South. Moreover, an irrepressible theme in African American folklore dealt with ocean voyages. Such trips did not turn out well. After all, the first such trip that the soldiers' African ancestors had experienced delivered them into slavery. It is understandable, therefore, that many of the black soldiers resisted when ordered to go to Texas. They became convinced that this reassignment was simply preliminary to their permanent exile, most likely in Haiti. Many ex-slaves, undoubtedly including some among Armstrong's troops, were aware that initially Lincoln had considered such emigration as part of his plan for emancipation.[41]

These resisters were deemed mutineers; and Armstrong, as regimental commander, was assigned to preside over their courts-martial. The experience was a classic example of Samuel's often unsuccessful efforts to accommodate authorities while nurturing those whom he had chosen to "serve." He lamented, "I cannot but feel for the poor fellows, who are now lying manacled, to see the sun rise but once more. . . . Well, the law must be obeyed; these fellows mutinied last May, near City Point, Va., along with a lot of others, and are shot as the ring-leaders; yet I, and every officer here, know that, morally their officers are even more than they to blame. . . . Had the officers been finer and bolder and quicker, the whole thing would have been crushed at the outset. In short, the moral guilt of these poor men is little; their legal guilt enormous."[42]

Like a missionary, Samuel Chapman Armstrong cared for the men whom he would have to order shot; but, as a soldier, he still ordered them shot. He carefully forbade any parading of the prisoners "through the ranks," as was customary. He allowed no "maudlin viewing" of the executed bodies. Nevertheless, he did his duty, and that was to kill men who had fought for their own freedom and for the North's survival but who doubted that their white Yankee allies would fulfill that promise of freedom now that the South had been defeated.

Samuel Chapman Armstrong agonized over such repugnant duties, yet he rebounded quickly. He soon discovered ways to enjoy his Texas assignment, visiting the generals of the Mexican "liberal forces" and their daughters. He and his fellow officers enjoyed many a gala evening entertaining and being entertained by their Mexican counterparts. Curiously, Armstrong retained the antipathy toward most Latin Americans that he first expressed when crossing the Isthmus of Panama on his way to Williams College. Of his location and its people, he wrote: "Rio Grande City is three quarters of a mile off, and a dull, dirty, sleepy place . . . mostly 'Greasers' or Mexicans—a filthy, low, trashy race, just such as are always to be found on a nation's border." He was prepared to be tolerant, however. He added, "I understand that further in the country [Mexico] the people are far superior to these. . . . One of these days, a party of us expect to make a trip into Mexico about 150 miles. . . . To this end, we are studying Spanish a little every day."[43]

Though he enjoyed the social opportunities provided by his Texas assignment, Armstrong felt the burdens of his command and of deciding his own future. Finally, in a cathartic letter to his closest sister, Carrie, he tried to explain himself and his vision of his future: "I find that I am not polite and accomplished—I aim rather to be just and manly and patiently seek to realize the higher, more heroic qualities;—these are a guarantee of success. . . . This inner strength is the great thing, and it is completed, perfected and made glorious by religion." Such reasoning allowed Armstrong, the poor son of a missionary, to conceive of a great future for himself. He continued, "Thus one, though poor and unnoticed[,] may be greater, grander and far more beautiful than anything that is made of the costliest stone."[44]

Armstrong employed the peculiar logic that allowed missionaries to impose their will on those whom they claimed to "serve." Defining his role in the hierarchy of man, he argued, "Men as a rule are heathen. . . . a greasy, dirty Mexican fighting for the liberty of his country inspires me more than the whole faculty of Andover Theological Seminary would. Don't let us pity the Zulus and the Esquimaux [sic] too much—we are almost as blind as they—they by darkness, we by too much light." The crucial phrase here was "almost as blind." That codicil gave Armstrong the opening to pursue his vision of "uplift for backward races." He proclaimed, "I wish to be in the great social revolution."[45] "[T]he only really good thing in this world is a noble strife."[46]

For Samuel Armstrong, "noble strife" was not garrison duty along the Mexican border, commanding black troops who wanted to go home, be with their families, and celebrate their justly earned freedom. The government in Washington recognized the dilemma, but from a different perspective. The Johnson Administration and all but the most radical among Republicans did not intend black freedom to mean equal capacity to defend hard-won rights through force of arms. The black troops from free state regiments were to be discharged, as were their officers. So Sam, on 20

October 1865, could write to his mother, assuring her, "This is last of my Army letters. In a few days, I shall be a civilian." On 10 November 1865, the 8th Regiment of the USCT was mustered out. It was transported to Philadelphia and, on 10 December 1865, discharged.[47]

Samuel Chapman Armstrong's problem in the winter of 1865 was that he had no particular inclination toward a profession. For the immediate future at least, he opted against going into business with either of his older brothers. He did not yet know how to do what he felt impelled to do, but—like his father—he had a strong sense of what he must do. He said it best to his mother: "My purpose is to serve the Great Master in some way—as well as I can—to be of use to my fellow man; to give the life so marvelously spared and wonderfully blest to the source of all mercy and blessing. I shall not, probably, enter the ministry—am not made for a preacher. I would rather minister than be a minister." Casting about for an occupation, he speculated, "I shall probably go into the Freedmen's Bureau—my chances are good for it."[48]

November 1865 was Thanksgiving time in the North. One immigrant, having discovered that, because of his wartime service, he now was a citizen of the United States, had special cause for celebration.[49] Samuel Chapman Armstrong was now an American, a man, and a brigadier general! Yet he retained the boyish exuberance, the adolescent anxiety and studiousness, the young man's ambition and seriousness. At age twenty-six he had had experiences that would have allowed men twice his age to die in peace, feeling that they had lived fully and well. He had grown up in a kingdom that was "an island paradise." There he had learned both reverence for hard work and delight in play. He had also learned to know and to feel affection for people of other races, although not necessarily to consider any of them his equal. Upon the death of his father, he had traveled a quarter of the way around the world, leaving his Hawaiian home for new circumstances in an American "New England" that he never had seen. Nevertheless, he had adapted and found in his teacher, Mark Hopkins, a new mentor who guided him through both his acculturation and the completion of his education. His service in the American Civil War compelled him to test himself and all that he had learned in ways that none of his previous education or experience had done.

War often is destructive of the body and the spirit. Although Samuel Armstrong suffered permanent disabilities (contracting malaria and crippling his right hand) as a result of the Civil War, he found his experience spiritually ennobling. His service in the war provided the means by which he could realize all the goals—both conscious and subconscious—that he had shaped for himself. On the one hand, Samuel very much wanted to be accepted by those members of the northern elites whom he had encountered. On the other hand, he wanted to fulfill commitments that he surely felt but did not yet fully comprehend. He risked the disdain and possible hate of his northern white colleagues to cast his lot with the freed slaves and the United States Colored Troops. Perhaps he had no choice. For the devoted son of a missionary, especially one as unconventional as Richard Armstrong, the choices probably were predetermined.

Richard Armstrong had died knowing that legal efforts to protect the freedom of indigenous Hawaiians had proven useless to most of them. Samuel Armstrong ultimately may have concluded that full realization of the freedom promised to Americans of African descent was impossible to achieve, at least in his lifetime. In 1865, he settled upon a course that throughout history invariably has proved the undoing of missionary enterprises. He tried to change and make more able, in terms of both intellect and practical skills, those whom he sought to serve. He did not, however, challenge or set out to change the racist mindset of those whom he presumed were his peers, nor of American society as a whole. His missionary experience and therefore many of his basic instincts were alien to most white Americans. The dilemma thus created would be revealed for the first time during Armstrong's tenure in the Freedmen's Bureau.

These were matters for the future, however. In 1865, Armstrong's instincts and inclinations told him simply: "Go Ahead." He wanted to be a part of the "struggle for right and wrong." He was ready to engage in "a noble strife." He went to call upon Gen. O. O. Howard, commissioner of the Bureau of Refugees, Freedmen, and Abandoned Lands.

6

TO REALIZE FREEDOM'S PROMISE

Freedmen's Bureau Agent, 1866–1868

Well—he owes a great deal to a good father, good blood, good training. The Lord seems to have taken him in hand to train him for His work.

—O. O. Howard, 1889

In the summer of 1865, as Reconstruction began, white America finally was forced to face the question it had assiduously avoided for most of this nation's history: What was to be done with the black population if it was no longer in slavery? The blacks' agenda was clear—they wanted land, political rights, education, and social autonomy.[1] Ironically, slavery had proven to be a "school," just as white slaveowners had claimed, but one markedly different than they had intended. Slavery had taught blacks what freedom meant in America, and now the freedpeople wanted that kind of freedom for themselves. It was far less clear that white Americans, even the blacks' northern white allies, really wished them to have these things that would make them, for all intents and purposes, equal to white men. The debate over the extent of the rights to be permitted blacks raged throughout Reconstruction. The fact that there was a debate at all boded ill for the freedmen. In the end, the majority of white Americans agreed that blacks were to become a permanently inferior caste and be confined to the South.

The items on the black agenda were not all of equal weight, as all parties involved understood. What blacks needed most was land. Without it, they would be forced to remain subservient to the very landowners who had held them in bondage for generations. But it was land that white America proved incapable of granting. Despite the fact that every other major interest group in America—from homesteaders to railroads and timber companies—was getting government land, and despite the efforts of Republican Radicals in Congress, no major land reform program was ever implemented to aid freedmen. Thus, essentially within the first year of Reconstruction, the first step in reducing the freedmen to serfs was accomplished.[2]

The denial of political rights, the second most important item on the black agenda, took longer. In fact, enfranchisement was proposed in part as an alternative to land reform. Blacks with political power in their states might pass laws that would facilitate the acquisition of land. More important, granting black men the right to vote and hold office would give blacks the same political rights as whites. It would be up to the blacks to prove whether they could make proper use of them. Although many blacks voted and held office during Reconstruction and thereafter until the 1890s, the franchise proved ineffectual. Black voters constantly were subjected to every form of intimidation, from economic to terroristic coercion.[3]

Into this maelstrom of conflicting agendas—while the outcomes were still uncertain—entered young Gen. Samuel Chapman Armstrong. He had matured considerably in his years as a Williams College student and Civil War commander of white and black troops. Nevertheless, Samuel had one more apprenticeship to complete—as Freedmen's Bureau superintendent—before he found his own voice and vision.[4] It was in this role that the adult Samuel Armstrong, the man long on energy and short on reflection, fully emerged. He captured many facets of his complex character when he described his work to his sister Jennie, also a missionary teacher, during his tenure in the Freedmen's Bureau: "There seems a prospect of my staying here and fighting all the rest of my life—for the poor darkies. My combative disposition will be (if I stay) taxed enough, I assure you.—I never exhausted as fully my resources in strategy and diplomacy."[5] Here was the quintessential Armstrong: the dedicated missionary, the patronizing paternalist, and the indefatigable commander who never would yield the field.

Strategy brought Sam Armstrong, in the spring of 1866, to the offices of Freedmen's Bureau Commissioner General Oliver Otis Howard. Armstrong's first inquiry about a position was rebuffed; there was nothing available. Persistence resulted in an appointment as Freedmen's Bureau assistant subcommissioner for the Ninth District of Virginia. To give young Armstrong additional clout among the primarily military men whom he would supervise in the bureau's work, he was confirmed in his rank of brevet brigadier general and forever thereafter would be known as "the General."[6]

The Ninth District of Virginia included nine southeastern counties of the state: Elizabeth City, York, Warwick, and James City on the Lower Peninsula; Charles City, New Kent, and King William further up the James River; and Mathews and Gloucester across the York on the Middle Peninsula.[7] Fortune once again had brought Armstrong to an area of great natural beauty, a land of gently flowing rivers and streams that empty into Hampton Roads, the huge estuary between the Peninsula and the Southside. Hampton Roads itself connects with Chesapeake Bay and then the Atlantic Ocean (see map). The

Peninsula is formed by the James River on the southwest side and the York River on the northeast side. The rivers converge at Old Point Comfort; nearby are Fort Monroe and Hampton—the town in which Samuel Armstrong would spend most of the remainder of his life.

The Peninsula is a land of great historical significance. It was at Old Point Comfort that British settlers first stopped on their way to that first disastrous winter at Jamestown in 1607. The great colonial plantations that produced Virginia's early wealth were situated along the banks of the James. The surrounding rivers and bay also provided a bounty of fish, crabs, and

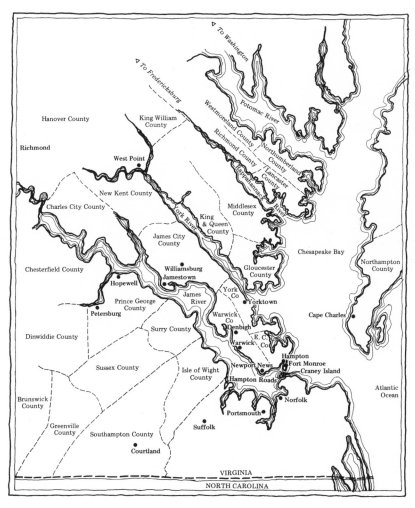

The Virginia Peninsula. From Engs, Freedom's First Generation.

oysters. From the colonial capital of Williamsburg in James City County came many of the ideas and much of the rhetoric that guided the American Revolution. During the years between Revolution and Civil War, the Peninsula became something of a backwater. With its soil exhausted, agricultural production declined. Its political and economic importance diminished as the state capital moved upriver to Richmond and the center of commerce relocated across Hampton Roads to Norfolk.

The Peninsula's importance in American history was restored somewhat with the coming of the Civil War. Fort Monroe commanded the entrance to one of the largest and best natural harbors in the world. The fort became one of only three southern coastal strongholds that the Union managed to retain throughout the war. In Hampton Roads, the battle between the *Monitor* and the *Merrimac* raged. Throughout the war, the Peninsula was the staging ground for assaults up the James River toward Richmond; it also was a principal locus for the settlement of wartime refugees.[8]

When Samuel Chapman Armstrong returned to Hampton Roads in 1866 (the previous year he had spent time in the army hospital there), much of its natural beauty had been obscured by the ravages of war and overpopulation. The village of Hampton had been burned by Confederates at the beginning of the war; roads and farmland had been destroyed by the constant movement of troops during those four years. There had been less than ten thousand blacks on the Peninsula in 1861; by 1866 there were over forty thousand. Most were refugees from inland counties; many were the wives, widows, and children of freed slaves who had fought in the Union army.[9]

In these trying circumstances, Samuel Armstrong found ways of making his tenure in the Freedmen's Bureau as pleasant as possible. He engaged in what might be called "Williams College, Class of '62, nepotism," hiring his best friend, Archibald Hopkins, and another classmate, Billy Ball, to work for him in the bureau. The latter was consumptive, and Armstrong hoped that Hampton's sea air might help him. Two other classmates, one a military surgeon and the other a missionary with the AMA, also shared his house. "I'm keeping bachelor's hall here and a merry old hall it is—college fellows—songs and jokes—lots of fun—pleasant house by the sea," he told Jennie.[10]

Armstrong kept up his playful courtship of the northern ladies he had become so fond of during his Williams years and the war. He delighted in picnics and rides with the missionary teachers in his district. He also procured an old mailboat which he used for recreation and business. True to character, he renamed the vessel *The Quakeress,* bringing blushes to the cheeks of Quaker lady teachers in Yorktown, who tried unsuccessfully to discover which of them had been so honored.[11]

It is well that Samuel found means for recreation, for his duties in the bureau were onerous. His principal assignments were to aid in the re-establishment

of the economy and to see to the removal of that portion of the black population designated "excess" by bureau officials and local white residents. Characteristically, he exulted in this newest challenge. "I am to have the Ninth District," he wrote to his brother Baxter. "My post is the hardest in the State; for
I have not only to take charge of the ordinary colored population but of several thousand vagabonds who have, during the war, fled to the Coast and are
now squatting lazily about Hampton. Howard told me it was the most delicate position in his Bureau and himself assigned me to it."[12]

In Hampton, the freedmen's affairs were in disarray. Because the area
never had been held by the Confederacy, many of its black inhabitants had
enjoyed quasi-freedom since 1862. They had squatted on abandoned farms,
making them productive once more. Many of the men had gone off to fight
for the Union cause. Those who remained behind had found allies in the
northern white missionaries and teachers, primarily from the American
Missionary Association, who had come down to assist them; and in Capt.
C. B. Wilder, local chief of the Bureau of Negro Affairs, predecessor of the
Freedmen's Bureau. In these circumstances, the ex-slaves had begun to work
out their own definitions of what freedom should mean. As for ex-slaves
throughout the South, it meant that blacks should enjoy all the privileges
given free white people in America.

By spring of 1866, the freedmen and their allies were at loggerheads
with state and national bureau officials, as well as with returning Rebels.
The heart of the conflict was the Johnsonian policy of restoring land to
former Confederates. From war's end to the reconvening of Congress in
December 1865, Andrew Johnson alone presided over the reconstruction
process. His goal was to restore the southern states to the Union as rapidly
as possible, and he insisted that the responsibility for doing so belonged
solely to the president. Part of his policy, with which the Republican Congress never would have agreed, entailed pardoning former Rebels who were
willing to take an oath of allegiance to the Union. The "ringer" here for
the freedmen and their white allies was that restoration of confiscated property other than slaves came along with a presidential pardon.[13]

The freedmen believed that the lands abandoned by their masters
during the war rightfully belonged to them. After all, the blacks had fought
for Union victory, their masters for disunion. Moreover, they had farmed
much of that land and made it more productive than it ever had been. And
certainly it appeared that Congress, through its Confiscation Acts and the
Reconstruction Act of March 1865, had meant for the ex-slaves to receive
land. Moreover, Freedmen's Bureau Circular Order Thirteen, of 28 July 1865,
actually specified procedures by which confiscated land was to be distributed among the freedmen.[14] But before C. B. Wilder could begin imple-
menting that order, Circular Order Fifteen, written at the command of
President Andrew Johnson, was issued. It directed bureau agents to return

confiscated land to pardoned Rebels and to encourage them to set aside small plots for the black laborers they employed.[15] Wilder, believing that Congress would reverse the restoration orders, attempted to hold onto as much confiscated land as he could. He also resisted forcing the return of refugees to their home counties. He had considerable evidence that they would be mistreated if he did so.[16] Because of his intransigence on these matters and his insubordination, Wilder was court-martialed on charges of illegally retaining and selling restored Rebel property. Although exonerated, his effectiveness as bureau agent had been irrevocably damaged, and he was forced to resign.[17]

The Johnson appointees to the Freedmen's Bureau had a vision of its purpose quite different from that of the freedmen, the missionaries, and officers like C. B. Wilder. As Orlando Brown, assistant bureau commissioner for Virginia, wrote in his Circular Order of November 1865, "The principal function of this Bureau is not to supply a channel through which government or private charity shall be dispersed, but to make the Freedmen a self-supporting class of free laborers, who shall understand the necessity of steady employment and responsibility . . . for themselves and families. Where employment is offered on terms that will provide comfortable subsistence of the laborers, removing them from idleness and from dependence on charity, they should be treated as vagrants if they do not accept it."[18]

Blacks were to be forced, by the very bureau they believed had been created to serve their interests, to resume a role subservient to their unreconciled and bitter former masters. Orlando Brown assured the missionaries and his bureau subordinates that the freedmen "must and will be protected in their rights." But he insisted that they had to earn this protection through "these first and most important conditions of a state of free men, a visible means of support and fidelity to contracts."[19]

Freedmen and their friends were enraged by the fallacies in Brown's argument. Many blacks had proven their ability to take care of themselves and their families during the war. Many others could not do so only because of Union actions, such as sending husbands away to war and leaving their families without support. In addition, many blacks who agreed to sign contracts with white landowners were being defrauded and mistreated. Their protests, appeals, and occasional physical resistance were to no avail. The bureau's first priorities were to restore order and economic productivity. Blacks were to submit to whatever policies the bureau deemed correct in the achievement of those policies. Bureau officers who resisted were discharged or, like C. B. Wilder, court-martialed and driven from the military.[20]

Samuel Chapman Armstrong arrived in Hampton in late March 1866. He was saddened by what he saw and wrote to his mother: "Here we raised several colored regiments, which took the men and left the women helpless—and oh, the misery there has been—it can never be told! . . . The men came not back, since most were killed, disabled or died, and here are their families in my charge; and they are a great care; we issue 18,000 rations a day to those who would die of starvation were it not for this; and keep their children at school, and get them work, and prevent injustice." He concluded, "Take us away and the Negroes might as well all be hanged at once."[21]

Given the unhappy circumstances that had surrounded Capt. C. B. Wilder's dismissal, the freedmen's allies were surprised and pleased to have Samuel Armstrong as his replacement. They were well aware of his family background, education, and military service. They thought of him as a known quantity and certain ally. As noted, Armstrong previously had met George Stuart, president of the Christian Commission, and a Mr. Leigh, executive agent of the New York Freedmen's Aid Society, during his recuperation in the North in March 1865. On the packet journey back to Virginia that same month, Armstrong had become acquainted with George Whipple, secretary for the AMA. Samuel's sister Jennie had worked as an AMA teacher in Norfolk.[22] D. B. White, editor of the pro-freedmen *True Southerner*, heartily approved of Armstrong. He editorialized: "The President, his servants, and his liberal co-laborers have chosen the wrong man for their purpose. The general is a man of much ability and too keen to be duped by men whose hearts have so recently been in sympathy with secession."[23]

Armstrong and the missionaries were able to work together, thanks to their common language, heritage, and goals. The general made full use of that other resource he had mentioned to Jennie, "diplomacy." Armstrong's great charm, energy, and ability obscured some other aspects of his character which the missionaries would not always find to their liking. He had become, first of all, a military man. He obeyed orders. Second, he shared the philosophy of freedmen's work espoused by Orlando Brown and other more conservative bureau agents. He wanted justice for the freedmen, a result that could be achieved only with the restoration of stability to the region. The sanctity of property had to be reestablished, and a stable work force had to be restored to the land. Although General Armstrong doubted the good intentions of the common white southerner, he had great faith in "men of property." He considered their interests and those of the freedmen compatible. The two needed each other. They would be able to work together, once the freedmen learned respect for contracts and acquired proper working habits.[24]

Here was another early manifestation of Armstrong's lifelong infatuation with men of property and power. It was an attitude that poorly served him and many of the blacks whom he sought to assist. Unlike his predecessor, C. B. Wilder, Armstrong never quite grasped the reality that men of power and men without power—in this case, white landowners and freedmen—most frequently were rivals with inevitably conflicting agendas.

As would be proven repeatedly during his years at Hampton Institute, most men of power did not share Armstrong's altruism or his goals. Often quite the opposite was true.

As bureau agent, Samuel Chapman Armstrong considered himself a great friend of the freedmen. It was not his feeling, however, that the freedmen were the best judges of who their friends were and what these friends ought to do. Certainly not all white men cared about the black man, but Armstrong never doubted that a well-intentioned white man could determine what was best for blacks better than most blacks were capable of doing for themselves.[25]

It is useful to note that Armstrong invariably treated people of lower status than his own as undifferentiated members of groups, not as individuals. Whether he was discussing his white and black soldiers during the war, his freedmen clients during Reconstruction, or, later, his black pupils at Hampton Institute, he seldom ascribed individual characteristics to them unless they were causing him problems or served to illustrate an anecdote.

On the one hand, while in the bureau, Armstrong delighted in his servant, "old Simon," who took care of his needs. Simon was a "funny, simple, kind old fellow—humble, yet paternal. What is there like an original darkey?"[26] On the other hand, Armstrong had little patience with blacks who meant to assert their freedom as they defined it. For example, the freedmen of York County were told that they could elect their own representative to the local Freedmen's Court established to adjudicate cases between freedmen and native whites. Quite logically, blacks assumed that "their own representative" meant one of their own race, and they elected Daniel Norton, a black lawyer native to the area and just returned after years in the North. The bureau disallowed Norton's election and instructed the freedmen to elect a white man. Instead the freedmen stubbornly reelected Norton. Much displeased, Armstrong ordered that his subordinate in York County appoint a white man of his choosing, and directed that any blacks causing trouble be expelled from the county.[27] In that same spirit, he refused to acknowledge established black leaders of Hampton, such as William Thornton, William Taylor, and Daniel Norton, with whom he was contending for the loyalty of the freedmen, because he perceived them as interfering with his efforts.[28]

It was with this combination of arrogance and paternalism that Armstrong set out to fulfill his orders. He would reduce his district's black population and insist upon black fidelity to contracts. He also would try to achieve fair treatment of freedmen who returned to their former homes and to assure equivalent white fidelity to labor contracts with blacks. He had considerably less power over whites, however.

Armstrong faced an enormous task in reducing the black population. Most of the refugees simply refused to go back where they came from. Though Armstrong was much irritated by such resistance, he understood the reasons for it. Whites were physically attacking blacks in surrounding rural districts and even in upcountry counties of Armstrong's own district. Whippings, court injustices, and outright murder were occurring as close as adjacent James City County. To justify his slowness in reducing the black population, Armstrong argued to his superiors that "some masters have threatened to shot [*sic*] returning ex-slaves who . . . left them, especially if they had joined the Army."[29]

Following the pattern learned from his father in Hawaii, Samuel Armstrong conducted periodic tours of the region and the people for whom he was responsible. After one such inspection tour of Northampton County on the Eastern Shore, an area from which many of the refugees had fled, Samuel returned despondent. "Often, as I rode along, some of my old soldiers from their cabins along the roadside recognizing me would jump out and call me by name," he wrote. "It has been very pleasant to meet them— now tending their patches of corn on shares—trying to feed and clothe their families, and struggling nobly against the greatest difficulties. They own no land, are at the mercy of whites who intend to keep them down, prevent their getting property and keep them ignorant. . . . [T]hey have lost much of their manly bearing—poor fellows, they didn't fight for this."[30]

Like his predecessor, C. B. Wilder, Armstrong resisted the resettlement policy when it threatened to place the refugees in actual danger. But the pardoned Rebels had better friends in the Johnson administration than the freedmen had. Whites in Armstrong's district wanted the population reduced; landowners in upcountry counties wanted their cheap labor back. As orders from Washington and Richmond became more insistent, Armstrong obeyed them. He applied draconian measures that never could have been used with people who were truly free. The bureau gave black families in the overpopulated counties only enough rations to prevent starvation, thereby encouraging them to leave. Strong, healthy women with families were denied rations altogether and "given tickets to anywhere they think they can find work." Blacks employed by the government were offered transportation to their home counties; those who refused were dismissed from their jobs. The new policy was so stringent that even self-supporting freedmen from outside the Peninsula were denied the right to have their families join them there.[31]

Given the poverty and violence which the blacks probably would face if they returned to their pre-war counties, Armstrong tried to develop alternatives. One rather impractical scheme was to have commanders of black troops migrate to Florida or Texas with their units when they were mustered out. The strong ties and acquired discipline of military experience would, Armstrong believed, make such regiments excellent colonization teams, particularly if led by their former white commanders. Given the disasters and insubordination he had experienced with his units in Texas, it is rather remarkable that Armstrong would propose such an idea. Clearly, he was grasping at straws.[32]

An almost equally impractical idea was to send many of the refugees north as servants or laborers with "good" white families. Armstrong appealed for help from his northern friends, arguing, "The daytime of our labor for the freed people is short. The North has not as yet done its full duty in this matter. . . . Their future is dark[,] for the bureau cannot last long and then they must choose between starvation and crime. . . . I wish some society at the North would undertake to find places for some of them, also for their children, and then communicate with me."[33]

Armstrong once again manifested considerable naiveté about racial attitudes in his adopted country. He seemed unaware of the intense northern hostility to an increased black presence in their region. Moreover, some northern agents clearly were as willing to exploit the freedmen as were their southern white brethren. One such character, O. P. St. John, even proposed sending boatloads of refugees to New York. There prospective employers who had contracted with him would "go onboard the boat . . . and select and take home the freedwoman or boy wanted immediately. In this way a vessel load of two hundred could be disposed of in three or four hours." St. John probably knew nothing of the slave trade "scramble" as a procedure for selling bondsmen. (Or, still worse, perhaps he was using it as a model.) Some northern blacks were no better. One former missionary teacher "of color" in Boston charged prospective employers five dollars a head for the transportation of a refugee servant and then absconded with the money. To his credit, Armstrong quickly realized the outrageousness of such schemes and put a stop to them.[34]

By the end of his first nine months in Hampton, Armstrong claimed, he had reduced the black population by 2,500.[35] How genuinely successful his efforts were is difficult to determine. If the estimates of bureau and civil officials of thirty to forty thousand refugees on the Peninsula in 1866 are accurate, the removal policy accomplished its goal. The 1870 black population of the four lower Peninsula counties was 13,654, only four thousand more than in 1860. It must be noted, however, that the black population in Elizabeth City and York counties, in which conditions were best for freedmen and in which most of the black schools were located, remained at twice its pre-war level, while the other two counties—Warwick and James City—experienced declines in the black population. Armstrong may have forced many of the freedmen to leave the Peninsula, but it is unlikely that most returned to their counties of origin. The rapid increase in Norfolk's black population during this period suggests that many may simply have crossed Hampton Roads to that city in search of greater opportunity and less harassment.[36]

General Armstrong was only somewhat more successful in restoring order and economic stability to his district. In 1866, over half the land remained out of cultivation, due to lack of capital and an unsettled labor force. Relations between landowner and laborer were acrimonious. Written contracts still were uncommon; whites complained, "Niggers won't work," to which blacks responded, "Whites won't pay." Wages were low, usually providing the barest subsistence for the laborer and his family. Often even these paltry wages were not paid, sometimes because the owner had no money but more often because the owner was defrauding his workers.

Touring his district, Samuel informed his mother that "the rebels are extremely poor and very much disheartened; they barely make out to live. There are a good many well-disposed, sensible ones among them—but the rebel politicians . . . exasperate all good men by their abuse and palpable spirit of treason." Of the blacks he added, "The darkies are poor; some are striving—some are shiftless—the only thing is to educate them."[37]

Poverty and ignorance only exacerbated already hostile race relations. Civil order threatened to collapse. "County court days bring trouble," the general wrote. "Whiskey is plentiful; there is drunkenness, rioting, and invariably 'a war of the races.'" In the aftermath, civil officials arrested the blacks involved, while the whites were allowed to go free. Freedmen's Bureau officers lacked the authority to intervene. As a result, blacks were denied any chance for justice in disputes with whites. Some frustrated blacks resorted to vigilante justice. Two black schoolhouses were burned in Northampton County; a few nights later, two *white* schoolhouses burned down.[38]

Two years later, in 1868, conditions were more peaceful but hardly better for the freedmen. Relative calm had been achieved through the evisceration of the Freedmen's Bureau and the repression of the freedmen. Armstrong complained, "The condition of freedmen in this sub-district is unchanged. . . . They are barely getting along, the chief end of life is to subsist; there is no progress, no chance of any, as things are now. Financially he receives nothing more than enough to get him through the following winter. He never gets ahead. The freedmen are precisely, in a pecuniary point of view, where they were two years ago."[39]

As General Armstrong composed those comments, he knew that the bureau's life was winding down. Except in its educational endeavors, the bureau would cease to operate in the southern states in January 1869. Armstrong seemed unaware of the national weariness regarding race and the woes of the freed people. Instead, he blamed Bureau Commissioner O. O. Howard for the bureau's demise. He wrote to Emma Walker, a young woman whom he had begun to court, "You ask why the Bureau is to be discontinued: it is because Gen. Howard is unwilling to ask Congress to expend any more money for its support. . . . I think he is not up to his position: that he is yielding to discouragement instead of making a strong stand for organized educational work in the South which the States are too poor to sustain themselves. It seems to me a sad mistake to leave all to them when there is such prejudice against negroes' education. The country will suffer quite as much as the freedmen."[40]

At first, Armstrong had envisioned black suffrage as an alternative to the bureau. Under the Congressional Reconstruction Acts of 1867, reorganizing the former Confederate states, black men were given the right to vote. "I am delighted with the new reconstruction bill," Armstrong told sister Jennie; "it is based on truth and justice. . . . Negro suffrage if it is allowed will become a fact without trouble or noise; and it's coming soon."[41] The promise of black suffrage, however, ultimately proved ephemeral. Men beholden to others for their livelihood were forced to vote as they were told, not as they wished.

Recognizing the limited utility of suffrage, Armstrong pleaded for some sort of permanent agency to assist the blacks in their transition to freedom. In his final report to the bureau as its full-time agent, Armstrong argued, "The few years that have passed since the slaves were liberated have no more than served to well arrange the forces, mental and moral, that should be steadily applied for generations."

Sounding much like his father, Richard, describing the natives of Hawaii, he continued, "They are children:—but are in the hands of an educated, shrewd, hostile race." But the situation of blacks in America was even more problematical. "The educated white looks with contempt upon the enfranchised colored citizen; the poor white is bitterly jealous of him. If such men are chosen the judges and juries that administer the laws and decide the destinies of the freedmen. . . . No outrage upon the virtue of colored females or violation of freedmen's rights receives any general condemnation from Southern society."[42]

The continued repression of blacks seemed fully to awaken Armstrong's missionary instincts. He decided to dedicate his life to the uplift of the ex-slaves. He came to this decision only gradually. A year earlier, in 1867, Samuel had been less certain about his future. At age twenty-eight, he was still undecided about his life's vocation. He had written his friend Archie that "my stay here [in Virginia] I cannot but consider uncertain though there is a likelihood of its lasting a while longer. I hold myself ready to fold my tents at the call of destiny or duty, and go to fresh fields and pastures new."[43]

Armstrong already had rejected some options proposed to him. He repeated to his mother that he was certain he did not want to enter the ministry. He also had decided that he would not return to Hawaii and rejected a business opportunity there. In fact, he had become quite alienated from his first homeland. He was so sharply critical of corruption in Hawaii and the dissipation of the royal family that his sister made him promise to keep his opinions strictly inside the family. To justify his decision to stay in America, Samuel quoted his brother Will's critique of Hawaii:

"'The Islands are a very small . . . hill, and it needs but a very little rooster to crow there."[44]

Armstrong also explored the possibility of remaining on the Peninsula, going into business, becoming a landowner, and entering politics. "[B]eing known as a land holder . . . will make my position socially far more pleasant and dignified, and my political chances greatly improved. Nothing is so bad for one in political life as to be dependent entirely on his office."[45] He soon decided, however, that politics was not to his taste. His brother Baxter had been encouraging such a career for him. "I have no intention of going to Congress," Sam cautioned Jennie in 1868, "Please tell Baxter this. There's too much dirty work to be done to get in."[46]

In truth, Samuel Armstrong was less than candid with his friends and family when he claimed uncertainty about his future. He did have a specific goal in mind. He wanted to create and operate a new sort of school for freedmen. He was merely biding his time until the opportunity appeared. He hinted of his plans to Jennie: "By and by my labors will be more in the educational line—shall be out of the Bureau—have less power but do more good. . . . Shall have to raise, probably, a large amount of money—for I shall not go into anything halfway or that shall be half supported."[47]

To his sister Clara, he had written earlier, "I will do only what comes in my way to do as part of my purpose, which is, so far as I can help accomplish it, the regeneration of Virginia by the establishment of right institutions in her; the first of which in importance are common schools."[48] What Samuel Armstrong was maneuvering for was the principalship of the new normal school that the American Missionary Association intended to found in Hampton. It was the kind of task that he had been pursuing, if not always consciously, since his arrival in Hampton two years earlier. Finally, in October 1867, Samuel was able to confide to his friend Archie, "I have been asked to run the Normal School here—have consented to take it *in addition* to present duty if that will suit—I will do nothing else."[49]

7

"To Teach and to Lead"

Founding Hampton Institute

*We negro teachers have a stimulus that the world knows
little of, in the enthusiasm of our students, whose opportunities in most cases, have cost a struggle . . . We are not like
those who fire into the air; we see our shot strike.*

—*Samuel C. Armstrong, 1877*

The new normal school for freedpeople in Hampton, Virginia, that Samuel
Armstrong was invited to lead was part of a larger response to the various
forces shaping the future of black folk in postbellum America. By 1868, black
freedmen and their white allies no longer could deny a profoundly disheartening truth. In many ways, white America had not been ready for black
emancipation. Despite the Reconstruction Amendments, the myriad Congressional acts, investigations, and military interventions, it was becoming
apparent that white Americans had no intention of allowing black people
to be as free as white people.

Blacks would receive almost none of the government land grants being
showered upon every other interest group in the society. Their right to vote
was fatally compromised by corruption, violence, and their economic dependence on white employers. Racism and fear overwhelmed all Consti-
tutional imperatives and any national tradition of fairness. Unlike whites,
blacks were to be required to prove their entire race worthy of freedom
before any individual member would be granted such status.[1]

These harsh realities left ex-slaves and their allies with a troubling
conundrum. What were they to do while white America grew out of its
bigotry? What could be done that might speed the process? After prolonged
and sometimes rancorous debate, a majority of the freedmen's allies settled
upon *education* as the realm in which they could best assist the former
bondsmen. Education would uplift the black man while helping him to
appear less of an "uncivilized threat" to white society.

From the very beginning of their endeavors to help the escaping slaves in 1861, freedmen aid workers, both religious and secular, had made black education one of their highest priorities. This was entirely appropriate, because the freedpeople made clear from the beginning that education was one of their foremost goals. Northern workers for secular aid societies anticipated the need for an educated southern citizenry, black as well as white. Religious missionaries shared that goal and added the evangelical Protestant imperative—a good Christian must be able to read the Bible. Indeed, the largest of the religious missionary groups, the American Missionary Association, had been founded in 1846 to bring Christianity and education to slaves, fugitives, and free blacks. It had even dared to found Berea College in Kentucky, a slave state, as an interracial school six years before the Civil War. It was only natural for it to continue its dual mission of education and racial—or, more accurately stated, *Christian*—equality in the Reconstruction South.[2]

Most of the freedmen's allies concurred with the AMA in its focus on education, but serious disagreements developed over the blacks' educational needs and abilities. As hopes for widespread black land ownership and meaningful black political participation faded, plans for freedmen's education became weighted down with ancillary matters. Decisions about educational content and goals became intertwined with disputes about the South's political and economic future, and about the nature of ultimate post-Reconstruction racial adjustments. For example, secular aid workers' support for the recreation of the New England common school, complete with northern lesson plans and textbooks, optimistically envisioned a reconstructed, integrated South with schools and teachers much like those in northern communities.[3]

Some freedmen's aid workers, particularly the religious ones associated with the AMA, were less confident about the future of the ex-slaves and the South. These missionaries tended to be those who had served longest in the South. They had been quite euphoric about the acculturation and capacities of the escaped slaves they first met. Many of these escapees were urban slaves or free Negroes who were skilled and partially literate. As the missionaries had encountered the more oppressed and isolated bondsmen of the southern interior, they had become less optimistic about the freedmen's intellectual and moral potential.[4] Reluctantly, missionaries began to acknowledge that "many Freedmen are ignorant, vicious and degraded."[5] Rev. S. R. Dennen of the AMA added that "the warm and sensuous nature of the African race" needed the drill of the school "to steady and poise it, . . . to make it effective."[6] These more pessimistic aid workers concluded that the freedmen would require an education tailored to their unique needs, including specially designed textbooks and curricula, and specially trained teachers.[7] Recognizing that the initial goal of achieving black equality simply would not be possible in the foreseeable future, they also argued that freedmen's education should prepare them for the kinds of lives they were likely to lead in the post-Reconstruction South. "Blacks, now released from the disabilities of bondage," the *American Missionary* editorialized, would have to "somewhere find and maintain [their] appropriate social position."[8] Such phraseology clearly anticipated an *inferior* "position" in southern society.

Questions about the most appropriate pedagogy and social status for southern blacks would be central in the evolution of black schools—especially Hampton Institute—during the remainder of the century. But in the early years of Reconstruction, the freedmen and their allies had a larger immediate problem. There were four million mostly uneducated ex-slaves in the postbellum South. The issue of what to teach them had to be subsumed within the dilemma of *how* so many could be taught at all.

Reflecting the growing northern disinterest in southern blacks, by 1866 northern aid—both governmental and private—was declining sharply. The supply of northern teachers likewise was evaporating. The missionaries who continued to go South stayed for shorter periods and often returned with less than salutary opinions of southern blacks. There were not enough northern white missionaries to educate the freed blacks, and those few were subjected to frequent abuse by hostile white natives. The freedmen's allies also were certain that, if white southerners were left to teach the Negroes, they would only use education to return them to slavery. Clearly the blacks would have to be prepared to educate themselves.

It was fortuitous that the freedmen's aid groups were learning these lessons about black education. Those they intended to educate were reaching the same conclusions at the same time, albeit via a somewhat different line of reasoning. As noted, freedmen supported education even before initial emancipation. They had hoped for universal, integrated public education as the surest method of adequate education for themselves. That vision quickly faded as the new southern public schools were segregated from the outset. Experience also had led to growing dissatisfaction with and distrust of white teachers, including many of the northern teachers and all of those supplied by white public school authorities. Faced with these setbacks, blacks sought to control their schools, particularly in the areas of content and instructors. They, too, concluded that the best method to achieve their ends was the training of black teachers.

A solution was found that was tolerable to both northern benevolent groups and the freedmen. It also was an outcome that shaped the rest of Samuel Chapman Armstrong's life. A small cadre of dedicated white teachers would remain in the South to train the most able of the black freedmen, so that they could become the teachers and leaders of their race.[9]

Toward that end, freedmen's aid societies, missionary associations, and the Freedmen's Bureau joined together in the creation of black normal schools and colleges in the South. The federal government sponsored the creation of Howard University in Washington, D.C. The American Baptist Home Mission Society, the Freedmen's Aid Society of the Methodist Episcopal Church (North), and the Presbyterian Board of Missions all established other schools that in the next half century developed into black colleges.[10]

Foremost among these groups was the American Missionary Association, which, in 1867 and 1868, founded eight teacher-training schools in Macon, Savannah, and Atlanta, Georgia; Charleston, South Carolina; Louisville, Kentucky; Nashville, Tennessee; Talledega, Alabama; and Hampton, Virginia.[11] All of them began as advanced grammar schools; and all, save one, ultimately aspired to collegiate status. In fact, the schools in Atlanta (Atlanta University) and Nashville (Fisk), from the very beginning were titled "Universities."[12] The school that would be different was the one in Hampton, Virginia. Its differences were primarily the result of its founder and first principal, Samuel Armstrong.

Armstrong had joined the debates about how to best educate the freedmen when he arrived as head of the local Freedmen's Bureau in 1866. One of the principal duties of a bureau agent was to facilitate the educational work of northern benevolent societies like the AMA. For example, the bureau built or renovated schoolhouses for the freedmen; northern aid groups supplied the teachers, and the bureau agent coordinated the process.[13] In June 1866, Armstrong toyed with one vision of the school he later would create and head. In his "Letter of Appeal" to northern philanthropic groups, he had said in passing, "There is another and most important field for philanthropic effort. It is the building up of industrial schools." At the time, he simply had in mind the dispatch of a few additional northern teachers to train freedwomen in the art of making cloth, so that they might support themselves.[14]

Later in 1866, Armstrong met in New York with prominent businessmen and philanthropists to elaborate upon his vision for a normal school that incorporated industrial education. The meeting occurred in the parlor of Robert Ogden, a manager for department store mogul John Wanamaker. Ogden later became one of Armstrong's closest friends and a trustee of Hampton Institute.[15] The young general also involved his mentor, Mark Hopkins, and fellow Williams alumnus, James Garfield, in his planning for the school. When George Whipple, corresponding secretary of the AMA, seemed to procrastinate about the idea, Armstrong connived to bring Edward P. Smith, also an AMA secretary and liaison to the Freedmen's Bureau, down to help select the land to be purchased for the new school. The site agreed upon was 125 acres of a former plantation called Little Scotland, or, less elegantly, Wood's Farm. When Whipple still hesitated, Armstrong wrote that he would come north himself to raise the money. Faced with such determination and carefully orchestrated support from the very people upon whom the AMA itself depended for its resources, the association gave in and purchased the desired property.[16]

Although he had not yet been invited to lead the new Hampton normal school when the AMA purchased the land for it, Armstrong was fully prepared to present his analysis of the freedmen and of how best to educate them. He had reflected upon his experiences as a wartime commander and as peacetime guardian of blacks during the chaos of early Reconstruction. He also clearly had leavened his conclusions with remembrances of his youth with native Hawaiians.[17]

Armstrong was much given to comparisons of blacks and Hawaiians, never entirely comprehending how different the two groups truly were, and much to the disservice of both. In his *Lessons from the Hawaiian Islands,* he argued:

> The negro and the Polynesian have many striking similarities. Of both it is true that not mere ignorance, but deficiency of character is the chief difficulty, and that to build up character is the true objective point of education. It is also true that in all men education is conditioned not alone by an enlightened head and a changed heart, but very largely on a routine of industrious habit, which is to character what the foundation is to the pyramid. . . . Morality and industry generally go together. Especially in weak tropical races, idleness, like ignorance, breeds vice.[18]

Hampton Institute Waterfront, c. 1868. "Mansion House," the principal's residence, is on the right. In the center is the U.S. Army Hospital barracks, first used as dormitories and later demolished. At the left is a house, also later demolished for construction of Virginia Hall. Courtesy of Hampton University Archives.

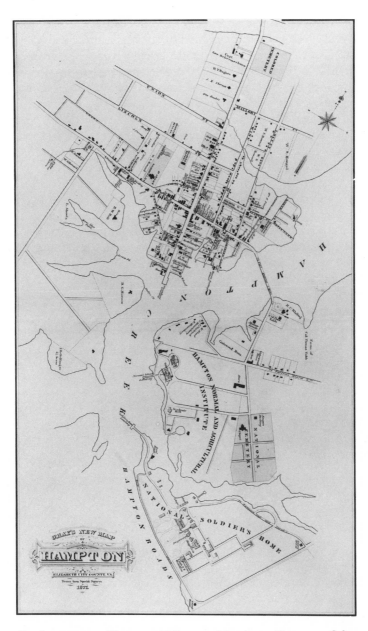

Grey's new map: Hampton Village and Institute. Courtesy of the Library of Virginia.

This logic led Armstrong to discount the fact that the southern blacks, unlike the native Hawaiians when they first encountered white men, were already Christians and relatively acculturated. For him, like his father, the true work of civilizing backward races began where the missionary effort to Christianize them ended.[19] Most important, it also meant that it would be up to men like Armstrong, rather than to blacks themselves, no matter how extensive their achievements, to decide when the latter had acquired enough of the requisite character.

Armstrong was willing to concede that there was "negro blood among those in the higher ranks of success of many kinds." But for him that was not the issue. "What does the race, as a whole, need most and need now? How shall their weak points be made strong?"[20] Armstrong reasoned that, "single handed, the Negro is full of resource; as a unit he is strong, but as a unity or race he is weak." The uplift of the individual might be speedily accomplished, that of the race would take much longer. "Too much is expected of mere book-knowledge; too much is expected of one generation. The real upward movement, the leveling up, not of persons but of people, will be, as in all history—almost imperceptibl[e,] to be measured only by long periods."[21] Armstrong hinted how long that period might be for blacks in a quip to his friend, Archie: "The parts of the 25th century will excite. The coming man will have woolly hair. The white man is intelligent but not pious—and is doomed. The races take their turns." In short, white men would not need to worry about black equality for generations to come.[22]

Armstrong's Hawaiian upbringing had not enabled him to avoid either racism or paternalism, but had made the manifestations of both in him rather singular. His racism contained none of the latent guilt about past injustices or the fear of righteous retribution by blacks that characterized white American racism. His paternalism never was tempered by the awareness (largely repressed in white American paternalists) that black inadequacies might be not inherent in the race, but rather consequences of disabilities imposed upon it. As a result, there was little restraint or caution in Armstrong's paternalism. He never would be able to perceive that his work actually might harm those he wished to help, nor that others might embrace his methods for entirely different motives.

For example, the general, in his vision for Hampton Institute, was prepared to acknowledge positive attributes of black people and their history. When reflecting upon the nature of African Americans and their culture, Armstrong was most open in correspondence with his wife, Emma, whom he married in 1869. In 1878, after listening to the "natural eloquence" of a black preacher in Richmond, he wrote to Emma, "It makes the matter of civilization a puzzle. . . . Should we educate them out of all of this . . . that was needed to carry them through slavery?"[23]

Armstrong sensed the power and poignancy in the culture black

Americans had developed during their enslavement. In another missive to Emma, he said:

> I have been sitting in Miss Bacon's parlor listening to the singing of our girls. . . . Few people have any idea of the deep and essential music there is in these people: there is a fascination about it. As they sang in their peculiar cadence, in perfect time, either in a plaintive music or cheerful major key one could detect the stamp of slavery on their lives.—These songs are but the cry of their desolate hearts unto their God—once uttered in the long agony of their oppression and now sung by their children as the songs of their home and nation.
>
> The imagery of the words is quaint, mild, and full of genuine poetry, but words and music are bound together—indeed the words are subordinate to the music which has the deepest expression and rather is the truest expression of the negro heart—and a tender beautiful story it often tells. In a few years these songs will be lost and some of the finest poetry and music in the world will thus be forgotten.[24]

Samuel Armstrong, the white missionary from Hawaii, obviously felt the beauty in black culture and sensed that music was central to it. The dilemma for Armstrong, and for the black people who benefited from his efforts, was the notion that this cultural richness would have to be sacrificed for a supposedly "higher" good. Even more problematical, Armstrong and his successors continued to attempt the preservation of this music and to insist that their black students sing it, long after a new breed of Hampton students had decided that such songs were not a symbol of culture but rather a "badge of slavery."[25]

The foundations for this misappropriation of black culture were laid by Armstrong in his original rationale and plan for his school. Armstrong argued that the black man's primary faults were "improvidence, low ideas of honor and morality, and a general lack of directive energy, judgment and foresight." "His deficiencies of character are, I believe," Armstrong continued, "worse for him than his ignorance." There was no reason to despair, Armstrong believed. "But with these deficiencies are docility and enthusiasm for improvement and a perseverance in pursuit of it, which forms a basis for great hope."[26]

What the black race needed immediately was "elementary and industrial education." Armstrong believed that "the race will succeed or fail as it shall devote itself with energy to agriculture and the mechanic arts, . . . and its teachers ought to be men inspired with the spirit of hard work." Here, for once, the general restrained his rhetoric, stating the problem and its solution succinctly. The circumstances he described were ones he had observed at first hand among his former soldiers and other downtrodden blacks in his Freedmen's Bureau district. He believed that the South's future would be primarily agricultural; therefore men were required who were skilled in modern farming methods and in the use and repair of farm machinery. His prescription for training in these areas was appropriate not only for the ex-slaves, but also for the impoverished white yeomen of Virginia.

Unfortunately but characteristically, Armstrong immediately cloaked the problem and its solution in paternalistic rhetoric. Armstrong continued his outline for the Hampton school, arguing, "Power, character, manhood, is [sic] the ultimate end of education, of experience, and of life. The best, most practical training is that of the faculties that should guide and direct all the others—the moral and religious part of our nature."[27] In two sentences Armstrong had moved his proposition from the tangible and clearly "do-able" to the metaphysical and most likely unrealizable. Success would be measured not by a bountiful corn crop but by "character" and "manhood," as assessed by potentially hostile white men. In 1868, however, such concerns were hazards for the future, and Armstrong's words seemed to impress his missionary contemporaries.

To provide his special education, Armstrong proposed the creation of a novel form of normal school which would train teachers who in turn would train other teachers and the common black people of the South. "The normal school graduate of the South should be of the people," Armstrong insisted, "—above them yet of them—in order to make natural or probable a life-long service in their behalf."[28] Armstrong intended, quite literally, to educate the entire black race by creating those who would be its leaders and teachers.

His school would omit the classics taught in traditional secondary academies. Greek and Latin would be of little use to the ordinary freedman who had to eke out his living from the land. To offer such subjects to his students would merely alienate them from the people they were meant to teach. Armstrong argued that "an English course embracing reading and elocution, geography and mathematics, history, the sciences, the study of the mother-tongue and its literature, the leading principles of mental and moral science, and of political economy, would, I think, . . . exhaust the best powers of nineteen-twentieths of those who would for years come to the institute."[29]

This specially designed curriculum was not be the only feature that would distinguish Hampton Institute from other AMA schools and traditional normal schools in the North. Another was the "home" aspect of the school. "The Christian home is the point of departure of civilization," Armstrong reasoned. "Without it, schools and churches can do but little, as among the heathen who may be converted to the truth, but so long as they live like savages, no matter what they profess, they only obtain a low standard of morals and easily backslide." At Hampton, teachers would have a much more powerful *in loco parentis* role to play than at northern schools. They would teach their students about *life* as well as book learning.[30]

In a similar vein, Armstrong insisted that the school be coeducational. In an age when most northern colleges and normal schools were single-sex institutions, Armstrong's commitment to coeducation was a bold departure from the norm. His rationale, however, was based not on some inclusive pedagogical ideal, but rather on the special needs he perceived in his black students. Armstrong believed that immorality was a major weakness of the black race. Therefore, women would have to play an equal role in uplifting the race. By teaching men and women together under the close supervision of their teachers, the school could inculcate the habits and values that had to be passed on to their pupils and communities.[31]

The most controversial of Armstrong's proposed innovations was Hampton's manual labor aspect. Industrial education and manual labor education both were concepts familiar to American educators in the mid-nineteenth century. Although Armstrong and other advocates of freedmen's education tended to use the terms interchangeably, important distinctions existed between the two as they had evolved in antebellum America.

Industrial education developed as a strategy for teaching useful skills to the children of the poor and to marginal elements of northern society, e.g., "orphans, the deaf, the blind, the feeble-minded and the Negroes."[32] The status of these youngsters would remain the same, but they would grow up to be docile "working" poor, rather than "disaffected" poor, a dangerous and disruptive element in society.

Manual labor in higher education, in contrast, evolved primarily as a means to provide healthful exercise and financial support for students of a higher strata in American society. Some of the nation's most innovative colleges experimented with this approach in the 1830s. The labor done—most often work on a school farm—provided physical exercise for students who too often got very little, and financial aid for needy students who otherwise might be unable to obtain a college education.[33] Andover, Amherst, Oneida, Oberlin, and Wesleyan were among the schools that experimented with the manual labor system in the antebellum period. Most of them, however, had abandoned the experiment by the Civil War because student labor proved inefficient and the school farms unprofitable.[34]

Some historians, noting the similarity between antebellum industrial training schools and the industrial education programs in black colleges at the turn of the twentieth century, have seen a direct relationship between the two. They have assumed that the technique was applied at Hampton Institute under Armstrong, then refined and brought to maturity at Tuskegee under Booker T. Washington. As will be seen, such analysis ignores the centrality of Armstrong's missionary background in his plan for Hampton, the ambiguities within his paternalism, and the duplicity of many with whom he and his protégé, Washington, aligned themselves to sustain their institutions. What industrial education at Hampton Institute became after 1900 was not necessarily what Samuel Chapman Armstrong set out to create in 1868.[35]

The young General Armstrong was familiar with both the industrial training schools and the manual labor movement. Indeed, he cited the manual labor program at newly founded Cornell University in his argument for a similar plan at Hampton.[36] But neither of these educational methods truly served as the basis for the Hampton Institute design. To Armstrong, the industrial training schools stifled ambition and did not offer the "home-like" and Christian atmosphere he had in mind. The manual labor schools were inefficient and did not place enough emphasis on the "character-building" potential inherent in manual labor. The true basis for the Hampton model was Richard Armstrong's missionary schools in Hawaii. Industrial education institutions like the islands' Lahainaluna Seminary incorporated both the atmosphere and the curriculum Armstrong sought for his new enterprise in Virginia.[37]

For Armstrong, manual labor and industrial education was far more than merely the acquisition of skills. When he spoke of "industry," he was using the parlance of the missionary, not that of the new industrialist. He meant the development of "industrious habits," of self-discipline, which he thought most freedmen sorely lacked. "The advantages of the industrial system are manifold," he argued. ". . . The real financial question as to manual-labor schools is this: Shall the expenses of teaching a student a trade, and making him self-reliant and manly, be met in the same way as is that of teaching him mathematics and Greek? It may cost twice as much to train the hands and head together as to train the head alone. Of course it will not pay in a money way but it will pay in a moral way. It will make them men and women as nothing else will. It is the only way to make them Christians."[38] Clearly Armstrong was not envisioning a less expensive shortcut for black education. He openly acknowledged that his method might cost more, because it sought to accomplish more.

In truth, a very practical concern informed Armstrong's manual labor design for Hampton. The institute was an unendowed school for impoverished black students. Some means had to be found so that they could support themselves during the three years of their education. Work on the school farms and in the school shops provided that opportunity. Moreover, Hampton graduates were supposed to go out to educate their race. It was a noble ideal, but southern black schools usually were in session less than six months a year. Hampton alumni needed to learn other skills simply to support themselves and their families during the remaining months. In short, manual labor education at Hampton was, originally, a means to important ends. It would provide graduates with moral character and additional skills needed so that they could pursue their primary task of teaching others.[39]

Samuel Armstrong was fully aware of the risk he was taking, and of the criticisms that might be hurled at his plan. He relished the challenge. He explained to his future wife, "It is only by tremendous activity for two or three years that this concern can be made to go[.] [I]f it does go it will be a grand success—conspicuous in causational history as the first success of a manual labor school; everyone else has failed. I must not[;] the reward will come[;] we will have a good time by and by."[40]

After the purchase of the Little Scotland plantation, it was certain that there would be a new AMA normal school in Hampton. But, despite his transparent lobbying for the position, Samuel Armstrong was not the AMA's first choice as leader of the new institution. Sam wrote to his friend Archie in the fall of 1867, "E. B. Parsons of '59 or '60 at Williams has been secured by the American Missionary Association, to run the machine. They are going to send a fine corps of teachers—I am fitting up, whitewashing, etc. for an active campaign."[41]

It is unclear why the AMA passed over the obviously willing Armstrong in selecting Hampton's first principal. It clearly was not age alone; E. B. Parsons was only two or three years older than the twenty-nine-year-old Armstrong. Conflicts between the AMA and Armstrong over educational philosophy were more apparent than real. Armstrong tended to trumpet his unique approach, while differences between himself and other freedmen's workers actually were relatively small. For example, coeducation and a modernized curriculum which omitted the classics tended to be the rule rather than the exception at the new normal schools for freedmen. (Even as freedmen's school organizers had few funds to pay for the luxury of instruction in Greek or Latin, classics teachers in places like New England and New York had little incentive to abandon comfort for the harsh life of a Yankee schoolteacher in the South.) The sometimes suffocating *in loco parentis* atmosphere at most black colleges remained characteristic well into the last quarter of the twentieth century. Even industrial education was not unique to Hampton. Many black schools experimented with the idea; Howard University even briefly (1884–88) instituted an "Industrial Department" on its campus.[42]

General Armstrong's tendency to cater to southern white opinion in some of his analyses of the freedmen's condition certainly discomfited other allies of the freedmen. Illustrative of this trait was Armstrong's analysis of the southern political situation by 1870. "The plastic character of the race puts them [blacks] completely under the control of their leaders. . . . A most unfortunate result of this blind leading the blind is already seen in the belief that political rights are better obtained by political warfare than by advancement in knowledge and in ability to care for themselves."[43] Simply put, blacks were to be denied the right of political "warfare" until well-meaning men like himself agreed that they were prepared for such arduous combat with the ordinary whites of America.

This was not yet the official AMA position in 1868, but by 1873, in an effort to gain the good will of the men then controlling newly "redeemed" southern states, the organization conceded that most blacks had not been ready for the franchise.[44] Armstrong's only fault in this regard was that his candor had been premature.

Nor did the elite northerners who were selecting the heads of the new black colleges seem to have any qualms about Armstrong's leadership abilities. Twice the Howard University Board of Trustees offered Armstrong that university's presidency. Twice Armstrong turned the post down, later explaining to his wife, "I wouldn't be connected to it for anything. It needs to be thoroughly cleaned out and start anew."[45] Armstrong probably disliked several things about Howard. These may reveal a good deal about the general and perhaps suggest why he was not offered the Hampton position initially. First, there was Howard's original conceptualization as a "Normal and Theological Institute." Armstrong was a deeply religious man, but he also was devoted to what he styled "Practical Christianity." He never was much interested in formal religious training for himself and was persuaded that the last thing the freedmen needed was "more preachers." Second, Howard clearly was intended to serve a more advanced, and therefore smaller, segment of the black population than Armstrong conceived of reaching with his Hampton design. Finally and probably most important, Howard already had a well-established Board of Trustees composed of prominent men, including George Whipple of the AMA. Armstrong clearly wanted to run his own show; he could not have done so under the supervision of Howard's powerful board.[46]

In the final analysis, the reason the AMA at first hesitated to offer Armstrong the leadership of Hampton probably was because it feared it would be unable to control him. If that was the case, the AMA was absolutely correct. When E. B. Parsons declined the invitation to lead Hampton, George Whipple and the AMA turned to the obvious choice. Samuel Chapman Armstrong accepted the offer with alacrity. Within four years, he made Hampton Institute virtually independent of the AMA.[47]

To achieve that independence and many of his other goals, the man who would serve as principal of Hampton Institute for the next twenty-five years created for himself an extraordinary public persona. In the *Courant,* widely read in freedmen's aid circles, he was described as "a man particularly adapted for the work, by nature, education, and grace. . . . He is a man of astonishing energy, and of boundless faith. In these degenerate days it is well worth a trip to Hampton to see a really earnest man, earnest in a noble cause, and carrying it along chiefly by the force of his personal magnetism and restless energy. He carries with him an atmosphere which makes his spirit contagious."[48] At the same time, he was able to disarm former critics in the local press. The white-owned *Norfolk Journal,* which earlier had opposed black education, wrote of Hampton Institute and its principal in 1871, "The place indicates the most perfect system and the proficiency of the scholars demonstrates a higher capacity for knowledge than is generally accorded the negro." General Armstrong, it continued, "is an active, energetic man, polite, gentlemanly and dignified in his manner, . . . admirably fitted for the duties of his office."[49]

General Armstrong emphatically saw himself as different from most of those involved in freedmen's uplift. In 1865 he had told his sister Ellen, "Men with good intentions are often great nuisances both to the body politic and social—a plea that he means well is all moonshine."[50] Armstrong tried to differentiate himself from such men and from others he thought of as more able. To Archie he wrote, "My order of capacity is inferior to that of those calm steady ones who, in a few words and with balanced minds and powers, are the true kings and queens of the earth. . . . [P]ermit me to express a frequent comment of my own upon my own doings? 'd—n fool.' In humility and sincerity I say it—alas. I know it." Happily Samuel had difficulty remaining entirely serious for very long. He continued, "The truth is the devil is after us and sometimes he overtakes us—lets go and chases again, I suspect just for the fun of it. Let us give the beast a hard pull of it." Armstrong then concluded the letter with a remarkable piece of self-fulfilling prophecy: "I sometimes think that there is a ghastly falseness about our conventional circle of elect ones and wonder what Christ would say, were he to revisit the earth. . . . But I am getting intolerant and am reminded of the besetting sin of all who find fault—that they are apt to be guiltiest of all of those things they declaim about."[51] Two decades later, Samuel Chapman Armstrong would be one of those conventional men of "good intentions." And there would be those who claimed that his product was "all moonshine."

But in 1868, Armstrong was blazing a new path. To free himself and his school from AMA control, Armstrong mounted a shrewdly planned campaign to ingratiate himself with the white leaders of postbellum Virginia and with other philanthropists in the North. Armstrong charmed State Superintendent of Public Instruction William Henry Ruffner. He lobbied Gov. Gilbert Walker for state aid to Hampton. Ever the prankster, when visiting the governor's office, he stole one of Walker's cigars and commented to his wife about Walker, "Alas, like the monkey, he has, I fear not much 'personal piety.'"[52] Lamenting the political machinations he had to endure to win over the Virginia General Assembly, he added, "The darkey question is a bad, ugly thing to manage and much trouble."[53]

It is ironic that part of Armstrong's success among white Virginians was his critique of blacks' participation in politics. The truth is that help from Hampton's black state legislators, whom he had scorned while in the Freedmen's Bureau, enabled Armstrong to win one-third of Virginia's

Morrill Land Grant funds for Hampton Institute.[54] Armstrong, of course, carefully avoided acknowledging that assistance to his white allies.

Armstrong displayed even greater political acumen in outmaneuvering George Whipple and the AMA. He assiduously cultivated his old friendships with men like O. O. Howard, James Garfield, and Mark Hopkins. He won the support of prominent northern families such as the Bacons and Woolseys. Daughters from such families were some of Armstrong's first faculty appointments.[55]

Armstrong's *coup de grace* was forcing the AMA to relinquish direct ownership of Hampton Institute. He warned his wife, "I have got to have a scrimmage with the Trustees and must beat them—I mean the AMA." In fact, he had rigged the game. He elicited a letter from Henry Whittlesey, adjutant general of the Freedmen's Bureau, threatening suspension of any further funding by the bureau until the deed for Hampton's property was vested in an independent board of trustees. This enabled Armstrong to solicit a similar letter from his great-uncle, Reuben Chapman, former chief justice of the Massachusetts Supreme Court, warning that the deed to the institute's land was in George Whipple's name, so that, upon Whipple's death, title would pass to his heirs, not to Hampton's Board of Trustees. Armstrong's tactics worked. The transfer of title was made. Although George Whipple remained president of the new board, Armstrong's maneuver and his receipt of the Virginia Land Grant funds made him virtually independent of the AMA after 1872.[56]

By 1868 Armstrong had become the man that his roommate, John Denison, described years later: "[H]e took in the organic value of a New England deacon, a Boston millionaire, a Quaker philanthropist and a Virginia legislature; he understood the gearing by which they could be united. . . . [H]e made the wolf to lie down with the lamb[.] [H]e combined the energies of the skeptic and the believer. To some this seemed a want of genuineness on his part. The fact simply was that he saw and made for those broader unities in which all good men stand together."[57]

Denison knew his man and recognized his greatest vulnerability as an educational leader. The machinations and intrigues that Armstrong found it necessary to undertake in order to make Hampton Institute succeed easily led many to question his "genuineness." The concern Samuel Chapman Armstrong held for black people, and his commitment to helping them, cannot be questioned. The wisdom of some of his strategies for accomplishing that goal can be.

Armstrong's design for Hampton Normal and Agricultural Institute was a cogent, appropriate response to the needs of the freedmen in southeastern Virginia in 1868. Armstrong created a school that would give members of the black masses skills that would enable them to achieve gradual progress in the political, social, and economic circumstances of their time.

Moreover, it would prepare these graduates to go out and teach these same skills to larger numbers of the black population. The major fault in this design was that it was static. Blacks would progress more rapidly than Armstrong imagined; the conditions under which they lived simultaneously would worsen in the resurgence of racism in the post-Reconstruction South. Armstrong never foresaw such things. The alliance that Denison described Armstrong creating to sustain Hampton had a fatal flaw. Among those New England deacons, Boston millionaires, Quaker philanthropists, and the Virginia legislature, there were *no black people!* Over the years, Armstrong gradually forgot to consult those whom he claimed to serve. He became one of his "men with good intentions."

But in 1872, all that was in the future. As Armstrong promoted Hampton Institute, he could proudly claim, "We negro teachers have a stimulus that the world knows little of, in the enthusiasm of our students, whose opportunities in most cases, have cost a struggle . . . We are not like those who fire into the air; we see our shot strike."[58] Hampton was a grand success, overwhelmed by applicants. Students were to be "of good character," able to read and write at the fifth-grade level, and between fifteen and twenty-five years of age. Students who had a trade were encouraged to "bring your tools along."[59]

Concurrent with the opening of his school was a more personal event in Samuel Chapman Armstrong's life. He confided to his mother in 1868, "I am beginning for the first time since I left the Islands to have a home feeling, about this place."[60] The general was in love and planning to marry.

8

A More Personal Armstrong

Sam, Emma, and the Missionary Ladies, 1868–1878

What are women after all—a bother, yet a blessing—a burden, a trap, yet a treasure.

—Samuel C. Armstrong, 1867

Samuel Chapman Armstrong married twice, yet, by choice, he spent most of his adult life as a widower. Although he enjoyed the company of women enormously, he never proved successful at incorporating one into his life until illness made him a semi-invalid and in need of a helpmate.

As with so many other aspects of Samuel Armstrong's character, his understanding of the "proper roles" for women in society were shaped very much by his Hawaiian and missionary upbringing. The adult women whom Armstrong had known as a boy were the wives of missionaries. Their burdens were many. Not only did they have the expected roles of wife, lover, bearer of children, and nurturer of both spouse and offspring, but they were also expected to perform special functions in the accomplishment of the missionary enterprise. Their special sphere was acculturation of the native women and their female children.

The lives of missionary women were quite complex. While they remained subservient to their husbands in the Euro-American fashion, both they and their spouses were appalled by what they considered to be the subjugation of the indigenous females in the traditional societies they sought to Christianize. Thus, while Richard Armstrong ministered to all Hawaiians, both he and his wife Clarissa assumed that she would play the central part in teaching hygiene, housewifery, and childcare to Hawaiian women and girls. On the one hand, the missionary wife was charged to help civilize the youth of the indigenous people; on the other hand, she was expected to see that her own offspring were not "corrupted" by the looser morals and discipline of the native people. Clarissa took all these responsibilities quite seriously. She was the epitome of the missionary wife. She was also, of course, Sam Armstrong's most important female role model, and he remained devoted to her throughout his life.

As principal of Hampton Institute, Samuel Armstrong expanded the roles that women were permitted to fill beyond the Hawaiian missionary model. During his tenure at Hampton, his chief assistants—especially in terms of the academic program and the structure of the school's community life—were female. Women were charged with guiding *both* sexes toward the level of civilization deemed appropriate in Armstrong's vision. And when Armstrong chose a wife, he selected a woman who, at first, seemed to have many of the same qualities as his mother and his largely female staff at Hampton.

In assembling his staff, Armstrong characteristically kept at least one eye on the potential to bring greater glory to Hampton (and to himself). He selected his teachers not only because of their capacity to educate his pupils, but also because of their connections with prominent potential donors. His first assistant principal was Rebecca Bacon, daughter of the distinguished Congregational minister, Leonard Bacon, of New Haven's First Church. Jane Woolsey, from a prominent New York family, became manager of the Girl's Industrial Department. Other faculty included Rebecca Bacon's sister Alice and Mary Frances Mackie from Vassar College.[1]

Most of these women were single and from New England or New York. Most were graduates of northern normal schools. The day-to-day operations of the institute were directed by these women, especially during Armstrong's prolonged absences. Mary Mackie, who succeeded Rebecca Bacon as "Lady Principal," was in charge of the academic program. Armstrong's recruitment of her in 1871 was typical of his style in attracting able teachers. When he offered her a position, she reportedly responded, "You forget, General Armstrong, that I am teaching at Vassar College!" Armstrong's retort was, "Anyone will be glad to teach in Vassar College; you come here, where you are needed!"[2]

Albert Howe, farm manager of the institute, claimed that "[Miss Mackie] did the work of five of six women. . . . She did as much for the school as General Armstrong."[3] Students remembered her with equal fondness. "She was stern," George Davis (Class of 1874) recalled; "when she said a thing she meant it. If she wanted a thing done, she wouldn't rest till it was done, but she was perfectly just. She had a very strong personal interest in all the students."[4] Mackie may have terrified young Booker T. Washington in her demand that he clean a classroom as an admissions test, but she was no less demanding of herself. She shocked her students by rolling up her sleeves and cleaning along with them when a job needed doing. Few of them had seen a white woman work with her hands before.[5]

Samuel Armstrong with mentor Mark Hopkins (2), teacher Alice Bacon (3), and two unidentified others, c. 1870. Courtesy of Hampton University Archives.

Alice Bacon became another of Armstrong's most valued staff members. She originated a nursing program for the institute's women students. Her problem was that Hampton village had no hospital in which her nursing students could develop their skills. In the late nineteenth century, hospitals were seen as places where one went to die, not to be cured. (The terrible mortality rates at the Peninsula's army hospitals—located on the very grounds where the new institute was rising—undoubtedly reinforced this perception.) Miss Bacon struck upon the idea of persuading two of the most prominent women of the community, one black and one white, to enter her new hospital for treatment. She hitched her beloved horse to a buggy and ostentatiously paraded the two respected ladies through the village on their way to her hospital. Thereafter, her facility had many willing patients. In celebration, Alice Bacon named her hospital "Dixie" in tribute not to the South's Lost Cause, but to her horse "Dixie," which had played so central a role in her public relations maneuver.[6]

Armstrong was very clear about what he expected from his teachers. "We need a teacher who shall take up the general field of science . . . in order that our graduates shall have a simple but clear and comprehensive idea of the kingdom of nature from their own bodies out to the fixed stars," he advised applicant Martha Waldron, later Hampton's physician. "Your teaching power is peculiar and needed," the general continued. "You have force of character. Power to interest and inspire."[7] He was also ever eager for innovation. He invited one potential teacher to Hampton in order to create a kindergarten program in which his students could practice-teach. He wanted a "clear headed woman" and reminded the candidate, "What is just the thing for the German child may not necessarily be just the thing for the negro child."[8]

In any enterprise led by a powerful personality who surrounds himself with similar types, conflicts inevitably arise. Such was the case at Hampton Institute. Some of the early faculty members, such as Rebecca Bacon, felt exploited. She became convinced that Armstrong had hired her as much for her family's standing as for her own talents. She complained frequently about the general's use of her name in soliciting funds from potential donors connected with her family. Once, at Armstrong's behest, she asked her father to solicit twenty-five thousand dollars for Hampton from Freedmen's Bureau Commissioner O. O. Howard. Ultimately, in 1871, she resigned in protest.[9]

Conversely, even Armstrong's hand-picked teachers sometimes exasperated him. In 1870, the general complained to his new wife, Emma, "September is passing and the saints are coming. I dread it[.] They have so many wants and are so all the while on the eve of explosion that I tremble." Of Jane Woolsey, he added, "I hope Miss W won't come with a tomahawk as she did last year. . . . I don't want to be with them at table. I think I'll eat only once a day so as to keep out of their way."[10] Such outbursts by Armstrong were rare, however, for he did not tolerate dissension within his "home." In the next few years, most of the "saints," including Miss Woolsey, were replaced.[11]

With his school established and his career determined, it was only logical for a man of that period and station to begin to seek a wife and start a family. It is not entirely clear, however, whether Samuel Armstrong first decided to follow convention and seek a spouse, or whether he fell in love and then pursued the expected course of courtship and marriage. The latter seems to be the case, given the abiding legend that all the lady teachers of Hampton Institute had crushes on the general. If this was true, there was no reason for Armstrong to venture as far from home as Stockbridge, Massachusetts, to find a willing bride.

Armstrong always had been a romantic, but he had seemed more in love with the idea of love than with any particular woman. He claimed that the "fair sex" mystified him. He and his best friend, Archie, exchanged numerous letters on the subject. "Be happy, but beware; steel your heart or 'twill be stolen," he cautioned Archie. "Love is awful—stronger than life—or death; angels be near—the battle thickens—the fire burns deep."[12]

After years of demonstrating his charm among numerous appreciative young ladies, Armstrong finally found his "treasure," Miss Emmeline (Emma) Dean Walker of Stockbridge, Massachusetts. Sam first met Emma in 1867 during one of his visits to Stockbridge, the hometown of his great-uncle, Reuben Chapman. Emma was an orphan. She had been born ten years after Samuel, the daughter of George and Harriet Walker. Her mother died two years later, in 1851, and her father soon thereafter became an invalid and was forced to live with his father until his death in 1860. As a consequence, Emma was raised by her father's younger sister and her husband, Frances Mary and Daniel R. Williams. During her youth, Emma attended the normal school of a Miss Brace in New Haven, Connecticut.[13] In background and upbringing, Emma was remarkably similar to Samuel's mother, Clarissa, and to the lady teachers he was hiring at Hampton. In his letters as suitor and new husband, Armstrong clearly thought of Emma as a partner in his endeavors, as well as his wife and the mother of his children. Tragically, Emma was able to fulfill the partner role only during the earliest years of their short marriage.

The courtship between Emma and Samuel was a passionate one, conducted mostly by mail but augmented by periodic visits by Samuel to Stockbridge. Sam's travels frequently took him to New England, where the couple took long buggy rides and visited mutual friends in villages near Stockbridge.[14] When separated, Sam and Emma exchanged letters almost daily.[15] Armstrong's duties with the Freedmen's Bureau and creation of the new normal school kept him in Hampton or on the road raising money. "I love you with a love that fills my being," Sam told her, but he cautioned her about what the future might hold. "I owe it to myself to mention this— that in the day of doubt and danger [Gettysburg], I felt an assurance that I was spared for other work—which I sought and have seemed to find— and that following duty though with weak and faltering step, I cannot leave my work—not even for love."[16]

Sam claimed to be overwhelmed at his good fortune in finding Emma.

Emma Dean Walker, the first Mrs. Samuel C. Armstrong, c. 1869. Courtesy of Hampton University Archives.

He professed doubts about his worthiness of her. "When I look at her, I say 'Angel'" he wrote Archie. "When I look at myself, I say 'Ass!'" His daily letters tried to inform Emma of the life he led and that she would soon share. "Don't you want to come?" he wrote her. " I know you do because you love me so. . . . I'll take up the song of all songs . . . 'Emma loves me' . . . that makes the world beautiful when before it was dreary and lonely. She is coming, my life, my fate." She was his "darling," his "own dearest Emma, far lovelier and purer than I have right to ask—more than I ever dared to ask for." He concluded, with his typical mixture of muted passion and religion, "I must go right to bed—but not without a kiss from you and a prayer for you."[17]

In November 1867, almost two years before their eventual wedding in October 1869, the smitten Armstrong proposed: "This will bear to you a simple, but probably surprising revelation. . . . I will not linger in useless words but at once let the sacred utterance of the heart be given and tell you that I love you with a love that fills my being." That said, Samuel rambled on for several paragraphs full of "useless words" before he managed: "Promise to be mine."[18] The proposal made, the appropriate Victorian rituals were then invoked: Sam wrote to Daniel Williams, Emma's uncle and guardian, asking permission to court his niece. Emma and Sam's mother, Clarissa, exchanged letters. In his own letter introducing Emma to Clarissa, Samuel's practicality seemed to weigh as heavily as his passion. He wrote of Emma, "She is young but very womanly, of unusual grace of manner and self possession, has a fine mind and disposition—and I am more and more convinced that we are suited and intended for each other." Ever the social climber, Armstrong could not resist adding, "The circle she moves in is one of the best in New England."[19]

Emma may have had reservations about the marriage she was agreeing to. Responding to one of her letters, Armstrong pleaded, "[B]anish from your heart all thought or fear lest you be unequal to all the needs of my life. Come and sit on my knee and promise you'll never indulge this doubt again."[20] Finally a wedding date, 13 October 1869, was set. In Hampton, Sam saw to renovations of "Mansion House" on the Hampton campus, so that he could accommodate his future bride. Although other teachers continued to share the building, a section of the house was separately enclosed to provide four small rooms facing the river. Armstrong furnished these with mementos from the Hawaiian Islands, including a Hawaiian flag.[21]

Emma, at home in Stockbridge, was left to handle all the wedding arrangements except for the minister who would conduct the service. Sam insisted that his old mentor, Mark Hopkins, do the honors. It was to be a small wedding, attended by only a few close friends. Some of Sam's previous romantic adventures in the area may have necessitated such a modest scale. In one cryptic note, he advised Emma, "On the whole I prefer that Mrs. Felton should not be invited: the hints of intimacy hardly permit it."[22]

The wedding in Stockbridge was a festive one, held in the home of Emma's aunt and uncle who had raised her. The new couple could afford only a brief time for a honeymoon. Within a few days, Armstrong and his bride left for Hampton.[23]

The early years of the marriage between Samuel and Emma were happy but enormously busy ones. Armstrong was immersed in his efforts to raise funds for Hampton. Emma quickly became pregnant and, after a difficult delivery, gave birth to their first child, Louise Hopkins Armstrong, in July 1870.[24] The new baby hardly slowed the pace of the young couple. In the summer months, Armstrong took his little family with him when he journeyed north to "beg," as he only half-jokingly called his efforts to solicit donations for Hampton.[25] Emma and the baby stayed in Stockbridge while Samuel made pleas for money to members of elite circles in New York, New Haven, and Boston. The arrangement allowed him to spend whole weeks at a time with his wife and daughter. When they were separated, Sam and Emma corresponded daily. Sam wrote loving letters, often augmented with cartoons to illustrate "Daddy's work" to his infant daughter. Emma, in turn, referred to her husband as "my busy boy."[26]

This almost idyllic period of Armstrong's first marriage was short-lived. In August 1872, after another difficult delivery, a second daughter, Edith Hull Armstrong, was born. Emma never fully recovered from this second pregnancy. She developed—in the opaque language of the Victorian era—"a severe nervous disorder" from which she suffered for the remainder of her life. In addition, Emma discovered that the Peninsula's climate, especially its hot, humid summers, was bad for her health. She suffered from problems with her eyesight and respiratory system. As a result, Emma began to spend more and more time in Stockbridge or visiting other relatives in the North. Often when she was in Hampton, Samuel was away raising money.[27]

Ironically, it was Samuel's health that first caused concern in the mid-1870s. His hectic travel began to take its toll. Emma confided to her friend Mary Anna Longstreth, "I sometimes feel a little troubled about him. . . . At times I fear he will break down completely, but when he rallies from these occasional attacks of exhaustion, he seems hearty and like himself again. It is impossible for a man of his temperament, impelled constantly by a strong nervous energy, to do things moderately. He must work in his own way, and we must make up our minds to the consequences. He is quite unconscious of being imprudent until there comes a sudden check; then he makes as many resolutions as anybody else."[28]

These brief bouts with ill health would slow the general's pace momentarily. There were also occasional happy and leisurely times at Mansion House. After the birth of Edith, Mansion House once again was renovated, and the remaining teachers moved to newly completed Virginia Hall. All of the Armstrongs' rooms now were on the first floor, to spare a weakened Emma from climbing stairs. The upper story was made over for guest rooms; these were in frequent use, due to the stream of northern visitors who came to view Armstrong's "experiment." The new family parlor was furnished by Mary Longstreth with small chairs and a table for the little girls, larger furniture for the parents, and a chaise lounge for the increasingly unwell Emma.[29]

The Armstrong family loved the warm fall days of Virginia's Peninsula. Miss Mackie described one such occasion at Mansion House with "General Armstrong . . . lying on the grass down by the edge of the creek, his wife . . . sitting beside him. . . . [The] little ones, of course they cannot be still, . . . making constant journeys between the house and the group on the grass. . . . It is such a pleasure to see the Gen[eral] enjoying his family once again here. He always does all that any mortal could do in the way of his work; few people spend less idle moments than he. . . . It certainly does go a great way toward resting one to sit down at night with those you love."[30]

These peaceful interludes in the Armstrongs' family life became increasingly rare after 1874. The general remained driven in his effort to make the institute self-sufficient and debt-free. Emma, still weakened by her second childbirth and now encumbered by two babies, no longer could travel with Samuel on promotional tours. Armstrong continued to think of his spouse as a partner in his work as well as in marriage. When he was away, he often would include, in his otherwise affectionate letters, detailed instructions for her to convey to the institute staff and advice on how to manage the diverse personalities within it.[31]

Armstrong family portrait, c. 1874: standing, rear: Samuel Chapman Armstrong; seated, from left: Edith Armstrong (Sam and Emma's second child), William Armstrong (Sam's brother), Mrs. William Armstrong, Louise Armstrong (Sam and Emma's first child), Emma W. Armstrong, and, looking away, Emma's unnamed nurse. Courtesy of Hampton University Archives.

Increasingly, however, Emma was unequal to such tasks. She was able to spend the winter of 1874–75 at Hampton with her family, but her health continued to decline. She was forced to spend long periods of time seeking medical treatment for her various ailments. In the fall of 1875, she underwent "electric and Hydropathic" treatments in Somerville, Massachusetts, for her nervous condition. Her eyesight continued to deteriorate, and she became unable to write. In January 1876, she began to cough up blood. Increasingly, General Armstrong found it necessary to juggle his travels so as to spend as much time as possible with his ailing wife.[32]

There were a few brief periods of recovery, as in May 1875, when Emma was able to host a reception for the senior class; and in May 1877, when she entertained the wife of President Rutherford B. Hayes during Commencement. But in the fall of that year, a Philadelphia physician pronounced that one of Emma's lungs was "entirely useless." He ordered that Emma seek recovery in a warmer climate. Arrangements were made for her to spend the winter in Thomasville, Georgia, and later in Aiken, South Carolina. She was accompanied to Georgia by the general and by Clara Fields, one of the teachers at the institute.[33]

Emma's illness brought Hampton's "family" closer together. The lady teachers, of course, were concerned about the worry General Armstrong felt, but they truly embraced Emma in her decline. There always had been warmth between the teachers and the general's wife, but there also had been some distance. She was deferred to as an extension of her husband; she always had been "Mrs. Armstrong," even "Mrs. General Armstrong." In Emma's final months, the nomenclature did not change, but actions did. The lady teachers devoted themselves to Emma's comfort whenever she was on campus. They took turns staying with her during her sojourn in Georgia and South Carolina. Clara Fields served as her companion and secretary during the winter of 1878. When Miss Fields had to leave, the wife of the institute's treasurer, J. F. B. Marshall, replaced her.[34]

Throughout the winter, Armstrong visited Emma as often as he could, sometimes combining his trips with tours of nearby black schools. This attention was deemed insufficient by some of Emma's fiercely protective women friends. Mary Anna Longstreth chastised the general for neglect of his wife and for his own overwork. "How can [one] not see his wife in her very delicate state of health for four months!?"[35] In fact, Armstrong was nearly distraught because of Emma's illness. He seems to have thrown himself even more energetically into his work as his only solace. Mrs. Marshall observed, "The general will feel that the sunshine has all gone out of his life when she goes; but . . . he will find at least occupation for his busy brain and hands in the great work he has undertaken and that is a blessing. . . . But how his heart will hunger and thirst for the presence of his beloved wife no one will know."[36]

Emma returned to Hampton for the last time in May 1878. Although she was somewhat improved, it was clear that she had become a permanent invalid. Her "nervous stress" had become so severe that she could not abide the hustle and bustle of Mansion House. She and Samuel moved to an isolated cottage on the campus, where she was attended constantly by a nurse. Her daughters were permitted to visit her only a few hours a day. Even watching them play exhausted Emma.[37]

Once back in Hampton, Emma almost immediately contracted pneumonia. It was clear that she could not endure the festive turmoil of the institute's tenth anniversary celebration in late May. She left for Philadelphia on 21 May. There her condition continued to decline. She was moved to Stockbridge and later to Lenox, Massachusetts, to stay with relatives. She was bedridden, unable to read or write, frequently incontinent and in pain.[38]

Samuel Armstrong managed to spend most of the summer at his wife's bedside. He was devastated by her illness and reconciled to her impending death. He wrote to Mary Longstreth, "It is inexpressibly sweet to be with Emma these days. . . . She never seemed so rare and pure and lovely a woman. . . . 'Thy will be done' is the great lesson of life, and is hard for our rebellious hearts to learn." Sam faulted himself as a husband: "I realize more and more the depth of her character and the strength of her heart. . . . I feel so unworthy of her. She has needed a tenderer care than mine."[39] On 26 September 1878, Samuel was forced to leave Emma to oversee the opening of the institute. He planned to return to her by 13 October, their ninth anniversary. He never saw her alive again.

Upon his arrival in Hampton, Armstrong learned of a new crisis. The institute had been given Wildwood, a plantation in New Bern, North Carolina. The manager there had lost two daughters to malaria and was himself gravely ill. He had lost the will to live; his wife pleaded with Armstrong to come and intercede. After telegraphing the family in Stockbridge and being assured that Emma's condition was stable, Armstrong rushed to New Bern and successfully persuaded the manager to rise from his depression and get on with life. As he hurried back to Hampton, Armstrong received a wire that, at eleven P.M. on 10 October, Emma had died. Nurse Reinertsen reported her last words as: "My dear Sam! So I shall not see you once more; poor boy, how sorry you will be!" Armstrong rationalized his absence as best he could. "I was in the right place," he argued. "Never was I so greeted by the helpless and afflicted. An unusual life and force filled me that day. . . . Emma would have wished me to be there. I know her heart."[40]

On 16 October, three days after what would have been their anniversary, Samuel Chapman Armstrong stood at his wife's grave, accompanied by his older daughter, Louise, and family members. His mind wandered back to a similar scene sixteen years earlier in faraway Hawaii, when he had buried his father; and to a more recent interment there in the Armstrong family plot. His brother, Richard Baxter, who had helped oversee the construction of Virginia Hall, had died in California in 1871 and had been buried beside their father. It seemed to Samuel that too many of those he loved had died.[41]

Samuel returned almost immediately to Hampton, accompanied by his daughter Louise. His younger daughter, Edith, sick with pneumonia, remained in Massachusetts. He spent Christmas with both daughters a few months later in Stockbridge, and the girls lived with him the following spring at Hampton. But Armstrong's pace and frequent travel left him little time to be a parent. In the years that followed, his daughters would be raised largely by their relatives in Massachusetts. Samuel mounted a portrait of Emma on his bedroom wall in Mansion House. "I see Emma's sweet face as soon as I open my eyes in the morning. . . . Friends are helping. . . . All is well here. A sweet, pure presence and influence seems to pervade the place."[42]

Saddened by the loss of his wife and perhaps chastened by his failure to devote time to her, Armstrong did not remarry until 1890. By then, his own health was failing, and his second wife, Mary Alice Ford, often served as his nurse as well as his spouse. In the interim, Hampton Institute, its faculty and students, were Armstrong's home and family.

9

"EDUCATION FOR LIFE"

Early Years of Hampton Institute, 1868–1878

Of course it cannot pay in a money way, but it will pay in a moral way! . . . It is the only way to make them Christians.

—*Samuel Chapman Armstrong*

When Samuel Chapman Armstrong returned to Hampton from Emma's funeral in the fall of 1878, he must have felt a befuddling combination of sorrow and joy. Behind him, in Massachusetts, was the grave of his young wife, to whom he had dedicated his life and work but who had proven too frail to stay with him as he pursued his course. In contrast, ahead of him, as he traveled westward from the Fort Monroe docks, were the towers of Virginia Hall (even at the time of this writing, one of the Peninsula's most distinguished Victorian buildings), Academic Hall, and Mansion House, home to his family and the institute's many guests. As he drew closer, he could see the foundations for the Wigwam and Winona Lodge for Indian students, and the new industrial building for female students. Off in the distance was the sawmill; surrounding him as he entered the campus were the increasingly productive fields of grain and truck crops his students were growing. There were now Native American students, as well as blacks, nurturing all these enterprises. Most important, waiting at Hampton's gates were his "children"—colleagues and students who depended upon him in much the way many Hawaiians had depended upon his father.

Once he was on campus, however, perhaps the differences between him and his father emerged more starkly. The students faded away to take up their strict regimen in the dormitories. The faculty also respectfully withdrew, and Samuel entered his empty apartment, accompanied only by his older daughter, Louise. It was a place very different from the abode full of loving relatives and children who had returned to "Stone House" in Hawaii after the burial of Richard Armstrong.

Hampton Institute cadets stand in review in front of Mansion House, c. 1880. Courtesy of Hampton University Archives.

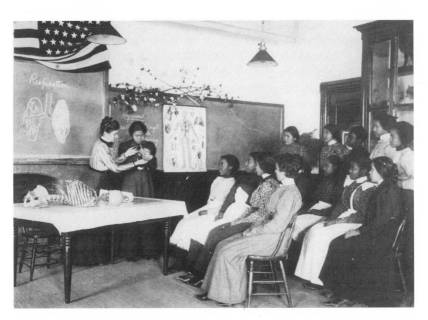

Girls' science class at Hampton Institute, c. 1890. Courtesy of Hampton University Archives.

Hampton Institute Waterfront c. 1890. A view from the river. Mansion House is in the center, Virginia Hall is on the left, and the new chapel is on the right. Courtesy of Hampton University Archives.

Nonetheless, Samuel Chapman Armstrong had come home to the little world he had made into his own mission station. Despite the anguish in his personal life, Armstrong between 1868 and 1878 had created a remarkable academic enterprise. The pioneering years of any venture often are the most important and exhilarating. This certainly was the case with Hampton Institute. In the Hampton school, Samuel Chapman Armstrong truly had found his niche. His enthusiasm and energy were infectious. Students flocked to Hampton; benefactors began to shower it with funds. An efficient and effective blending of academic and industrial education evolved.

There was much progress but too little reflection and evaluation. General Armstrong's tendency simply to "go ahead" began to betray him. Once the philosophy and structure of his institute were in place, Armstrong gave little thought to major reappraisals. He fine-tuned, he expanded his student body, but he never reconsidered his first principles. Nor did he respond to the changing circumstances of blacks in the American South. In Hampton's first decade, however, such reassessment seemed unnecessary. Hampton was a demonstrable success.

When Hampton Institute opened its doors in 1868, applicant demand proved that the need for advanced schooling was felt widely among both black and white southerners. The new southern racial order had not yet solidified; for some whites, integration still was conceivable. Officially, the institute was open to all races, and many whites as well as blacks initially showed interest in it. One white father wrote, "I felt that God in his providence had opened a way for me to educate my children. . . . My son will soon be eighteen years old; a fine looking strong and healthy lad, but very backward in his studies. . . . He has no bad or vicious habits that I know of. . . . How large a place where your school is and is it free from temptations of the young[?] . . . How large a share of the school will probably be white?" Evidently, in 1868, not all white Virginians were yet imbued with the belief that the races had to be educated separately.[1] In fact, however, the only white young people to attend Hampton during its early years were relatives or offspring of Hampton's white teachers.

More typical of early applicants was the son of a black minister recommended by a white man, E. F. W. Baker, from Dorchester, Massachusetts. Thinking that he was paying a compliment, Baker said of the father: "No one would think he was a colored man from his *traits* of character!" Of the candidate, Samuel Ford, he added, "A good brain and so young[,] Samuel seems to come of a good stock[,] and education may develop a fine, useful man. Sam is right musical, and an earnest intelligent Christian. . . . he is industrious but very poor, . . . he has been a member of the church for two years."[2] Other candidates for admission were like the children of P. Henkel, a white missionary to Gabon who had married an African woman and now sought a place to educate his children.[3]

A significant portion of the early student body were the offspring of the "contraband" of wartime Hampton. Not all their parents were thrilled with Hampton's industrial education design. William Roscoe Davis, a former slave, wartime fundraiser for the AMA, and pastor of the black Baptist church in Churchill, scoffed, "If Negroes don't get any better education than Armstrong is giving them, [then] they may as well have stayed in slavery!" Nevertheless, he sent his children to Hampton; and one of his grandsons, in the twentieth century, served as longtime treasurer of Hampton. Another, Arthur, became a prominent scholar of black literature.[4]

In those pioneering years, Hampton students were to be "of sound health, good character, age not less than fourteen or over twenty-five, ability to read and write intelligently; knowledge of arithmetic through long division; [have] intention to remain through the whole course of three years and to become a teacher."[5] Most of Hampton's early students were like the young Booker T. Washington, who simply arrived at Hampton's gates and sought acceptance. He later would claim that his admission examination was how well he swept and dusted classrooms.[6]

Some supplicants seeking a Hampton education were so pliant that they would surrender their identities for admission. One young man presented himself as "Robert Russell Morton." The northern teacher who recorded his registration was baffled by the boy's southern accent. She heard and wrote down "Robert *Russa Moton.*" And that was what the second most prominent graduate of early Hampton, and the second principal of Tuskegee, came to be called for the rest of his life. It was an innocent mistake, but one illustrative of the power Hampton teachers could exert over hapless students.[7]

The Hampton Institute entered by those first students was a far cry from the handsome buildings and grounds that students only a generation later would enjoy. The natural beauty of its waterfront location was obscured by the remnants of wartime devastation. It consisted of only the old Wood Farm plantation mansion, a few barns remaining from the antebellum era, portions of the Chesapeake Female Seminary buildings, and the barracks of the wartime military hospital. In between were mud flats, trod over for three years by the Union soldiers stationed there. Female students were housed in the seminary dormitories, the men in the old barracks. As the number of students increased, many of the men, including young Booker T. Washington, were reduced to sleeping in tents even in the middle of winter. Nevertheless, their morale was reported to be high, primarily because of Armstrong's dedication to making that the case. He would visit the tents of the young men early in the morning to cheer them up and get them energized for the long day ahead of them.[8]

Hampton's curriculum was demanding for those students with only the modest prior training Hampton anticipated. Armstrong cautioned that "the first year . . . is probationary; about twenty per cent are dropped, principally for weakness of character or for dullness of intellect. Most of these are benefited by their short course, and work for such is not considered as wasted."[9] The "good English course" Armstrong had designed entailed high school–level courses in language; mathematics; history of the United States and England, and "Universal History"; natural sciences; and other courses in civics, "moral science," Bible teaching, pedagogy, music, and business.[10]

During their three years—the "Junior," "Middle," and Senior"—students completed the equivalent of a high school education. In addition, students were encouraged to spend a year working in their home communities between the first and second years. Seniors were required to engage in practice teaching at the "Butler School" for black youngsters on Hampton's campus. The intention was that graduates would be able to "teach the rudiments of knowledge in the best manner." It was expected as well that graduates would be equipped to take a leadership role in the black communities that they served. Such additional duties included spreading the Hampton philosophy of hard work, frugality, temperance, and political abstinence. Graduates were expected to teach Sunday school and see to "the spread of Christian morality and *Bible* truth."[11]

Central to the success of this educational vision was manual labor. Graduates should be able to understand and perform the same kinds of labor as those they taught. "Our work is to civilize quite as much as to impart book-knowledge," Armstrong wrote. "Students' labor is generally faithful, but school boys' work is not equal to that of hired hands. It is, however, paid at the price of the latter, regardless of the demand for it, not only as needed stimulus but as necessary to their support." In these early days at Hampton, industrial education still was a means to a larger end. Armstrong explained, "Employment is given on the oft-stated plan of this Institute, that instruction is prior to production."[12]

In fact, Armstrong found it difficult to supply useful work for all of his students in the early years. Products like brooms, produced in the student shops, were not competitive on the open market. Useful and profitable work for women was especially hard to design. Female students were taught to sew and cook; some were assigned to the laundry room or to the truck garden outside the women's dormitory. Recognizing these realities, Armstrong began to admit students who would not work but who could pay their own fees.[13]

When Hampton first opened, students spent each morning on the school farm or in the kitchens and laundry; afternoons were devoted to classes and the evenings to study. Such a program quickly proved inadequate in terms of both mastery of academic skills and proficiency at mechanical or agricultural techniques. Armstrong was forced to confront the same fact encountered by earlier manual labor colleges in the North—i.e., student labor was terribly inefficient. School farms did not require the large numbers of students available at a particular time but needed the continuing attention that part-time labor could not provide. The northern schools simply abandoned the experiment. But for Armstrong, acquiring the discipline of labor was a transcendent goal. "Of course it cannot pay in a money way," he reiterated, "but it will pay in a moral way."[14]

In truth, Armstrong's resolution of his dilemma had far more to do with practicality than ideology or morality. What he did was expand Hampton's curriculum to include an "Agricultural Course," a "Commercial Course," and a "Mechanical Course." "Studies of the Normal Course" were "at discretion." By 1879, this alternative curriculum was articulated fully in what became known as the "Trade School Course" or "Night School." It was four years in length. During the first three of those years, boys spent forty-nine hours a week in "Shop Practice" and a total of sixteen hours in academic pursuits, along with eight hours in activities such as mechanical drawing, mechanics, gymnastics/drill, and trade discussion. Additionally, they spent twelve hours a week in "Supervised Study." Only in the fourth year did students spend the bulk of their time pursuing the Normal Course curriculum.[15]

Armstrong had found a way to make industrial education work. For a large portion of their Hampton experience, participants in the trade school were primarily workers, not students. A mitigating factor in what might appear to have been a system of exploitation, rather than education, was the success of Night School students. Hampton's records do not allow an

HAMPTON INSTITUTE CURRICULUM, C. 1880

Normal Course of Study for Full-Time Day Students:

LANGUAGE	MATHEMATICS	HISTORY	NATURAL SCIENCE	MISCELLANEOUS
Spelling Reading Sentence Making English Grammar Analysis Rhetoric	Mental Arithmetic Written Arithmetic Algebra Geometry	History of United States History of England — Readings from English Writers Universal History	Geography — Map Drawing Physical Geography Natural History Natural Philosophy Physiology Botany	Science of Civil Government Moral Science Bible Lessons Drill in Teaching Principles of Business Vocal Training Instrumental Music

Agricultural Course	Commercial Course	Mechanical Course
Studies of the Normal Course at discretion *Lectures on the following subjects:* Formation of Soils Rotation of Crops Management of Stock Fruit Culture Cultivation of Crops Drainage Market Gardening Meteorology Practical instruction in the routine of farming and market gardening	Studies of the Normal Course at discretion Instruction in Book–keeping, Single and Double Entry, in Business Letters, Contracts, Account of Sales, and other Business and Legal Papers, and in Commercial Law Each Student is required to keep his account current with the Institute in proper form	Studies of the Normal Course at discretion Practical instruction in the different varieties of Sewing Machines in use, in household industries, and in the following: Penmanship Free Hand Drawing Mechanical Drawing Printing

Course of Study by Year

CLASSES	MATHEMATICS	LANGUAGE	NATURAL SCIENCE	HISTORY
JUNIOR CLASS	Arithmetic, from Long Division to Percentage	Spelling Reading English Grammar Sentence Making	Geography, with Map Drawing Natural History	
MIDDLE CLASS	Arithmetic completely Book-keeping	Spelling Reading English Grammar, with Analysis of Sentences Composition	Physical Geography Natural Philosophy Outlines of Astronomy	History of United States
SENIOR CLASS	Algebra Geometry	Spelling Reading Rhetoric Composition	Physiology Botany	Universal History History of England, in connection with Readings from English Writers Science of Civil Government Moral Science

SOURCE: Compiled by author from Hampton catalogs, 1876–85.

exact tabulation of how many Night School students finished the Normal curriculum. School tradition has it that many did so and went on to earn places among Hampton's most successful alumni. Certainly the institute's most famous alumnus, Booker T. Washington, began his education in a prototype of what evolved into the Night School, and he later came back to oversee it.[16]

The manual labor program was only one of the methods by which Armstrong tried to make his students into "good Christians." His institute has been condemned for inculcating middle-class values while discouraging its students from aiming at middle-class attainments. The reality, however, is more complex.

Although most of Hampton's early teachers could be described, in modern parlance, as members of the middle or upper class, they did not conceive of themselves in such terms. They thought of themselves as "civilizers, missionaries, and teachers." Their role was to instill in their black students those values and forms of behavior that would enable them to advance in the "civilized white world." Like their leader, Samuel Chapman Armstrong, they seemed far more adept at finding fault with blacks than at criticizing the civilization they themselves represented and insisted blacks should emulate. Nonetheless, these teachers were sailing against the prevailing winds in postbellum America. They were striving to facilitate black survival and black progress during an era in which further black degradation or even extermination was entertained by a remarkable number of white Americans.[17]

Accordingly, Hampton's teachers instituted a rigid set of behavioral regulations and an almost draconian disciplinary system. Hampton students were regimented from "Rising Bell" at 5:15 A.M. until "Taps" or "Lights-out" at 9:30 P.M. Each half hour or hour of their day was programmed. After breakfast at 6 A.M., their rooms were inspected. They attended chapel twice daily. Male students were organized into a corps of cadets. Uniforms were required of all male students (a boon for many of them, who otherwise could not have afforded decent clothing). The men marched to classes, meals, and work details. Women were not so regimented but were supervised as closely by their teachers and matrons in the dormitories. Students were allowed only one afternoon a week to go into nearby Hampton village for necessities, a day carefully chosen so that it did not coincide with "market day," when local rowdies might be around to corrupt them.[18]

Although coeducation had been insisted upon by Armstrong, Hampton's system required strict sexual segregation except in the classroom. Women, of course, lived in accommodations separate from those of the men. Men and women did separate work. Once Virginia Hall was completed, students were able to eat in a common dining room, but women sat on one side, men on the other, and faculty and matrons in the middle.

Only on special occasions, such as Founders' Day and holidays, were male and female students allowed to come together for socials in the living-rooms of dormitory matrons; even then, they remained under the watchful eyes of the latter.[19] The institute's rules were so restrictive partly because of the youth of so many of the earliest students. The ages of accepted students gradually rose, but Hampton's rules remained the same.

Armstrong had said that the first year at Hampton was "probationary." Nonetheless, expulsion of a student meant that Hampton had failed. The young person would return to his or her community little better off than upon arrival, and return without the ability or inclination for racial improvement that Hampton intended to instill. To enforce its many rules, Hampton established an elaborate disciplinary system under which students accumulated demerits. Excessive demerits could result in fines (an impractical device, since most students had no money); exile to the almost primitive conditions on the school farm at Shellbanks, several miles from the campus; or incarceration in the campus guardhouse.

A campus "jail" for recalcitrant students may be inconceivable in modern collegiate education. But Hampton was not a college, nor were its early students like those who attended colleges even in that day. Washington and Moton were not atypical of Hampton students in their poverty, but a significant number of their colleagues had considerably less self-discipline than those two model pupils.

The guardhouse was established as a last resort short of expulsion for the most troublesome students. It was the product of Armstrong's military background; he had, after all, organized the male students into a quasi-military "corps of cadets." Only men were confined there. Its existence also reflected Armstrong's determination to "save" as many of the black masses as he could. So the guardhouse was, in a sense, *in loco parentis* carried to an extreme. It was an extralegal means of incarceration carried out by private parties who presumed the right to intrude in the lives of free black men and women in ways that never would have been tolerated among free white people. It was, however, also a means of protecting Hampton students from the penalties they were likely to suffer if they were remanded to the local white civil courts.[20]

Early Hampton students were a feisty group. Most seriously sought further education, but not all had acquired the maturity that would make that goal possible. There was much bickering and sometimes actual fighting among the students. They stole from each other on occasion. The adjacent Soldiers' Home gave students access to liquor. Young women of the town encouraged the male students to do with them what they were forbidden to think of in relation to Hampton's female students. Two students were expelled in 1878 after being "corrupted by outside girls" at the "very gate" of the institute. Two others followed shortly thereafter, for peeking into the bathroom of the girls' dormitory.[21]

Some disciplinary problems were far more serious. In November 1885, Armstrong lamented that two students were incarcerated in the local jail, one for "cutting with a knife" and the other for "pure unadulterated badness."[22] Usually, however, even the most serious discipline problems were handled on campus. One such case involved a male student who systematically terrorized another, threatening to beat him up. Since he had taken no physical action, he was given demerits and threatened with expulsion. Finally, he attacked his antagonist with an ax in a classroom. The victim avoided serious injury only by hitting his attacker with a desk. The faculty disciplinary committee confined the ax-wielder to the guardhouse and found that the other student had merely acted in self-defense. The prisoner apparently conspired with some of his friends to break him out, and they were prevented from doing so only by a teacher who observed the conspirators acting in a suspicious manner in front of the guardhouse. The young prisoner finally was expelled, but his collaborators were merely given additional demerits.[23]

Expulsions did occur at Hampton, but Armstrong agonized over each one. "I expelled Carrie last eve at prayers so he has gone home hard as ever," the general told his wife. "God forgive me if I did wrong. I hated to take quite so much responsibility, too much like an execution."[24] In those early years of Hampton, Armstrong was the final arbiter on disciplinary matters and wrote almost all expulsion letters personally. Actually, there were usually two letters. The first, clearly designed to elicit remorse, went to the expelled student and set out his or her transgressions in detail. The second went to the student's parents. It was less specific about the student's problems or misbehavior. Most interesting about both sets of letters is that they—even the one to the young man in the ax-swinging incident—held out the possibility of readmission if the expelled student did well and "made something of themselves" during their enforced absence.[25]

Hampton's disciplinary procedures provoked the earliest extant protest letters, one from an alumnus and the other from a student group. J. M. Moody wrote to Armstrong to protest the fact that expulsion was the only punishment given to a girl thought to be guilty of setting fire to Academic Hall, which housed the main classrooms and men's dormitory. Moody felt she should have been turned over to local authorities and criminal charges brought against her. He argued that this leniency reflected badly on the institute and could not be justified. "Blacks should be taught to obey the law like all others," Moody grumbled.[26]

The student protest took an entirely different tack. In 1874, Armstrong created a "Senior Cottage" for male students, complete with its own student court to oversee disciplinary problems. When one student was expelled for smoking without the case coming before the student court, its members protested to Armstrong: "Sir: We as members of the Senior Cottage and its court feel that the case of D. F. Douglas was not carried to you in the proper form and that it was not by consent of the court but rather by a great abridgment of our rights, we therefore petition for said case for a legal trial. We feel that our rights should be respected as long as we are recognized as a court but we cannot think that our court has any authority where cases are wrested from us as at present."[27]

Twenty-two members of the student court, including a nineteen-year-old Booker T. Washington, signed the letter. Armstrong, always one to insist that rules be obeyed, admitted his error. Dennis Douglas was reinstated, graduated with his class, and was one of the Commencement speakers. Armstrong so respected those students who had reminded him of the rules that, within five years, he had hired five of them as staff members of the institute. Two of them, Booker T. Washington and Warren Logan, later became principal and treasurer, respectively, of Tuskegee Institute. A sixth, W. M. Reid, became one of the three curators of Hampton Institute, appointed by the governor of Virginia to oversee the school's use of state Land Grant funds.[28]

Despite its problems of poverty, overcrowding, and discipline, the early Hampton Institute was far from a joyless place. Teachers and students alike were dedicated to a most serious enterprise; nevertheless, in a reserved fashion, they found ways to have fun. Holidays and special occasions, such as the dedication of a new building, were times for celebration and socializing. Armstrong himself set the tone: "At Mansion House, on a Friday, there would be 'the frolic' at which teachers and neighbors would gather." Here Armstrong was "Peter Pan," the boy who never grew up. The general would insist upon rollicking and irreverent singing of hymns and popular songs. He continuously organized picnics and sailing parties on his little boat. It was, Robert Ogden's biographer claimed, that "golden period when all was hope and zest and risk; the splendor of pioneering; the covered and sometimes uncovered wagon."[29]

Nor were the institute teachers and students disconnected from "respectable" black elements of Hampton village. Staff and students regularly attended Sunday school at local black churches. Hampton staff members such as Booker T. Washington helped to organize community temperance societies. Students organized photography and folklore clubs to record the histories of the contraband residents of the village.[30]

As always, it was Samuel Armstrong who set the standard. Until a stroke prevented him from doing so, the general regularly rode through the black section of Hampton town, stopping periodically on the excuse of watering his horse. He would ask the residents at each stop two questions: Did they own the house they lived in, and were their children in school? If the answer to the first inquiry was negative, he instructed them on procedures for buying property, on where property might be for sale, and on how to save money for the purchase. If the answer to the second inquiry was also negative, Armstrong offered a more immediate solution. Taking any of the children who were of school age up on his horse, he delivered them to the Butler Freedmen's School on the institute campus. Many a black Hampton youngster's first memory of school was arriving there aboard Armstrong's stallion. As noted earlier, Alice Bacon, head of the institute's nursing school, used a similar tactic to promote the school's new hospital.[31]

Everything about the institute, from its admission standards and curriculum to its manual labor requirements and disciplinary procedures, was a product of the personality and energy of its founder and principal, Samuel Chapman Armstrong. He oversaw everything, even when away from the school. He approved the payment of all bills, gave instructions on employment and policy, even wrote and forwarded expulsion letters by mail.[32]

Armstrong left little to chance. He actively solicited support from prominent men in both North and South. He received approval from men like W. H. Ruffner, superintendent of public instruction in Virginia. He orchestrated a letter of support from famed abolitionist William Lloyd Garrison. He brought William Still, leader of the antebellum Underground Railroad, down to Hampton's Commencement in 1874. To spread Hampton's message more widely, Armstrong founded the *Southern Workman* in 1872. Its aims were to report on progress at Hampton, to spread the values and teachings of Hampton among southern blacks, and to solicit support from philanthropists in the North. The motto of the *Southern Workman,* "devoted to the industrious class," reflected Armstrong's antebellum conceptualization of the word "industry."

The general left no stone unturned in seeking subscriptions for the *Workman.* He offered a free picture to each member of a Hampton black church who subscribed, and he promised the minister a forty-cent rebate to the church for each member who paid the one-dollar subscription fee. In another instance, he wrote to the editors of the major northern college newspapers, proposing a swap of the *Southern Workman* for copies of their papers.[33]

Armstrong's intimate oversight of everything associated with Hampton was its greatest strength, but also a potential weakness. If Armstrong strayed from Hampton's original educational purposes, or if his overweening ambition began to divert his attention from his initial goal, Hampton Institute might begin to lose its focus and definition. The impetuous Armstrong was, after all, ever ready to embark upon another "grand adventure."

The first signs of this danger emerged early, albeit innocently. Armstrong's primary problem was Hampton Institute's status as an unendowed school for impoverished black youth. It cost far more to run than its students could pay. The only solution was to establish a network of benefactors who regularly would contribute to the school's survival. As will be seen later, Samuel Chapman Armstrong became an incredibly skilled and original educational promoter, but his first major venture in fundraising borrowed an idea from Hampton's sister AMA school, Fisk University in Nashville.

Armstrong created a choral group, "The Hampton Singers," modeled after Fisk's successful "Jubilee Choir." Through concerts in major cities, primarily in the Northeast, the choir sought money to erect a permanent women's dormitory at Hampton. The effort proved most successful. The problem was that Armstrong devoted an inordinate amount of his time to the "Singers" campaign. Administration and teaching at Hampton were delegated to his staff.

Armstrong traveled about Virginia with his music director, Thomas Fenner, searching for talented singers in the fields and in the tobacco factories of Richmond. "Yesterday we found in one of the tobacco factories[,] a wonderfully rich soprano voice—a Delia Smith—very dark—plain: rolling up tobacco in a dirty dress," the general wrote his wife. "She has the best voice yet found." He also discovered a man named Mills who was "the finest African tenor I ever heard—soft notes and strong. He is a treasure. I have hopes of getting him."[34] It was only a small sign, one to which General Armstrong apparently gave no thought. Nevertheless, it was a disturbing precedent. He was recruiting these young people not because of their academic ability, not because they wanted to be teachers, but because they could sing; they could raise money for Hampton.

Armstrong joined the "Singers" on their northern tour. Here the general was truly in his element, socializing and soliciting support from members of the northeastern elite whom he considered his peers. The tour was a grand success. The group received rave reviews in Troy, Rochester, and New York City. It did not fare quite as well in Boston, apparently because the concert followed a disastrous 1872 fire in that city, and philanthropists were giving their money to a cause closer to home.[35] The tour continued on through Philadelphia and reached its climax as the "Singers" performed in the Capitol Rotunda and before President Ulysses S. Grant on the White House steps. Later Armstrong was received by the president, to whom he presented a needle and thread. The two Union veterans sat on the steps, mending socks and trading war stories![36]

By 1879, Hampton Institute was a going concern. It had over 20 teachers and department directors, and 339 black students, 80 of whom were women, and 63 Indian students, 18 of whom were women. The Normal School curriculum was functioning at full capacity. The Industrial Department had grown to include a Printing Office, as well as Knitting, Girl's Industrial, and Tailoring departments. A Sawmill and a Woodworking Department also had been added.[37]

The previous spring, Armstrong's great coup had been getting President and Mrs. Rutherford B. Hayes to come for the institute's tenth anniversary celebration and its Commencement ceremonies. Reflecting upon Armstrong's efforts at Hampton, Hayes recorded in his diary, "[The] freedmen and women . . . need something more than the learning of the schoolhouse. Illiteracy must be overcome. But industry, self-reliance, self-control, economy, thrift—the virtues Dr. Franklin taught so well—are of still greater importance."[38] The proselytizing of those "virtues" and the conservative cast of Hampton's vision for blacks were clearly manifest in that year's student speeches, which included "Homes for Our People" and "The Dangers of Universal Suffrage." The commitment to spread Hampton's philosophy and methods was reflected in addresses on "The Present Conditions in the West Indies" and "Who Are Needed in Africa?" The student debate, presented for guests and graduates, likewise reflected Hampton's basic purpose. It was entitled "How Can We Do [the] Most Good for Our People?—As Farmers, Ministers, or Teachers?"[39]

Another assembly during the 1878 Commencement celebrations forewarned of problems Hampton would encounter as its black constituency became more sophisticated. The new alumni association met, and some members expressed dissatisfaction with the institute's curriculum. Some argued that Latin and Greek should be added to the course offerings. Others protested the strict regimentation of students at the school. According to one of Armstrong's most avid supporters, Mary Anna Longstreth, the general handled the criticisms with "forbearance and magnanimity." "With perfect coolness and kindness," Longstreth reported, "he told the alumni that he was pleased with their frankness, wish[ed] them to mention every grievance, and explained to them the reasons for the course he pursued. They saw their error, and next morning made a handsome apology."[40] As usual, Armstrong managed to diffuse criticism, but the incident clearly illustrated that at least some of Hampton's graduates were aspiring to a more advanced education than the institute offered and were in no mood to wait for it until the "25th Century," as the general jokingly had suggested to his friend Archie Hopkins.[41]

Successful Hampton alumni were not alone in their criticism of Hampton's direction. Other educated blacks also began to complain about the vocational focus of the institute. In 1876, John Wesley Cromwell, a black journalist from Alexandria, Virginia, complained that blacks were not allowed on the stage at Hampton's Commencement that year. In fact, a black member of the Board of Curators and the student speakers were on the platform.[42] More damning criticism came from Bishop Henry Turner, the prominent advocate of black rights. In 1878, he decried the absence of higher-level courses in "algebra, geometry, higher mathematics, Greek, Latin and Science." He also complained of the rudeness of the white teachers he encountered.[43] The plain-talking Turner was in error about the curriculum in mathematics, but it is quite likely that Hampton's missionary ladies were taken aback and spoke abruptly to a black man who approached them as an equal rather than treating them as his "betters."

Turner and Cromwell were not the only black critics of Hampton's educational program and faculty. The point these adversaries of Hampton overlooked was that they were not among the constituencies the institute and its principal sought to please. They wanted Hampton to be something

Principal Armstrong (and dog) with the class of Miss Cora Folsom, c. 1885. (Note that most students are wearing cadet uniforms.) Courtesy of Hampton University Archives.

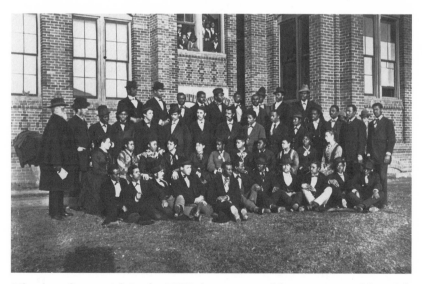

The class of 1875, with Booker T. Washington seated front row, second from left. Standing at left are Gen. John Marshall, treasurer; and Principal Armstrong. Courtesy of Hampton University Archives.

Robert Russa Moton and classmates, 1890. Courtesy of Hampton University Archives.

it emphatically said it did not intend to be. The black masses of Virginia and northern philanthropists found Hampton very much to their liking. The real problem was not the Hampton "model" per se, but the danger that Hampton would become the only model.

Just as he had done as Freedmen's Bureau superintendent, Armstrong ignored complaints from black leaders. He remained certain that he knew what was best for the black masses. The very success of Hampton, and the solicitude with which Armstrong was greeted in elite northeastern circles, began to seduce him away from his original goal of providing a school that responded to genuine black needs and facilitated black advancement. It was an unconscious evolution, but gradually the preservation and prosperity of Hampton Institute became the primary goal. The fundraising "cart" began to lead the educational "horse." The dangers were reflected in the growing strength of the trade school in relation to the normal school, as well as in the mounting criticism from some black leaders.

Ambition began to cloud Armstrong's original vision. Six years earlier, in a cryptic note to his wife, he had said playfully, "I am on the track of some more money—it will be necessary to prove that the darky is an Indian in order to get it: but I can easily do that you know. . . . Keep dark about it and send me your thoughts on the identity of the Indian and the darky—SAME THING, aren't they?"[44]

Armstrong was planning to incorporate more "backward races" into his student body. He set out to capture a portion of the money allocated for Indian education under America's new "Indian Peace Policy."

"EDUCATION FOR BACKWARD RACES"

Teaching Two Races

We expect the Indians next Monday. I want some Chinese and New Zealanders next.

—*Samuel Chapman Armstrong, 1878*

By 1878, Reconstruction was over, and the final conquest of the Western frontier was under way. At this juncture, the United States committed itself to two contradictory policies toward its most troublesome minorities: African Americans and Native Americans. American blacks had been thrown upon the mercy of their southern white brothers and sisters and were being pushed with ever-increasing vigor toward a status of permanent inferiority. For the Indian, whites had chosen an opposite destiny. Under the Peace Policy initiated by President Grant in 1868, the nation proposed moving the Native American toward civilization, citizenship, and assimilation. In this new policy, Samuel Armstrong saw an opportunity to expand the fame and financial security of his fledgling institute.

An indispensable component of the Peace Policy was educating the Indians to the white man's beliefs and customs. Indians were to learn English; they were "to give up the blanket," or their traditional dress; they were to abandon communal life for individually owned farms; they were to acquire the white man's habits of working hard, taking initiative, and practicing "Christian responsibility."[1]

There was much debate about how this educational process could best be achieved. Many whites, especially those operating religious missions for the Indians in the West, believed that schools should be created on the reservations, so as not to remove students too far from their own people and so that the educated Indian could have maximum impact on his parents and peers. Others argued that, in order to "civilize" the Indian, it was necessary to remove him entirely from the negative influences of family and tribe. Indian Commissioner Edgar M. Marble insisted that "the opportunity for teaching Indian children how to live as well as how to read and think is found only in the boarding school."[2] It was the advocates of this second viewpoint who, somewhat hesitantly, supported the creation of an Indian boarding school at Hampton Institute in 1878.[3]

At first glance, it may seem paradoxical that the federal government and advocates of its Peace Policy should support education of Indians at a school for the inferior black man. This apparent contradiction disappears, however, when the distinction between government rhetoric and popular attitudes is made clear. Americans were far from being of a single mind about the wisdom, or even the possibility, of Indian assimilation. Westerners wanted Indian land, not Indian neighbors. Easterners were more inclined to support the equality of Indians in the abstract, and in the West, than they were to welcome them in Boston, New York, or Philadelphia. In this sense, the northeastern elites approached African Americans and Native Americans in a consistent way. Members of the elite were solicitous of the well-being of such groups—as long as they remained far removed from their own doorsteps.

Samuel Armstrong already had established ties with this elite. He proposed that Hampton Institute also become a school for Indians. In truth, Hampton became an Indian school by default. It was prepared to act when other eastern schools were not. More important, Hampton had a proven record of training members of one "backward race" for useful participation in the dominant society. Hampton's principal and faculty were eager to try their methods on Native Americans as well.

It was under these circumstances that, in 1878, a most unusual effort in multiracial education began at Hampton Institute. During the thirty-four years of black and Indian education that followed, all the absurdities, hypocrisies, contradictions, and injustices inherent in American racial attitudes could be discovered at the institute and in the lives of its African American and Native American students. It is not that Hampton failed in its mission to civilize its students. Rather, American society refused to accept either blacks or Indians on the basis of equality, no matter how civilized they might be.[4]

As has been seen, Samuel Chapman Armstrong consciously designed Hampton Institute so that his black students would not be educated "out of sympathy with those they must teach and lead." He believed that black people's future lay in the South, and black graduates of Hampton were expected to accept both the limits and the possibilities that a society dominated by white southerners permitted.[5] Hampton alumni were to focus on the uplift of those less fortunate among their own race and not themselves intrude upon an unwelcoming white society. This strategy reflected the limited opportunities permitted to blacks in an abidingly racist South and an increasingly indifferent North.

Armstrong firmly believed that his philosophy at Hampton could be applied to all "backward races." Once his work with black students was well under way, he saw no reason why the school could not expand to serve other similar groups. But more than Armstrong's idealism and missionary zeal were involved here. Hampton was a school that lacked an endowment and was enormously expensive to operate. The general was perpetually in search of reliable sources of income. He thought he might find one in the national government's new Indian policies. "There's money in them, I tell you!" he wrote to Emma.[6]

Armstrong had been exploring the idea of an Indian education program at least since 1872. Not until six years after that did the Indian School at Hampton Institute actually begin to operate, however. The school opened despite widespread concern among Hampton trustees and advocates of Indian-assimilation policy; it operated under considerable criticism throughout its existence; and it ended amid claims that it was a failure and an insult to Indians. Whatever the justice of those charges, the story of Hampton's Indian school and of Armstrong's crucial role in its origin and operation is far more complicated than its critics or supporters understood.[7]

In 1874, some 150 Kiowa, Comanche, and Arapaho Indians who had participated in an uprising in the Indian Territory of Oklahoma were incarcerated at Fort Marion, Florida. Their warden was Lt. Richard Henry Pratt, a United States Army officer who had commanded black troops during the Civil War. The exiled Indians had been imprisoned without regard to actual degree of guilt in the uprising. Such injustice outraged Pratt. He barraged officials in Washington with letters begging for the release of those who were innocent and for some provision for "civilizing" the others. Finally, in 1877, the army and then Indian Commissioner E. A. Hayt agreed to the release of Pratt's charges and to their education in eastern schools if they desired it.[8]

Pratt immediately began seeking eastern schools which would accept his Indians. None could be found. Whatever the national policy of "Indian assimilation" was, eastern whites wanted no part of Pratt's partially tamed "savages." In desperation, Pratt turned to Hampton Institute.[9]

Samuel Armstrong leaped at the opportunity—and at the money potentially available for Indian education. Hampton's trustees were more reluctant, but, as always, Armstrong brought them around. Seventeen of Pratt's charges were accepted. On 14 April 1878, the prospective students arrived with Lieutenant Pratt and his family.[10] The general celebrated the event in a letter to his wife and two days later reported that "the Indians so far have scalped nobody." They had been given "food and religious instruction and set to hoeing onions." "[They] do as well as our darkies," Armstrong concluded.[11]

Pratt had taught his Indians to speak English, made them wear white men's clothes (which were called "citizen's dress"), and given them some religious instruction.[12] Armstrong continued this approach, adding classroom instruction in reading and writing, and assigning the Indians to manual labor tasks. Each Indian was given a black roommate, in order to aid in the acquisition of civilized manners. This process took some time, because blacks, too, had their prejudices against Indians; they feared that they might be attacked and scalped. It took Armstrong's persuasiveness and further proof that the Indians were disarmed and peaceable before enough black men volunteered to room with their new Indians classmates.[13]

Armstrong did not hesitate long, once the Indians arrived. He intended that Indian education at Hampton should become a permanent program, not an isolated, short-term venture. Moreover, he reaffirmed his commitment to coeducation, insisting that Native American women were as central as men to the envisioned civilizing experience.[14]

Armstrong had assiduously maintained contact with powerful men whom he knew from his army days, and these once again proved useful. The general arranged to have President Hayes and Secretary of the Interior Carl Schurz visit Hampton to observe the Indian education program. The ploy was effective. A government-financed program for 120 Native Americans a year at Hampton was approved. Hampton would receive $167 a year per student. Lieutenant Pratt was dispatched to go west to recruit more Indian students.[15]

This alliance between Pratt and Armstrong was short-lived. Pratt was a firm believer in the Indian's equality with the white man, and he objected to their education among "inferior" Negroes. A personal incompatibility also came into play. Both men were driving, aggressive, and ambitious, too much alike to work well together. Still, the brief alliance was fruitful. Armstrong got his Indians and a new, assured source of income; Pratt established the contacts with important government officials that enabled him to start the Carlisle Indian School in 1879.[16]

Native students could not be admitted to Hampton in the same manner as black students were. As has been seen, the latter often simply appeared at the school, were tested and interviewed, and, if qualified, were admitted on the spot to the Normal or Night schools. Indians, of course, could not come to Hampton; Pratt's journey to the West in search of Indian students was only the first of those undertaken by Hampton faculty each year while Indians attended the school.

Pratt toured primarily the Sioux (Lakota) agencies in Dakota. Most of these were supervised by the Protestant Episcopal church. The Episcopal church of that era never had been a stalwart friend of black people; and Pratt discovered that, at one agency, missionaries had discouraged students from going to a "colored institution." Pratt reported that he "found this prejudice more or less at several other agencies." This experience reinforced his conviction that Indians should be educated in a school of their own.[17]

Despite this problem, the quota of 40 students readily was filled. No accurate record was kept of the proportion of full-blooded Indians among the total Indian group at Hampton, but Pratt's first recruits included many Indians of white ancestry. At Fort Berthold, of 13 students, 4 were "half-breeds," and 2 were "quarter-breeds." Between 1878 and 1888, 301 of Hampton's 417 Indians students were Sioux. There were, in addition, some 56 Sac and Fox tribe members from the Indian Territory; 70 from Nebraska, mostly Omahas and Winnebagos; and a Pamunkey Indian from Virginia. In all, some seventeen tribal groups were represented at one time or another, including 3 Negro Seminoles who were ex-slaves.[18]

Indian students did not come "straight from the warpath" to Hampton Institute, but they were considerably less accustomed to white culture than their fellow black students. Most of them spoke little or no English upon their arrival. Conditions on their home reservations were changing rapidly, but most Native Americans still dressed in the traditional fashion, insisted on maintaining tribal institutions, and continued to hold their land communally. All of this irritated Indian agents, who were supposed to be helping their clients adjust to white culture. One, William Courtenay at Fort Berthold in the Dakota Territory, offered an apt description of what purported Indian "civilization" meant to white men in the field: "Indians are essentially conservative and cling to old customs and hate all changes. Therefore the government should force them to scatter out on farms, break up their tribal organization, dances, ceremonies, and tomfoolery; take from them their hundreds of useless ponies which afford them the means of indulging in their nomadic . . . habits, and give them cattle in exchange, and compel them to labor or accept the alternative of starvation."[19] Clearly, some intended that Native American "assimilation" be no less oppressive for the victim than "exclusion" was for the African American.

From the beginning it was apparent to Armstrong and his staff that the Indians could not be given the same education as was provided to the blacks at Hampton Institute. Most of the Native Americans were entirely unprepared for the standard Normal School program. A separate Indian School had to be established that taught basic language skills. As described by Helen Ludlow, Armstrong's alter ego and manager of the campus during his frequent absences, the first three years of the Indian School program concerned "oral training in English," with rudiments of writing. Only in the fourth year did students actually begin to study texts. History, mathematics, geography, and art also were included in the curriculum. The Indian students, she reported, had particular difficulty with mathematical concepts. On occasion, they also objected to the one-sided view of the nation's expansion in the West as portrayed in the standard American history texts.[20]

The Indian School program ran five years, at the end of which a student would be ready to enter the Normal program. But the government Indian

"Before" and "after" photographs of Indian students. Photos were used by Hampton publicists to demonstrate effects of "civilizing education." "Before" photograph recorded as November 1878. "After" photograph recorded as March 1880. Courtesy of Hampton University Archives.

scholarships allowed only three years' study for each student. Thus an Indian graduate usually returned to his reservation with only the most rudimentary knowledge of English, reading, writing, and arithmetic. The overwhelming majority of Indians went through this three-year program. Only ten to fifteen Indians a year were enrolled in the Normal program; these usually were supported by private charity rather than by government funds.[21]

Native American students, like the African American students at Hampton, were required to acquire manual as well as academic skills. Indians were assigned to the various shops along with the blacks. Regular Indian School students spent half the day in the classroom and the other half in a shop. A few Indians enrolled in the Night School and spent their full time in the trade departments. In 1884, Indian men were learning carpentry, tinsmithing, harness making, and painting. Together with the black girls, Indian women students were studying homemaking, sewing, cooking, and laundering. Greater experience with Indian graduates, however, demonstrated that opportunities for Indian employment in a specific trade were rare on the frontier. In 1887, the trade program was revamped. Indians studied in a "technical shop," in which they received a modest amount of training in a variety of trades.[22] As an aid in the pursuit of a trade upon return home, each Indian male was given a toolbox and tools when he left Hampton. The tools were paid for out of withheld wages that the students had earned during their time at Hampton.[23]

Samuel Armstrong's concept of the proper education for "backward races" had never been limited to the acquisition of academic and technical skills. Such skills always had been a means toward a more important end. "The difficulty with both races," he explained in 1880, "is not so much ignorance as weakness or deficiency of character; not lack of brains but of moral stamina. Both need drill throughout the range of living." To get that "drill," Indians, like Hampton's black students, lived a rigid, carefully supervised existence. Indians had to learn all the proper habits of "civilized" men, from how to make a bed to what clothes to wear. They also had to acquire the proper attitudes of respect for women— an area in which Hampton's northern white female teachers held Indian "braves" to be notoriously deficient.[24]

Armstrong began by giving each Indian a black roommate, by making Indian boys walk while Indian girls rode in wagons, and by holding up the behavior of the blacks as an example for the Indians to emulate. The difficulties were many. The black males had to convince their Indian roommates to sleep on top of, rather than underneath, their beds; and had to remind them to put on all their clothing before leaving the room. By using the formal and deferential way in which black men treated Indian girls as a model for Indian men, the school challenged the Indian concept of manliness and aggravated latent racial tensions between the races.[25]

These tensions soon forced the creation of separate living facilities for the Indians. The "Indian Cottage," later named "The Wigwam," was constructed for the boys and "Winona Lodge" ("Big Sister" in one of the Sioux languages) for the girls. Further separation was required in the Wigwam. The different branches of the Sioux and of other tribes did not always get along with one another, and there were great differences in the ages of the male students. In its original design, the building was divided into three parts, connected only by the sitting room of the resident matron.[26]

In each dormitory, a student janitor was appointed. Along with a teacher, he or she inspected each room daily. The Indian men were organized in separate companies of the school cadet corps and were inspected daily by student officers. As with black students, the process of teaching civilization continued into the evenings. Indian students attended their required study halls and participated in their own debate society, prayer meetings, temperance association, and social events at Winona Lodge. On special occasions, such as Founders' Day, they joined the black students in social affairs.[27]

Religion, of course, was an important civilizing ingredient. Indian students from Episcopal agencies were escorted to Saint John's Church in Hampton village. They participated in all church activities, including singing in the choir. Presbyterian or Congregational students attended the school chapel services. Catholics were escorted to mass at the Soldiers' Home adjacent to the Hampton campus.[28]

Unlike most African American students, Native American students suffered from many health problems. The Hampton climate, humid and warm, contrasted sharply with that of the western highlands from which most Indian students came. Most of the early students were described as suffering from "weak lungs." They frequently were plagued by scrofula, an early manifestation of tuberculosis, and many of them later contracted pneumonia and tuberculosis. Moreover, Indians had difficulty adjusting to the traditional southern diet provided for Hampton's black students; and it became necessary to provide a special Indian menu, including more fresh fruits and milk and replacing pork with beef. Special food and cooking requirements necessitated separate kitchen and dining facilities. Even these precautions were not entirely sufficient; of the 427 Indian students who attended Hampton between 1878 and 1888, 31 died. Another 111 had to be returned to their reservations because of poor health.[29]

Like the black students, Hampton's Indians sometimes broke school rules and required punishment. "They have quick tempers," Armstrong noted, and "a few have had bad dispositions."[30] But expulsion, "the all-sufficient, severest punishment" for recalcitrant black students, could not be used against the Indian. It would have meant sending the student back to the reservation without the benefit of civilization and perhaps with a greater inclination to "make trouble." (Not incidentally, it also would have meant loss of the government stipend for that student.) Indian students reputedly disliked being separated from their peers; thus, for them as for their black schoolmates, the common punishment for minor infractions was exile to the school farm at Shellbanks, five miles from campus. For more serious infractions by Indians, another guardhouse was established in the basement below the principal's office. It was an unlit room without furnishings. Although Armstrong was criticized severely for resorting to solitary confinement as a punishment for Indians, the room had the desired effect in eliciting confessions or reforming a student's behavior.[31]

With special discipline and separate classrooms, dormitories, dining facilities, and social activities, Hampton after 1878 was not a school for two races but rather two distinct schools, one for the black race and one for the red. Even the few Native Americans in the Normal School participated with their fellow Indians in out-of-class activities.[32]

The policy of separation evolved in part from the peculiar needs of the Indian students. More basic was the necessity of deferring to national attitudes toward blacks and Indians and to the prejudices existing on the campus itself. The African American and Native American students simply did not care much for each other's company. Black students claimed that they were more civilized than the Indians; the Indians retorted that they never had been slaves. In 1879, Armstrong prevailed upon his prize graduate, Booker T. Washington, to be the first graduate resident of the Wigwam. Washington was characteristically diplomatic, reflecting more upon the demands being made of the Indian students than upon the latter's responses to him. But in 1890, when R. R. Moton, another Hampton black graduate, became Wigwam supervisor, the Indian students protested. They petitioned for Moton's removal, arguing, "Many of the boys have spoken of disliking him here, not because they have any feelings against him personally but because they do not like to have a colored person over them." They pointed out that "colored boys" had no school officials resident in their dormitories and asked, "Why can't they trust us?"[33]

George L. Curtis, commandant of the cadet corps at the institute, glossed over the racial situation when he said, "There has been much pleasant intercourse, though little intimacy between them."[34] Helen Ludlow, who supervised the Indian School for a period, was more candid about student attitudes, and about the fears of Hampton's faculty, when she wrote in her first national publication on Indian education: "General social intercourse between the races of opposite sexes is limited and guarded. Trouble might come of it. . . . The effort is to build up self-respect and mutual respect. And we believe that education of the mind and heart tends to individual morality and race purity."[35]

Miss Ludlow emphatically reassured those who were concerned that the large black population of Hampton village would "contaminate" the school's Indians. Hampton's Negroes were "the most thrifty and industrious remnant of the 'contrabands.'" The school's holiday was set on Monday to avoid the

town's market day, "when there is more drinking and loafing." A former Indian student, Anna Dawson, wrote to add her reassurances. She was distressed
by "considerable and unfavorable talk concerning the Negroes and their
influence over the Indians at Hampton." She explained that Indians did not
"come into contact with the Negroes as most people suppose"; they had separate dormitories, dining rooms, and classrooms.[36]

As often was the case, what Hampton and Armstrong presented to
the contributing public was not *quite* the reality on or off campus. Indian
students, like their black peers, participated in community service programs
to assist black residents of Hampton village. Indian students participated
in biracial school sports teams, as well as mounting their own separate teams,
especially in men's basketball and football.[37]

Even Hampton's much celebrated "outing" system for Native American students had its parallel among black students. In this program, Indian
students (usually males) spent a summer or longer with a trusted white
family in the North. This program formalized Armstrong's continuing effort to connect his best black students with potential northern benefactors
and to enable students to earn additional money to support their education at Hampton. As will be seen, many of Armstrong's most successful
graduates of both races were participants in these northern employment and
acculturation experiments.[38]

One unique program was Hampton's inclusion of married Native American couples. Armstrong always had argued that "the family is the unit of civilization." The married-student experiment lasted only a brief time, from 1882
to 1894. It was, however, another example of how Armstrong incorporated
Native Americans into his overall philosophy. Neither age nor marital status
were central to his civilizing mission. If the goal of the group was accommodation to the priorities of the dominant society, ways had to be found to accomplish that task. Native Americans required appropriate role models. A
couple, educated at Hampton, possibly including offspring born at Hampton,
was exactly the unit that Armstrong envisioned for the Plains Indian.[39]

Hampton presented itself to potential public and private donors as a
school for the civilization, not the amalgamation, of its two minority races.
It claimed that the basic contact in the institute was an educational one
between white faculty and one of the two races, not between the two races
themselves. Though this was not an entirely candid portrayal, it was the
most expedient way to extract needed funds from a society with irrational
and conflicted perceptions about nonwhite people.

In truth, the segregation of African American and Native American
students was not merely an accommodation to reported hostilities between
the two nonwhite groups. Hampton's white faculty conceived of the two
races as being different and felt that these differences required separate
handling of each group.

The essential difference, of course, was that Indians could be candidates for amalgamation with the white race, while blacks could not. This did not make the aim of Hampton's education for Indians entirely different. The institute, Armstrong explained, was "to give the Negro and Indian races what they need most . . . a class of intelligent, earnest teachers, practical workers and leaders."[40] But, unlike their black counterparts, the Indian leaders had a specific goal to which they were to lead their race—amalgamation with the white race. The Indians, Helen Ludlow said straightforwardly, "like our foreign elements . . . are being absorbed into our common population. The Indian problem is likely to disappear in the next century for want of a distinguishable Indian race."[41] No one at Hampton ever postulated such a future for the black race.

This separate destiny for the Indian required that safeguards be established against romances between the black and Indian students. Racial purity apparently meant the absence of any taint of Negro blood in superior red and white people.[42] Miss Ludlow could speak glowingly of two of her "star" Indian girls who had married white men. There is no record that any marriages between black and white occurred; but if they had, Hampton's faculty certainly would not have praised the nuptials.[43]

Martha Waldron, the school physician, offered her own "scientific" evidence for the benefits of Indian-white amalgamation and the evils of Negro-white amalgamation. "The full-blood Indians have less endurance than the half or mixed bloods," she observed. "This is the reverse of the condition seen in the Negro race, in which pure bloods are less subject to phythisis [*sic*] than mulattoes and light shades."[44] Admittedly, Negroes had more physical stamina than Indians, "though much less than the Anglo-Saxon." On the other hand, the Indian race, "with all its weakness and wildness, possesses traits which would make no unworthy addition to the sum of American civilization."[45] A similar vision of the black future in America apparently was inconceivable for many of the institute's white teachers.

Armstrong, as principal of the institute, was particularly vocal in attempting to define the differences between African Americans and Native Americans. He had no question "as to the Indian's mind." It was "observing, shrewd, quick and persistent in directions where it had been trained for generations." The failures of Indian students, he argued, were "to be found not from innate causes but from surrounding influences."[46] Here Armstrong was referring to both the traditional culture of the Indian tribe and the failings of white culture on the frontier as those "surrounding influences." Strikingly, he had never been willing to condemn the failings of the white culture of the South in regard to blacks' problems.

Armstrong's motive in these arguments is transparent. The survival of the institute depended upon maintaining the goodwill of southern whites, so they could not be faulted for having enslaved and demeaned

African Americans. The survival of the Indian program in 1883 was relatively independent of the attitudes of western whites, so there was no worry about offending them. The program was dependent, however, upon northern benefactors who were temporarily enamored of Native Americans and favored their complete assimilation into white society; so it remained necessary to demonstrate that the Indians were assimilable.

These efforts to build up the Indian by comparison with the black were threatened by the indisputable fact that African Americans were more fully acculturated to white society than were Native Americans. In attempting to circumvent this problem, Armstrong carried his arguments to their illogical extreme: "The submissive Negro . . . has not thrown a pauper upon the nation. Of the proud Indians, about one-half are in the national poorhouse. . . . The superior personality of the latter is in the body whose habits are opposed to industry and whose weakness unfits him so far for competition with any other people. . . . [T]he severe discipline of slavery strengthened a weak race. Professed friendship for a strong one has weakened it."[47] Somehow the Indian was stronger than the black, even though all evidence seemed to prove the opposite. In addition, it was permissible to blame white men for the Indian's plight. Far from being guilty for the black man's condition, however, white men, by making the Negroes slaves, actually had helped them.[48]

The fatuousness of Armstrong's comparisons of Indians and blacks is an excellent illustration of his role as politicized educator. National policy makers had decided—at least for the moment—that the Indian was a potential equal but that the black would not be for generations. Given that premise, it was necessary to explain away the contradictory reality of black people's greater degree of acculturation. Having done so, Armstrong went one illogical step further. The education of blacks and Indians together could be a great advantage to both races. Blacks would serve as models for Indians. Evidently, once Indians had caught up with the Negro, they could strike out on their own and participate in white society.[49]

This reasoning many whites understandably had difficulty accepting. Why not let whites provide the model for Indian civilization? Armstrong had a ready answer. The "sentimentalists" of a New England–style college would fill the Indian with "useless knowledge." The Indian needed to be educated to aid his brethren back on the reservation. For the Indian as well as the black, civilization evolved in stages. At his present stage, the Indian had to learn to live simply, to acquire the rudiments of knowledge, to study the Bible, and to learn to obey orders. Hampton Institute could provide this training better than any white school.[50] Less openly stated, but equally important to the cause of racial coeducation at Hampton, was Armstrong's own ambition to "civilize" as many backward races as possible.

Not stated at all, but certainly of considerable importance, was the tremendous contribution that Indian education made to the fiscal and political security of the institute. The school was guaranteed an annual government subsidy of twenty thousand dollars for its 120 Indian students. In addition, wider sources of philanthropic support became available. Many people who had not the least concern for blacks would give for Indian education. In publications after 1878, Armstrong placed more emphasis on the education of Indians at Hampton than was merited by their numbers alone. Indian education brought many new contributions to the school coffers, and also secured greater fame and prestige for Hampton and its founder.[51]

Samuel Chapman Armstrong's defense of Indian education at Hampton did not convince everyone. Throughout its existence, the program came under intermittent attack. Some critics, particularly westerners, were opposed to the whole idea of Indian education, no matter where it took place.[52] Others, like Richard Pratt, were specifically opposed to Indian education at a school for blacks. The most serious attack came in 1888 from the Reverend T. S. Child, inspector for the Board of Indian Commissioners. Child rejected the argument that the education of Indians and Negroes together was beneficial for both races. Hampton was fine for Negroes but not for Indians. Child found the health problems of Hampton Indians severe, their diet inadequate, their careful regimentation into military companies unnecessary, and the guardroom used for confining errant students "a fearful place of punishment." The new technical shops for Indians, Child complained, prevented the development of competency in any trade, rather than preparing Indians for whatever jobs they might find on the reservation. The inspection report concluded, "It is a question whether it may not be wise and right that Hampton should devote itself entirely to the work for which it was founded—the education of the colored race—while the Indian is removed to some institution where he may have equal educational advantages at less serious risk of life and health."[53]

Armstrong's reply to this attack was lengthy and systematic. Indians at Hampton, he argued, were as healthy as those at the Carlisle Indian School. Most of those who died had been sick when they arrived. He presented testimony from the school physician and from a doctor in the village that the diet for Indians was entirely adequate and carefully formulated. Armstrong professed shock at Child's readiness to accept the Indian students' grievances at face value. "Indians," Armstrong explained, "are fickle, fertile in grievances, and often wish to change their work for no good reason." As for the guardroom, Armstrong presented evidence that the commissioner of Indian affairs had approved its use. The charge that Indians were only superficially trained in trades, Armstrong rejected flatly. Indians trained intensively in one trade, while they studied a wide variety of others in a more general fashion. Superficiality, Armstrong said pointedly, was a characteristic of the inspector's report, not of Hampton's training program.[54]

The general's defense was an able one, but his own cordial relations with the Board of Indian Commissioners, and particularly its chairman, Gen. Clinton Fisk, seem to have been the decisive factor. E. Whittlesey and Albert Smiley of the board visited Hampton and reviewed the complaints of Inspector Child. Their tour included a visit to the now-infamous guard-room. They had little defense against the charms of Samuel Armstrong; Child's recommendations were promptly rejected. In fact, it is unlikely that Child would have gone away so displeased with Hampton had Armstrong himself been on campus to act as his host. Smiley and Whittlesey wrote to the board that to close the Indian school at Hampton would be a "great calamity": "No other Indian school can show better results, no other has taken stronger hold of the people or done more to mold public sentiment in favor of Indian education."[55]

Armstrong won this particular battle over racial coeducation. But later, under principals who were less adroit educational politicians and publicists, Hampton was unable to justify educating a race that was preparing for assimilation in a school for a race that always would occupy a separate, inferior status. In 1912—a benchmark year in the resurgence of anti-black sentiment—pressure in Congress, particularly from representatives of Native American ancestry, forced the removal of the government subsidy and so brought about the demise of Hampton's Indian School. Indians, though in much smaller numbers, continued to attend the institute for another decade, supported by private charities.[56]

During Armstrong's lifetime, the Indian School at Hampton Institute was a financial and political success. It would be wrong, however, to suggest that these purely practical matters inspired Hampton's Indian program. Samuel Chapman Armstrong believed deeply in his proclaimed mission to facilitate the uplift of all "backward races." But in his enthusiasm, the ever-ambitious Armstrong neglected lessons from his own experience. He had designed his program for blacks at Hampton based upon two years' experience with black troops during the Civil War and three following years as Freedmen's Bureau agent in Hampton. In addition, he had borrowed unabashedly from his father's work in Hawaii. In other words, Hampton's original program was structured carefully to respond to realities that Armstrong himself knew intimately.

In contrast, the general initially tried to "graft" his Indian program onto the preexisting one for blacks. At the beginning, he knew nothing of the circumstances in which most Native Americans from the Plains lived. The Indian School format, at first, was "reactive" rather than "creative." It was the creature of government legislation, documents, and policies, not a response to the genuine needs of Native Americans in the place where they struggled to survive. That level of response was beyond Hampton's capacity—and indeed, as the continuing repression of Native Americans demonstrates, beyond the capacity of the nation as a whole.

There are positive aspects of Hampton's work with its Indian students. As will be seen in the following chapter, those Native Americans who came to the institute as well prepared as their black comrades achieved on an equal plane. Unfortunately, most were not so well prepared.

Equally important is the reality that Indian education at Hampton had costs that could not be perceived immediately. By incorporating a significant portion of students who were even less well prepared than its original ex-slave pupils, Hampton became even more wedded to its industrial education component. That aspect of Hampton's educational program originally had been conceived only as a means by which to facilitate the Normal School program and provide ancillary skills to its graduates, who would become teachers. The needs of Indian students dictated that industrial education would be given a more central role in the Hampton educational design.

In creating the Indian School, Samuel Chapman Armstrong became less and less an educational innovator and more and more an educational entrepreneur and publicist. He began to neglect questions about how the school should change in response to changes in black conditions in America and became and more concerned about how to expand his enterprise. One measure of the appropriateness of Armstrong's expansionist inclinations was the outcome for his students. Samuel Armstrong, above all else, was a missionary of nondenominational Protestantism and nineteenth-century America's version of capitalistic uplift. What became of his converts?

II

"GATHERED TO SCATTER"

Lives and Work of Hampton's Alumni

*I tell my girls that all good things have come to me that I
may pass them to others. General Armstrong always made
us feel that Hampton students "gathered to scatter."*

—*Mary Melvin, 1911*

Key measures of Samuel Chapman Armstrong's life and work should be the
fates of the Indian and African American students he educated, and how
they responded to their educational experiences. The views of Hampton
expressed by early alumni stand in striking contrast to evaluations of Hampton made by scholars later. The author of this book, like his predecessors
and peers, initially accepted the stereotype of the Hampton-Tuskegee system as producing black accommodationists who retarded the advancement
of black people for at least the remainder of the nineteenth century. Once
again, the evidence tells a more complex story.[1]

General Armstrong and his teachers at Hampton always considered their
efforts at the institute to be an "experiment." In 1878, Armstrong asked one of
his New England friends to recommend someone who could "correspond with,
and send reading matter to all . . . graduates during their teaching months."[2]
From that initiative evolved the institute's Department of Correspondence with
Graduates and Former Students. As documenters of this unique experiment,
Hampton's teachers became prodigious recordkeepers who tried to keep track
of their Indian and Negro graduates and former students. Periodically, these
records were published in the *Southern Workman* or in short bound volumes,
as testimony of Hampton's achievements.[3] Because these excerpts were in publications promoting the institute, they must be viewed with some skepticism.
However, the original records upon which they were based offer a revealing
picture of the impact that a Hampton education had on its students' and
alumni's lives. These documents still exist at Hampton University.[4] Data on
Indian and black former students and graduates were kept separately. Because

there were significant differences in the experiences of the two groups, they will be considered separately here.

To Samuel Chapman Armstrong, civilization was an incremental process that required generations and happened to races, although individual members of a race might achieve it sooner than others. In Armstrong's thinking, respectability was the most important characteristic of civilized men and women. He argued: "Respectability in a civilized society is in the air; it is a habit, we inherit it, it is the fashion, and it pays. Among savages, degradation is in the air and in the blood. . . . The civilized man is honest, not because it is good, but because it pays to be honest; but it took many generations to find it out. . . . Not till a race comprehends the practical bearing of integrity will it practice it."[5]

If the work of Hampton Institute is judged by this standard that Armstrong set, then the criticisms made after 1900 seem unfair. The problem did not lie in changing the values of Indian or black students while they were at Hampton. That was something Hampton's principal and teachers accomplished with remarkable efficiency. The dilemma was that most of late-nineteenth-century white America did not care whether Hampton graduates acquired integrity. Its prejudices remained entrenched, and any achievements graduates might make had to be realized within the narrow limitations established by white America.

This reality manifested itself most graphically with Hampton's Indian students. Thomas "Wildcat" Alford, a former student, wrote from his reservation that there were "a great many obstacles in the way of returned Indian students." The most formidable of these was the temptation to give way to "his natural propensities" toward Indian culture, which had been "dormant" while he was at Hampton. Work, Alford said, was the "great remedy" to this problem. Then he added, "Here we come to the worst feature of the case. There is not enough work for them [Hampton's Indian graduates] at the Agency or at home."[6]

Alford had identified the heart of the problem. Indian culture on the reservation remained so different from white society that even Hampton's avowed effort not to alienate the Indian from his people was insufficient. Armstrong and the Hampton teachers, who journeyed frequently to the reservations between 1879 and 1890 to evaluate their former students, complained of the same problems. Those who could find jobs with the reservation's Indian agent did well enough, but few had such opportunities. Usually, the Indian students had to make some accommodation with the tribal structure from which they had come. The problem was particularly severe for returning Indian women. They found themselves bound to marry the mate selected by their parents. He was usually a man without the "benefit" of a Hampton education and with little patience for ideas about the respect due women that Indian girls had been taught at Hampton.

Under such circumstances, the main criteria used to evaluate the Indian former students were whether they had "gone back to the blanket" and whether they had managed to stay aloof from other tribal customs. The record was mixed. Of those returnees who could be located, only 60 percent qualified for the classifications of "good" or "excellent." Of 460 returned Indian students, 143 were judged as "fair," "poor," or "bad." Three were "criminals against the law of the land."[7]

Whereas 90 percent of the school's black graduates taught school, only a small number of Indian graduates did so. The limited education they had received at Hampton left them unprepared to teach. Even those who had completed the Normal School found themselves handicapped. There were few openings for Indian-school teachers, especially for teachers who were themselves Indian.[8] The vast majority of Hampton's Indian male graduates became subsistence farmers. An overwhelming majority of the women became the wives of such men and the mothers of their children.[9]

There were, to be sure, some spectacular success stories among Hampton's Indian graduates. Susan LaFlesche, an Omaha, was salutatorian of the class of 1886. She went on to become the first Indian woman doctor and dedicated her life to treating patients on her home reservation in Nebraska. Anna Dawson, who continued lifelong correspondence with Hampton Institute, arrived at the school as a young child in 1878. She was of mixed parentage, white and Arikara. She graduated from the Normal program in 1885 and taught at Hampton in the Indian and Night schools. Dawson later enrolled in the Normal School in Framingham, Massachusetts, and devoted her career to serving as an extension agent at the Sioux reservation in Nebraska, and later at her home agency in Fort Berthold, North Dakota. She married a graduate of Carlisle Indian School and spent the rest of her long life caring for her children and others whom she took in. She died in 1968 at the age of 101.[10]

Some Indian men also achieved distinction after graduation from Hampton. Thomas Sloan, who was one-eighth Omaha Sioux, entered Hampton in 1884 and graduated as valedictorian. He returned west to the Omaha-Winnebago reservation, read law, and was admitted to the Nebraska bar in 1892. He was active in Indian reform work and served as president of the Society of American Indians and as a member of the Committee of One Hundred. That committee's work led to the "Merriam Report," which served as the basis of New Deal Indian policy in the 1930s.

William Jones, also of mixed blood, is acclaimed as Hampton's most illustrious male Indian graduate. After completing the institute in 1892, he attended Phillips Andover Academy, Harvard, and Columbia, where he received a Ph.D. in anthropology under Franz Boas, one of the pioneers in that discipline. Tragically, Jones's career was cut short. In 1909 he was murdered, and was rumored to have been consumed, by the "heart-eating" Hongot tribe in the Philippines, among whom he had spent a year and a half doing research.[11]

The achievements of Indian graduates like LaFlesche, Dawson, Sloan, and Jones are genuinely impressive, but they need to be seen in proper perspective. There were more black Hampton alumni professionals in the village of Hampton alone than there were Indian alumni professionals in the West. Neither Hampton's Indian School nor the opportunities available to Indians in the West enabled most Native American men and women to duplicate the achievements of those stellar graduates. Although Armstrong attempted to serve Native American students in the same way he did his African American students, the circumstances of the former—outside the Hampton Institute environment—were so different that his efforts had far less impact upon them than upon the African Americans.

Of his black students, Armstrong originally had said that the education he offered them would "exhaust the best powers of nineteen-twentieths of those who would for years come to the institute."[12] The actual figure is closer to nine-tenths. Of the 723 graduates between 1871 and 1890 for whom records exist, 67 went directly from the institute to northern colleges and universities. Seventeen others went first to northern prep schools and then to northern colleges. Several others "read law" with northern attorneys and themselves became lawyers.[13]

In any analysis of Samuel Chapman Armstrong, it is crucial to note that these students did not pursue advanced education in defiance of their mentor at Hampton, but rather had his enthusiastic encouragement. Most received their admission and scholarships at places like Boston University, Harvard, Oberlin, the University of Pennsylvania, and Yale through the mediation of Samuel Armstrong. Some, like George Washington Fields, became professionals more as a result of Armstrong's insistence than through their own initiative. After graduating from Hampton, Fields obtained several jobs as a manservant in prominent northern white families, all arranged for him by Armstrong. His last position was with Gov. Ezra Cornell of New York, who encouraged him to enter the law school at the university named for the governor. Though at first reluctant, Fields finally submitted to the persuasion of Cornell and Armstrong. He went on to become Cornell's first black law graduate and Hampton village's leading black attorney.[14]

George Fields is but one example of the variety among Armstrong's black graduates. A survey of all the graduates from Hampton during Armstrong's twenty-five years as principal is beyond the scope of this study. Nevertheless, a closer look at the graduates and former students who attended around same time as the institute's most famous and controversial graduate (and Armstrong's favorite protégé), Booker Taliferro Washington, provides insight into Hampton's educational methods and the results for its black students.

Armstrong always remained true to his missionary upbringing in the ways he dealt with Hampton's alumni. For his father, religious conversion had to be followed by education in the faith. For Samuel, in his process of secular conversion, refinement of belief and behavior continued long after completion of Hampton's academic program. For that purpose, Hampton Institute established an elaborate system of correspondence and support for its former students. It was possible to sever Hampton's umbilical cord, but not without determined effort. Armstrong and his teachers were incredibly tenacious in tracking down every former student. They used the network of Hampton Alumni clubs (and, after Armstrong's death, the "Armstrong Clubs" that became a part of the modern Urban League) around the country to seek out former students with whom contact had been lost. Most Hampton alumni seemed to welcome this continuing contact with their *alma mater*. Equally important, the institute provided important services to them that extended well beyond moral support.[15]

The operation of the postgraduate Hampton support system is well elucidated through close study of the graduates of Booker T. Washington's generation—the classes of 1874 through 1876. There were ninety-one students in those three classes; postgraduate records remain for seventy-one of them.[16] In their backgrounds as well as their post-Hampton careers, these alumni defy the easy stereotypes so often made about students at early Hampton Institute.

It is true that the majority were ex-slaves or the children of ex-slaves. Several of the former were also Civil War veterans. Nearly a quarter of the students in these classes were, in fact, northerners—from such states as Pennsylvania, New Jersey, New York, and Massachusetts. Most of the students came from backgrounds of dire poverty, but a few came from relatively prosperous families. One graduate, Frank T. Hyman ('75), was the son of a congressman.[17]

Just as the origins of Hampton students do not quite fit either Armstrong's vision or past stereotypes, the postgraduate careers of Hampton's black graduates were more varied than has been presumed. It is true that most of them became teachers, but very few were *only* teachers. They were also lawyers, like George Fields; they were ministers, newspaper editors, actors, musicians, Pullman porters, postal workers, and politicians. As noted, about 10 percent went on to advanced training in northern white schools.[18]

What these alumni had in common was a deep devotion to Hampton Institute and to Samuel Chapman Armstrong, as well as considerable admiration for their most famous fellow alumnus, Booker T. Washington. They absorbed Armstrong's teachings with a thoroughness reminiscent of religious conversion. As Mary Melvin ('74) wrote in 1911: "I so often say that I am glad I was born colored. Had I been born white and poor as I am, I should have had the 'door of opportunity' closed in my face. As it now is, no one can keep the best things from me. And I owe all of this to Hampton and the accident of being born Negro[.] I tell my girls that all good things have come to me that I may pass them to others. General Armstrong always made us feel that Hampton students 'gathered to scatter.'"[19]

Not all students were quite as impressed with Hampton Institute as Mary Melvin. William Adams, who apparently had been accused of stealing while at the school, made his point of view clear:

> I have only to say that I have not considered myself "a member of your School" since I was so unfairly turned out of it. . . . I was sadly disappointed in coming to the school. . . . I was not learning anything but going over what I had learned in primary school. It was not for want of a good school to go to at home that brought me here: but seeing in your catalogue that Scholars could learn trades I thought I would have the opportunity to learn the printing business. . . . I had been here but a short time when I found the School was greatly overrated. Had I been fortunate enough to have gained the good will of the teachers, I would not have been turned off for non-payment of $20—while others were behind doubly the amount. I determined the day I was turned off never to re-enter the School again![20]

More typical, however, were students who found Hampton's educational opportunities truly unique. An anonymous student wrote to Hampton: "The fact about Hampton that impresses me most [is] the power that there seem [*sic*] to be here of getting hold of seemingly worthless fellows and drawing forth the true worth that is latent in them. . . . When Hampton does not find out the secret, you may rest assured that the problem is difficult to solve."[21]

Almost all the alumni from early Hampton were deeply absorbed in their school and community work. For them, Hampton's requirement that they "uplift their race" was a sacred obligation. As a consequence, many undertook a scope of activities that would exhaust many modern-day reformers. Almost all had to pursue second careers (usually in farming or the skilled crafts) because of low teachers' wages and short school terms. In addition, they taught Sunday schools, sang in their church choirs, and organized literary societies, adult evening schools, YMCAs, temperance groups, and industrial training classes for young people. Many also found time to become involved politically, serving in local government or lobbying for increased funding for colored schools. One graduate, John Newsome ('75), paid the ultimate price for his political activism. He was shot to death in a political brawl in 1883.[22]

Although these alumni from the Booker Washington era greatly admired their famous fellow graduate, they did not necessarily speak with his voice. The comment of John Pool ('74) typifies alumni attitudes and sophistication in analyses of the South's problems: "A Republic cannot permanently advance while proscribing a constantly increasing citizenship to a caste or any other inferior plan. . . . If the [N]egroes are not educated, what shall be done with them? . . . This is the *white man's* problem. Will he learn more humanity by the presence of the [N]egro or shall his progress falter beneath the consequences of this prejudice?"[23]

These alumni of Hampton were able to work as hard as they did, and to speak their minds as freely as some of them did, in large part because of the continuing support they received from Hampton Institute. The school's alumni support system was constructed as carefully and was almost as effective as its educational program on campus.

Hampton Institute's first contact with a recent alumnus was one that would hardly surprise a modern college student. It was a reminder about unpaid bills. But, like all else about the Hampton educational system, this reminder served two purposes, the lesser of which was to collect the money owed. Primarily, this first letter gave the institute staff an opportunity to reinforce two of Hampton's basic teachings—frugality and responsibility for debt. These were lessons that most alumni seem to have absorbed well.

The debts owed Hampton usually were small, often as little as five dollars. But Hampton insisted that they be paid, and graduates were devastated if they were unable to do so promptly. As Sarah Hemmings ('76) wrote in 1877: "The school where I have been teaching has as yet only paid me for one month out of six. . . . But all the teachers that have been teaching . . . have had to wait so long before they received all their pay. I will pay my [bill] as soon as I get it."[24]

An alumnus's financial relationship with Hampton sometimes operated in more unusual ways. Armstrong frequently arranged summer jobs for both Indian and black students and alumni at northeastern resort hotels. In at least one instance, the grateful graduate sent most of his wages each week to Armstrong for safekeeping, so that he might have some savings with which to buy books and supplies for his school when the fall term began.[25]

Along with this sort of special correspondence with young graduates, Hampton wrote at least once a year to every alumnus or former student it could find. The number of letters varied according to needs and requests. One certainty was that, if a graduate did not respond to the annual Christmas letter, he or she soon would receive another one. Alumni from an area in which a missing graduate was thought to be living would be contacted and requested to provide information on the absentee's whereabouts and condition.[26]

There is an aspect of these early institute-to-alumni letters that might amuse today's college alumni directors. The letters asked not what they, the alumni, could give to Hampton, but what Hampton could do for them! To scores of alumni each year, Hampton sent issues of the *Southern Workman,* along with old books, magazines, and newspapers for use in their classrooms. The graduates were most grateful to receive such materials. Most were teaching in underfunded, undersupplied, isolated schools. Lorenzo Ivy ('75) wrote in 1885, "I received a bundle of papers sent by you a few days ago for which accept many thanks. After I look them over myself, I give them to my scholars, and they appreciate them very highly. . . . It seems quite a treat to the children to have selections from other than their regular textbooks."[27]

Hampton did more than simply share with its graduates materials for which it no longer had use. It was also a conduit through which alumni were able to receive aid from northern philanthropic groups. Through Armstrong's intercession, the schools of several alumni were "adopted" by northern charitable organizations, and each year gifts of books, clothing, and even food were sent to the adopted school. The gifts usually were small, but to a teacher with almost no resources, they were invaluable.[28]

Clearly, *in loco parentis* at Hampton did not end at the campus gate or upon graduation. It is revealing that the institute did not limit itself simply to sustaining graduates in their professional lives. Some alumni wrote requesting help with personal problems, and the institute seldom hesitated to provide what assistance it could.

One former student, Thomas Scott ('75), was a Civil War veteran who had suffered a hernia while moving a cannon during battle. He was continually plagued by pain and frequently was unable to work as a consequence. His letters also suggest a deteriorating mental condition. He constantly besieged Hampton for aid of one sort or another.[29] (Scott's file is the largest for this period, save the one for Booker T. Washington, the contents of which are quite different.)

Despite Scott's apparent instability, the Hampton staff tried to provide help for him. In one instance, Miss Sherman, then the Alumni Correspondent, solicited evaluations of Scott from other alumni in the area before deciding what assistance to give. One respondent wrote. "He is unable to work most of the time. When he is at his best he is able to do but little work. . . . Those who know him say his case is one to be pitied. . . . Even if he were given money, we . . . think it wise to put only a very small amount into his hands."[30] The recommended amount, five dollars, was duly sent to Scott.

The Thomas Scott story reveals a side to the Hampton alumni support network that is less than laudatory. It was judgmental and intrusive as well as inspirational and supportive. The system showed little respect for an individual's right to privacy, and it publicly condemned those who did not live up to Hampton's ideals. One graduate, reported to be running a "Gentleman's Bar-Room" in Ohio, clearly had passed beyond the pale.[31] The report on another member of these classes, added to his file in 1903, concludes with the terse comment: "Does not amount to much."[32]

Samuel Chapman Armstrong, of course, was intimately involved in the activities of his alumni. Indeed, while Armstrong was alive, graduates tended to address their letters to Armstrong, no matter who the official alumni correspondent might be.

This choice was well advised, for the general was at least as solicitous of his graduates' well-being as he was of that of his current students. He corresponded with southern state and local superintendents, soliciting jobs for his graduates. He annually toured schools in Virginia and other southern states in which his alumni taught. He sought to intervene when his alumni teachers were not being paid promptly. Armstrong firmly believed that his graduates should carry on Hampton's missionary work and spread both its religious and its secular visions. He constantly exhorted his alumni to work in the neediest areas of the South and encouraged some of them to become missionaries to Africa. But at the same time he asked sacrifices of them, he was insistent that their professional status be acknowledged. When a Boston friend asked him for "a good, honest, reliable girl" to be a house servant, Armstrong's curt response was, "None to send."[33]

Armstrong's role as surrogate father for his graduates extended well beyond their professional lives. He tried to assist his alumni in whatever ways they requested. For example, he helped arrange payment of pensions to widows of former students who were Army veterans. In another instance, a graduate had gone on to Oberlin College and then enlisted in the Navy. When he was summarily discharged, Armstrong wrote to Sen. Blanche K. Bruce, asking him to investigate whether the discharge was racially based. Armstrong even elicited help for a graduate who was in danger of losing his house. And, in at least one instance, he was asked to intervene in a graduate's marital dispute. On that occasion, even Armstrong was sensible enough to keep his distance.[34]

To one special set of alumni Armstrong gave more surreptitious assistance. Despite his public statements that blacks should refrain from politics, Armstrong nurtured his politically engaged graduates along with the others. In the 1880s, all the black delegates to the Virginia Legislature with more than elementary school training were Hampton alumni. Other alumni served in city and county governments. Armstrong depended upon these graduates to fund Hampton and to protect the school from hostile legislation, such as a bill to restrict Hampton's trade programs. Local whites had complained that the institute's programs competed with their businesses. Hampton's alumni politicians saw to the bill's defeat.[35]

One early Hampton graduate was the most political of all its alumni, and a man who "amounted" to very much indeed. Booker Taliferro Washington was Samuel Armstrong's prize pupil and chief protégé, a famous exponent of the Hampton Institute philosophy. Almost all previous depictions of Armstrong, in fact, have viewed him through the lens ground by Booker T. Washington. There are unfortunate ironies in this interpretation, for the two men were as different from each other as they were similar in certain beliefs. Moreover, Washington truly came into his own only after the death of his mentor forced him to find his own voice and his own methods to exercise his remarkable, if flawed, leadership.

In reality, the relationship between Armstrong and Washington may have been rather different than the latter's portrayal of it. To Armstrong, his association with young Booker seemed very much a replication of the role his mentors—his father and Mark Hopkins at Williams—had played in his own life. He tried to imbue Washington with all that he had learned from those older men, and he encouraged the ambitious young man to follow in their (and his) footsteps. In many senses, Booker Washington became a surrogate for the biological son Armstrong did not have until the final months of his life. Most remarkably, that "son" was *black*, and Armstrong very consciously was *white*.

In forming this unique relationship, Samuel Chapman Armstrong demonstrated that he was not an ordinary late-nineteenth-century white American. He made a black man his spiritual heir and the bearer of his vision for the people to whom he had chosen to dedicate his life. As noted, Booker T. Washington was unable to define his own path until after Armstrong's death. When he began to do so, his course proved much more precarious than that of his white mentor. Washington's color, and the resurgent tide of racism at the turn of the century, made his rise to leadership and prominence a balancing act even more delicate than that which Armstrong had performed for the preceding twenty-five years.

There is little evidence that Armstrong, at first, gave any particular notice to a new student from Malden, West Virginia. In Armstrong's records, only the Senior Cottage petition and Armstrong's response to it establish any early association between the two. In contrast, Washington, in his two autobiographies, *The Story of My Life and Work* and *Up from Slavery*, waxes eloquent about his years at Hampton and the role Armstrong played in them.[36]

Surely, though, Armstrong gradually became conscious of the remarkable young man in the Class of 1875. The general arranged summer employment for Washington in Saratoga Springs, New York, following his graduation. Four years later, Armstrong invited Washington to return to the institute to deliver the Graduate Essay at Commencement.[37] The speech was a great success, and the following summer Armstrong invited Washington to return to Hampton as a staff member. Hampton was beginning to integrate its staff (though not yet its teaching faculty); Washington was to be one of the first of its graduates to join his former teachers on staff.[38] Thus began the remarkable collaboration between Armstrong and Washington that would last the rest of the general's life.

It should be understood that the association never was one of equality. Armstrong emphatically was the senior partner—indeed, the *patron* in the relationship.[39] At first, Washington served as the teacher of the Night School. Later he was supervisor of the Indian men's dormitory. Clearly his work was more than satisfactory. When General Armstrong, in May 1881, was asked to recommend a white man to lead the new colored normal school planned at Tuskegee, Alabama, the only name he would offer was that of his black protégé, Booker T. Washington.[40]

For the next twelve years, Armstrong and Washington worked together intimately in creating the first of Hampton's "children," Tuskegee Institute. The voluminous correspondence between Washington and Armstrong illustrates both the closeness and the limits of their relationship. To the very end, Washington (at least in his letters) was the dutiful supplicant and Armstrong the aging wise man ready to dispense advice on any matter.

It is striking that very little of the correspondence concerns educational philosophy or pedagogy. Apparently Washington had internalized the Hampton philosophy to the satisfaction of his mentor. What Washington desperately needed in his first years at Tuskegee was a crash course in the mechanics of educational administration and fundraising. From the very first, Washington consulted Armstrong on every major decision he made at Tuskegee. In fact, Armstrong and his staff frequently made personal loans to Washington just to keep his school afloat. And Gen. John Marshall, Hampton's treasurer, instructed Washington on how to establish a bookkeeping system to keep track of his funds. "I hope you have a book of receipts—like a bankbook with stubs so as to keep account of your receipts," Marshall admonished.[41]

Washington clearly saw himself as an apprentice to Armstrong, the master craftsman. But it is also obvious that Washington learned many of his lessons well. Step by step, as he developed Tuskegee Institute, he tried to duplicate the process Armstrong had employed at Hampton. First he arranged for the purchase of land for the school and its farm. He solicited advice from Armstrong on how to make the property independent of state ownership and how to vest it in an independent board of trustees, just as Armstrong had done at Hampton. He then sought Armstrong's counsel about whom he should choose for his board. Hinting at frustration with his work in Alabama and with its differences from life in Virginia, Washington wrote to his mentor, "I know, General, that this is putting more on your already overburden shoulders, but our position towards the whites here is a little peculiar. We have to lead them along gently. They are still distrustful of 'Yankees.' You are one of the few Northern men in whom the southern whites seem to have complete confidence."[42]

Once Tuskegee was established, Washington constantly beseeched his old teachers to send their best graduates to staff his new school. He consulted with Armstrong on major acquisitions such as a sawmill and printing press, and asked for his help in paying for such items.[43]

The areas in which Washington most depended on Armstrong were promotion and fundraising. He constantly besieged the general for introductions to the philanthropists who were aiding Hampton and for advice on how to approach them.[44] Washington even attempted modest imitations of two of Hampton's most successful promotional devices, a singing group and a progress report to be titled *Ten Years' Work at Tuskegee Institute*. Characteristically, he consulted his mentor first. His singing group would be only a "quartet or quintet" and he wanted to be sure it would not compete with the Hampton Singers. He was equally eager to avoid siphoning off support for Hampton with his proposed pamphlet. He sent it to Armstrong for prior approval, saying, "Shall be glad of criticisms from you. Do you think we pressed our [i.e., Tuskegee's] *'Needs'* too strongly? I have tried to show that Tuskegee is *a result of Hampton.*"[45]

The personal relationship between Armstrong and Washington remained a strong one, even though distance and the enormous burdens each carried prevented frequent personal contact. Armstrong was unable to attend Washington's marriage in August 1882, but he did visit Tuskegee twice, once briefly in 1887 and for two months in the spring of 1893. By this second visit, Armstrong had been severely crippled by his second heart attack and a stroke in 1891. The highest honor to which a Tuskegee student could aspire during those months was pushing General Armstrong in his wheelchair up and down the hilly terrain of Tuskegee's campus.[46]

Despite the closeness of the Armstrong-Washington relationship, it remained clear to all that Tuskegee was an offspring of Hampton, not its equal. Tuskegee's students were less advanced than Hampton's when they matriculated. Washington solicited, and Hampton readily supplied, graduates to teach Tuskegee's students and staff members to evaluate Tuskegee's progress. Some strategies that might have been necessary for Booker T. Washington in rural Alabama clearly seemed inappropriate for the more sophisticated Hampton Institute. When Hollis Frissell, Hampton Institute chaplain and Tuskegee trustee, returned from a board meeting at the Alabama school, he waxed eloquent about the reception given the trustees. Students and staff had lined either side of the road into the campus with baskets, tossing flower petals before the trustees' carriages and reciting specially composed verse:

> We have saved our scant pennies
> to buy you garlands sweet;
> They're the price of needed footwear,
> But we cast them at your feet. . . .
>
> So here's to our TRUSTEES, bless 'em,
> They do the best they know,
> And if this glory suits them
> Why then we'd have it so.[47]

Frissell was so enchanted that he proposed at a faculty meeting that something similar be done for Hampton's trustees. Apparently the suggestion was greeted with stony silence and never was raised again. Clearly Hampton's faculty felt themselves and their students to be above such fawning.[48]

In the final analysis, the relationship between Armstrong and Washington was more extensive and intense than those Armstrong formed with his other most promising graduates. But it was not different *in kind*. In all these associations, he remained the mentor and they his protégés. He promoted their careers, publicly or secretly, whichever seemed more expedient politically. And they remained intensely loyal to Armstrong and his institute. In most cases, however, they remained more independent of Armstrong. What distinguished the association between Armstrong and Washington was greater personal affection and interdependence between the two. In his declining years, Armstrong came to depend more and more upon Washington to sustain his vision of black education.

Still, it was an unequal partnership. As Louis Harlan poignantly explains, Armstrong's death devastated Booker T. Washington, but it was also, in a way, his personal Emancipation Proclamation. It was two years—until his Atlanta Exposition address—before Washington developed his own voice in continuing the efforts upon which he and his mentor had worked together for over a decade.[49] Equally important to understand is that it was with his *own voice alone* that he now spoke. He addressed a new, and even more dangerous, age in American race relations. And he had to do so with few of the privileges permitted his mentor, an elite white descendent of New England missionaries to Hawaii. His choices may have been flawed, but the society in which he had to work was at least equally so.

The lives of Booker T. Washington and his fellow graduates reveal the promises and pitfalls entailed in Hampton's educational system. The alumni were, in fact, trained to function, progress, and lead in the post-Reconstruction world that existed when Armstrong founded his school in 1868. Evidence shows that remarkable numbers of them acquired the requisite skills and internalized both the message of ambition, commitment, and leadership; and the attendant message of conservatism in effecting change.

The difficulty for them, and ultimately for Armstrong, was that post-Reconstruction America was far from a stable society. Alumni had to adjust to the economic changes and the rising tide of racism that engulfed the United States in the last two decades of the nineteenth century. Once again, the evidence shows that large numbers of them did so successfully. It is useless to argue whether they did so because of, or in spite of, Samuel Chapman Armstrong. Polemical arguments can be—and have been—made for both sides. Very few Hampton alumni became black militants, but few became fawning accommodationists either. The most salient point to understand about Hampton's early alumni is that an overwhelming majority of them agreed with Mary Melvin: "As it is now, no one can keep *the best things* from me. And I owe all of this to Hampton." For them, Armstrong's institute had been a gateway into a fuller, more secure life.

12

EDUCATIONAL
PROPAGANDIST AND
ENTREPRENEUR, 1874–1886

*The story of Hampton is indeed one with the life of its
General.*

—*Francis Peabody, 1898*

From the perspective of his students, their employers, and the institute's
benefactors, Samuel Chapman Armstrong's work at Hampton was a splendid triumph. Yet, in his mature years as principal of Hampton, General
Armstrong appears to have fallen into a trap that also has snared many of
his educational, political, and business successors. They come to their re-
spective enterprises with great energy and clear ideas for innovation. But
once those innovations are implemented, their primary goal becomes maintaining their new system, even though new developments, inside and outside the enterprise, may necessitate change. Often, such changes are required
precisely because much that the innovator attempted has been successful.

These were the circumstances that confronted Samuel Chapman
Armstrong between 1874 and 1886. Hampton Institute was working extraor-
dinarily well. By 1880, Hampton graduates were teaching over ten thousand black pupils in the South and receiving accolades from their white
supervisors.[1] In sustaining such success, Armstrong had to be fully aware
of the conflicting constituencies he had to please.

At one extreme were the "unreconstructed Rebels," opposed to all
forms of black education. There also were southern white moderates, such
as Edward Joyner, president of Washington and Lee College, who instructed
Armstrong that "the work which your Institute is ingaged [*sic*] is devoted
to the interests of this Commonwealth[.] I trust that its continued success
may, among other good results, teach our Northern friends that *mixed
schools* in the South are not necessary to secure to the colored race even the
highest educational privileges."

W. W. Wyson, another southern white ally, warned Armstrong, "I have on several occasions had my temper considerably ruffled in defending your efforts in behalf of [N]egro education. . . . [They] can see but one side to every question of public policy. . . . Some of these parties, as you well know, are men of position and influence. They look upon the problem of Negro education with distrust, and regard it as the legitimate outgrowth of fanatical sentiment originating in the North."[2]

At another extreme were black critics. Bishop Henry Turner of the African Methodist Episcopal Zion Church, for example, was beginning to articulate a black nationalist vision for education and all else in the lives of African Americans. Turner reportedly was impressed by Hampton's discipline and neatness but distressed by the absence of teaching in "the higher branches." A white faculty member purportedly told Turner that blacks still were "too ignorant" for such studies.[3]

Positioned between these two extremes were the people Armstrong thought of as his most important potential benefactors. They included northern freedmen's advocates, who sometimes doubted the efficacy of Armstrong's industrial education format; and the growing class of philanthropic industrialists, who felt that "practical," rather than "academic," education should play the larger role in the education of all working-class people, especially blacks.

Armstrong's core constituency" was the "Hampton family." They were those men and women who wished to contribute, those teachers who were prepared to educate, and those students who were anxious to learn. It was this last element that Armstrong wanted most to satisfy; but to do so successfully, he had to accommodate all those other groups as well. His success in so doing was Armstrong's greatest achievement. It also—perhaps—became his downfall.

It may have been instincts honed during the Civil War that enabled General Armstrong to guide himself and his school through this minefield of conflicting agendas. More likely, it was his experiences in Hawaii, relating to a people with whom he had very few shared perceptions, that underlay Samuel's success. What he claimed was the native Hawaiian's talent for mendacity he elevated to high art. He lied to white southerners, missionaries, philanthropists, his teachers, his African American and Native American students, and—most of all—himself.

In his yearly "Principal's Report," Armstrong tried to include something that would satisfy everyone. For example, Armstrong sought to ingratiate himself and his school with white southerners by proclaiming, "[T]he intelligent people of the South are favorable to a real elevation of the negro. . . . The temporal salvation of the colored race[,] for some time to come, is to be won out of the ground. Skillful agriculturalists and mechanics are needed, rather than poets and orators."[4] At the same time, Armstrong offered northerners reassurances that the black population would remain in the South: "The Negro who wishes to do a man's work goes south to live. There is his empire. He may make, in some cases, more money in the North, but accumulates more in the South, where relatively he is more of a man, from his importance as a voter and laborer."[5]

Armstrong continually stressed the centrality of Hampton's industrial education program. "Labor, I say, again, is the greatest moral force in civilization, and the moral value of our industrial system is its chief excuse. Students who come to us with little or nothing can pay their school bills in labor, thus making their poverty a means of grace, for through this training in self-help can come skill, character and success."[6]

According to the general, "[Blacks] will never really own themselves or their homes or their votes, till . . . they can pay their debts and be free from control of rapacious traders. . . . A minority of both races [black and Indian] will be mechanics; this will be the better class. The more prosperous Negro farmers, with the carpenters, masons and blacksmiths, make, in the South, a middle class, whose thrift and good conduct command respect of all."[7] He argued further: "The hope of the race is in its desire for land and for education. . . . Owning an acre is the best cure for indolence and intemperance; it creates a motive for good conduct of every kind."[8] "Teach him, I say, that Grass is King over cotton, that the field of his agricultural industries must be broadened, if he is to get homes, attain manhood, and secure his rights as a citizen. . . . Cows and pigs can do more for him than Acts of Congress."[9]

Southern whites could not have been comforted by Armstrong's notion that their region was the blacks' "empire," nor by his advocacy of their ownership of property and exercise of the vote. It must be understood, however, that Armstrong's vision incorporated *class* as well as *color*. He was at least as demeaning toward poor white southerners as he was toward blacks and Indians. "I sometimes wish that the poor whites of the South had some such compelling force as that which has excited the Negro's pride and drives him to self-assertion, to organization and to self-development," the general wrote. He continued, "It has made him determined and cheerful. He owes much of his manhood to the hard cruel pressure of our civilization."[10] There is no better statement than this to demonstrate Armstrong's self-deception in ignoring the realities of southern life. All around him, especially in the 1880s, the white yeomen farmers were rebelling against their oppression through Farmers' Alliances and dissident factions of the Democratic party. Such events could not have escaped Armstrong's attention; rather, they were inconvenient for him to acknowledge, if his overall vision of southern race relations was to be plausible.[11]

Samuel Armstrong genuinely believed that upper-class white southerners supported his endeavors. He constantly reassured them that blacks understood them to be their best allies in the South. He told them, for example, that most blacks were "indifferent" to voting and that the growing use of literacy requirements was an appropriate strategy to disfranchise unqualified voters.[12]

In some ways, the general was similar to New South propagandists like Henry Grady, or his own protégé, Booker T. Washington, in his mature years. They told their audiences what they wanted to hear, in an effort to win support for their various schemes of southern development and for self-aggrandizement.[13] But Armstrong's mission and vision of himself were different. Both probably were unique. At the core of Armstrong's perceptions was an understanding of the world and of events that not only was not specifically southern, it was not even specifically *American.* Armstrong's philosophy and strategies were derived largely from his missionary upbringing and only refined by his education at Williams, his Civil War experiences, and his work in the Freedmen's Bureau. Armstrong's approach to what he saw as the "negro problem" was almost entirely in place by the time he opened Hampton Institute. Over the ensuing decades, he would fine-tune it, accommodating to certain political changes in the South. (For example, he de-emphasized black suffrage after 1890, in response to the rising white hostility toward black voting.) Nevertheless, Armstrong did not really change his basic beliefs about race, class, or education during the twenty-five years he presided over his creation, Hampton Institute. He periodically adjusted his rhetoric to satisfy white southerners or northern philanthropists; for better and worse, however, he did not significantly alter the school's educational design.

Because of that rigidity, it is possible to approximate Samuel Chapman Armstrong's understanding of society and race, and of the ameliorating role that education could play in reconciling the two. Armstrong believed that white Christian civilization—despite some acknowledged deficiencies—was innately superior to any other, primarily because it had been evolving longer.

In Armstrong's worldview, races were unique, separate entities. The "darker races" could aspire to, and ultimately attain, parity with the white race, but this change would take generations of paternal white guidance if it were to be realized. Individual members of a race might progress more rapidly and should be encouraged, but that did not change circumstances for a race as a whole.

In the American context, slavery had left blacks at a lower level of civilization than white men. Nonetheless, blacks could be improved. They had to acquire education, moral values, and property in order to advance. In addition, for generations to come, the vast majority of blacks would make their living from the land and in the South. Therefore, they had to develop strategies to maximize their possibilities for progress *in* the South.

In these circumstances, Armstrong embraced a paternalistic, rather than a class, analysis of southern society. Elite white men were blacks' best allies in the South, while the white masses were uncompromisingly hostile to black progress. Alliances with the latter were doomed to failure. But the good will of even the white elite in the South was limited. Therefore, given white hostility to black political participation, efforts at voting and office holding would merely distract blacks from their more important goals of education and property ownership.

Given the prevailing racial climate, blacks should expect to advance primarily through their own efforts. This was the juncture at which Armstrong's own paternalistic work fit into the South's future. Hampton Institute and schools like it (which admittedly were *not* colleges) could provide the most appropriate education for southern blacks for generations to come. They would inculcate academic knowledge, useful trade skills, and moral stamina through the industrial education needed by the leaders of the race. They would teach the teachers, who in turn would teach the masses of their own people. Northern white Christians, whose aid Armstrong solicited, were obliged to support this work to the extent that their resources would permit.

Samuel Chapman Armstrong devoted the rest of his life to promoting these beliefs, along with the school at which, he believed, they were being put into practice. Like the military man he fancied himself to be, Armstrong mounted a campaign and pursued it toward victory, seldom reflecting on the cost to his basic principles or to himself. In the process, Armstrong would traverse many obstacles and then guide his students through them, too. He had to see not only that they attained an education at Hampton, but also that they gained employment thereafter. In these tasks, the general characteristically put practical results ahead of principle.

During Armstrong's twenty-five years at Hampton, Virginia schools—especially those for African Americans—were characterized by isolation and poverty. Although black teachers might enjoy considerable autonomy in their shabby, ill-equipped schoolhouses, they first had to receive appointments. Local, white-dominated school boards controlled hiring.[14] Armstrong strove to ease the paths of his graduates toward employment and survival in these difficult conditions.

On certain issues, he could be quite straightforward. He successfully fought to change the Virginia teachers' exam so that it gave less emphasis to "technical grammar, . . . parsing and analysis of sentences." Hampton, he explained, would prefer to devote itself "to the proper use of our language by useful, practical exercises." Armstrong added, "In making this change, Virginia would only follow Connecticut, which has taken the lead in common sense methods in this matter. Getting at essentials and getting rid of non-essentials is, these days, foremost in the thought of educators."[15]

Other issues that afflicted Armstrong and his students were not so readily resolved. For example, the general first supported the proposed Civil Rights Bill in 1874. His southern white supporters immediately began to manifest their displeasure. William Ruffner, superintendent of public instruction of Virginia, cautioned Armstrong, "[I] have no hope for an attendance [at Hampton Institute's Commencement] of leading Virginians, owing to the exasperation of feeling produced by the Civil Rights Affair. . . . I am discouraged by the Congressional insanity. Still I shall not surrender as long as the negroes keep their senses as well as they have done."[16]

President Joyner of Washington and Lee added his advice on the issue: "The existence of a school like yours in the South ought to be a strong argument against the Civil Rights Bill. It is only as a separate school for the colored race that such a school could exist. . . . It seems to me, a supreme folly and wrong. . . . [I]f you agree with me, as I cannot doubt that you do, . . . will you not raise your voice, when it would be so influential, against the consummation of this act."[17]

Samuel Armstrong, Civil War veteran that he was, understood marching orders when he received them. He had already written to his schoolmate, Sen. James Garfield, expressing hope that Congress would realize that existing laws were adequate. Simply enforcing those laws, Armstrong argued, would cause influential southerners less anxiety. More important, those southerners were becoming reconciled to black education. New "punitive" legislation would only interrupt that process.[18]

Armstrong's opposition to the Civil Rights Bill won him Ruffner's continued help with allocation of Virginia state funds for Hampton. The general returned the favor five years later, in 1879, when the Readjustors gained control of Virginia government. These would-be reformers gained office through the support of blacks who remembered Ruffner's opposition to the Civil Rights Bill. Some of them, in fact, gained seats in Virginia's House of Delegates as a consequence of the Readjustors' victory. They wanted Ruffner fired. Armstrong interceded. He wrote the new governor, William Mahone, supporting Ruffner's retention. The superintendent and his subordinates, Armstrong reasoned, had been "generally favorable and fair to our colored teachers," and he should be allowed to keep his position.[19]

The general also pressured black legislator Peter Carter. He acknowledged that Ruffner "some years ago . . . inadvertently offended the colored people. . . . He made a terrible mistake. . . . But it is best to be magnanimous. . . . He is . . . a staunch friend of education for all classes." Armstrong tried to persuade Carter of his vision of two distinct classes of white southerners, writing: "He is a southerner of advanced ideas compared with many others. The true policy is to *stand by the progressive men of the South.* You cannot wholly agree with them; but to work together is most important even if you don't always feel like it."[20]

At the same time Armstrong solicited help for Ruffner, he tried to make clear that he expected the superintendent to help Hampton in return. The general sought to be diplomatic. He wrote, "The idea of building up the South by *moral forces* is grand and strong and sure to come in time. . . . Let us press the point through the press. Will you take hold?" He then concluded with some of the shameless flattery he showered on white southerners whom he knew to be susceptible to such an approach. "It is the winning idea[,] and the man who puts it on his banner will go to the top."[21]

Ruffner kept his job for a while longer, but there is no evidence that Armstrong's intercession made a difference. Nor is there evidence that Ruffner did any more for Hampton Institute than he had always done.[22] Samuel Armstrong was speaking with his father's missionary voice to men whose ears were not attuned to such words. Inexplicably, the general never seemed to catch onto white southerners' differing agenda. He remained persuaded that his good work and his trust in a just and practical God would carry him through. Somehow, Armstrong believed, Peter Carter and William Ruffner would find ground upon which they could stand together. Only Armstrong could have reached such a conclusion. Even the general, given what he clearly was observing in southern race relations, as opposed to what he hoped would develop, should have known better.

But with Gen. Samuel Chapman Armstrong, optimistic self-deception and not disciplined reflection prevailed. No episode in his life better illustrates that failing than his ambivalence about the Blair Bill. This legislation, first proposed in the late 1870s, would have used the surplus from tariff income to aid public schools throughout the nation. Those schools could be segregated where local laws so required, but aid would have to be distributed equitably between the separate systems. The bill outraged and terrified white southerners. The North had been inconsistent in matters concerning state-federal relations and in the protection of black rights. In response, southern advocacy of states' rights, especially in matters involving race, had seen a resurgence. If the federal government could be empowered to aid state public schools and stipulate how that money might be used, what else might it be able to mandate? If Congress had the right to give aid to local schools, even while allowing them to be segregated, so long as funds were distributed equally, could it not later force the South to accept such aid and *require* that those schools be integrated? White southerners took that possibility very seriously.[23]

At first, Samuel Chapman Armstrong failed to grasp the intensity of concern among southern whites. He lived among them, but he never could really become one of them, any more than he could become a southern black. The general was, however, a quick learner. Although he initially supported the Blair Bill, he changed course when white southern winds blew in another direction.

When the proposition for federal aid to southern education first surfaced, Armstrong argued that it was essential. He told a South Carolina correspondent that he distrusted the motives of both Democrats and Republicans when it came to black education. "I don't like the Democratic party. I am a Republican, but detest the party's neglect of one of its great duties: giving light to the benighted blacks whose freedom is valuable only as it is enlightened." Ever promoting himself and his vision, Armstrong continued, "Allow me to suggest concerted action at the next Congress to secure public aid for the free school system of the South. . . . You can reach Southern men. I can reach Northern men. Many can and would join me."[24]

General Armstrong had been seduced by the propaganda of the New South and, perhaps, by his own rhetoric. "Clear headed men know that the Southern Democrats are a better class of men than Northern Democrats and that the latter have led the former most unwisely."[25] Deliberately or not, Samuel Armstrong was learning the parlance and values of the white southerners around him. In 1877, he called out for federal aid to education; but by the time that year's *Annual Report* was published and Reconstruction ended, he had concluded, "I do not believe in the 'Blair Bill' as a wholesome measure."[26] Six years later, during the more promising period of Readjustor government in Virginia, he had changed his mind again: "The combined resources of northern charity and of southern taxation are wholly inadequate to the educational work to be done for the Negro youth." He proclaimed, "National aid is the need of the hour."[27]

If Samuel Armstrong had one skill that especially suited him to his southern environs, it was his capacity to say what others wanted to hear. Having twice switched on the Blair Bill, he reversed course once again when the forces of racism and reaction reasserted themselves in Virginia. By 1887, federal aid to education once again was anathema. Black education in the South, the general argued, was going well and being adequately funded by state taxes and private contributions. "National aid," Armstrong reasoned, "is certainly of doubtful wisdom." He even was quoted in the *Congressional Record* as arguing, "Apply the Blair Bill to the southern school system and it will check the growth of the best thing in Southern life, [i.e.] the effort of the people to educate themselves."[28]

A basic fallacy in Armstrong's argument for Hampton was his oft-repeated claim that manual labor education "could support itself." It could not. Armstrong knew that and had admitted as much during Hampton's formative years. It was true that most students were able to defray the costs of room and board through their labor, but they could not earn enough to pay tuition and other expenses. To keep Hampton afloat, the general had to raise enormous amounts of money. His ambition that Hampton educate as many black students as possible required ever more funds.

Some of Armstrong's most faithful allies cautioned him against excessive expansion. But the general was determined. He had confessed to Emma before her death, "I feel that a crisis in my life is before me. I am now unfit for such responsibility. . . . I wish I could 'climb where Moses stood.' . . . There is a grand position of moral leadership to be taken for the colored people. God is fitting the right man for it. If I am wanted I shall be summoned. . . . Meanwhile all that is to be done is to do the work today and let the morrow take care of itself. To be content to follow the call of duty wherever it points and lean on the Father. I do not mean to work for the new buildings. I shall ask for them and they will be given if we ask aright."[29]

Apparently Armstrong heard the summons and became most adroit at asking "aright." He was able to report to his Williams classmates in 1874:

> I have a remarkable machine for the elevation of our colored brethren, on which I mean to take out a patent. Put in a raw plantation darkey and he comes out a gentleman of the nineteenth century. Our problem is how to skip three centuries in the line of development and to atone for the loss and injustice of the ages. About $370,000 have been expended here since I took hold in the fall of 1867. . . . I have been in the travelling show business for the last two years—have given over three hundred concerts with the "Hampton Singers" (ex-slaves) in behalf of the School. This is a rough and terrible fight with difficulties, but I think I'm on top.[30]

Armstrong's extraordinary success at fundraising transformed him from an educational innovator to an educational entrepreneur. He began to devote large portions of each year to a northern campaign soliciting donations for Hampton and proselytizing for his educational philosophy. Increasingly, he spent only the fall and winter terms at Hampton, using spring and summer for promotional efforts in the North.

In everything he did, Armstrong kept at least one eye on the potential for bringing greater glory to Hampton (and himself). As noted earlier, he hired many of his teachers because of their connections with prominent families in the North. Others he selected because they could serve promotional or political purposes. Sometimes this strategy backfired. Thomas Fenner, the original music director of the Hampton Singers, felt undercompensated. His continuous complaints so annoyed Armstrong that ultimately he was fired.[31] Other staff members, like Capt. George Brown, who was detailed to Hampton from the U.S. Army to oversee the Cadet Corps, felt unappreciated. Despite Armstrong's complimentary reports to the army, Brown constantly complained about lack of authority and lack of respect from the students. Armstrong finally despaired of placating Brown and asked that the army reassign him elsewhere.[32]

Even though he entrusted them with the day-to-day operation of Hampton, Armstrong kept a close watch on his teachers. More problematical to him were the members of his Board of Trustees. Armstrong depended upon his trustees to facilitate his fundraising enterprises. Very quickly he freed the board from the legal control of the AMA. Thereafter he set out to attract a group composed primarily of secular men who would help him gain access to the philanthropists whose support could guarantee Hampton's future.[33]

Despite winning legal independence from the AMA, Hampton's board continued to be dominated by members of that missionary society. As late as 1875, six of the seventeen board members—including the board's President George Whipple—were affiliated with the AMA.[34] Even more unacceptable from Armstrong's point of view, the AMA for years remained a primary conduit through which Hampton's funding passed. Unseemly, even "un-Christian," battles broke out between Armstrong and his initial AMA patrons. Gen. John Marshall, Hampton's treasurer, accused the AMA of raising money specifically for Hampton and then distributing it equally among all the AMA schools. General Armstrong called an emergency meeting of the board to review the situation but neglected to inform board president Whipple until the very last minute. Ultimately, only Whipple's death in 1876 gave Armstrong undisputed leadership of this board.[35]

Armstrong wanted board members different from the AMA types. Christian faith was important, of course—so long as it was manifested in ways the general deemed "practical." What Armstrong had in mind was best evidenced in his offer of board membership to Bishop Henry Potter: "We need a representative of the Episcopalians—at least one!" He argued, "Our Board is not very strong. The new one[s] we need are hard to get[,] are too busy to take more work as I am afraid you are. . . . You could add force to our board. Trustees are not expected to contribute or to raise funds. [W]e do not seek rich men, but clean, strong men who stand for something. . . . [I]f they are wealthy[,] all the better."[36]

Armstrong's appeal to Potter was unsuccessful. Moreover, it was somewhat disingenuous. Because so many of his new Indian students came from reservations supervised by Episcopal missionaries, Armstrong wanted to diffuse criticism from such agencies by including one of their leaders on his board. He finally succeeded in 1886, when he persuaded Bishop William McVickers to join Hampton's board.[37]

General Armstrong's real targets for the board were not religious men unassociated with the AMA. Rather, they were primarily "all the better" for being rich. From his base at Hampton, Armstrong sought to share in the power and prestige of the men who where shaping America's future. After all, many of them had fought with him in the battles to preserve the Union. Now it was time for them to join him in guiding the transformation of the ex-slave into a free person.

Gradually, aided by deaths and resignations, Armstrong built the kind of board he sought. He began as merely the board's secretary, but he ended as its indomitable chief member. By 1874, he had added former generals James Garfield and O. O. Howard, as well as his trusted friend Robert Ogden, to the board. By 1890, Hampton's Board of Trustees consisted of men whom

Armstrong counted as his peers: northern businessmen like Ogden, philanthropists like George Peabody, and railroad mogul Collis P. Huntington. Astute politician that he was, Armstrong made sure to include one or two prominent local white men, like Col. Thomas Tabb, among his board members. Although Christian ministers still were well represented (seven out of seventeen), the board clearly was dominated by Armstrong's men.[38]

Robert Ogden of New York and Philadelphia, Armstrong's chief ally on the board, was an invaluable friend. Ogden was business manager for John Wanamaker in the latter's expanding department store enterprises. More important, Ogden often served as Armstrong's alter ego, counselor, and restrainer. The two men had met in New York during Armstrong's Williams College years. Ogden was older; he was already an established businessman when the two were introduced. It was in Ogden's home in 1866 that Armstrong gathered with members of the AMA to describe his plans for a new normal school at Hampton.[39]

Robert Ogden was intrigued by Samuel Armstrong's energy and vision but somewhat taken aback by both. The bond between them, despite the age difference, was based on their shared irreverence toward pomposity. Ogden felt Samuel was overly disdainful of "stuffiness," but he was delighted when he and the general could see silliness for exactly what it was. Events following Hampton's 1877 Commencement offered one such opportunity. Most of the AMA trustees became ill from overindulgence in the delicious crabs that could be had nowhere in their northern environs. Ogden, however, felt quite well and had the bad manners to show his amusement at their distress. "I'm afraid I disgraced your Board of Trustees by my lack of dignity," he reported. "Brother Hyde told me that Trustees should be known by their *dignity*." Ogden assured Armstrong, "Out of the Board or in it, you can count on me."[40]

Armstrong took his friend at his word, and soon Ogden began to discover that he would have to fulfill his promise in unanticipated ways. For example, Armstrong, when on a fundraising tour, often would arrive unannounced at the Ogden home in Philadelphia. Ogden, returning home from work, always could tell who his visitor was. There was the battered cloak, "thrown at rather than placed upon" the coat rack. And there also was hysterical laughter coming from the kitchen. Samuel Armstrong always delighted in joining people as they made meals. Whether they were black, white, or Hawaiian, he most enjoyed the communion involved in the process, more than the product. Still "Sam," he regaled the Ogden family servants with stories of life in the South, even as he wrote appeals for more money to their employer's friends on his host's kitchen table.[41]

Ogden indulged such behavior because he believed in Armstrong and his vision. Samuel could get generals and presidents to visit his campus. Among other responsibilities, Robert Ogden took on the burden of insuring that the general would be dressed appropriately. It was not an easy task. Characteristic of his missionary frugality (and his playfulness), Armstrong sent Ogden an old shirt "which has been through the wars, addressed audiences, mingled in society, wept over the wrongs of Indians and is now retired from active service." If it could not be repaired, Armstrong asked for a half-dozen in the same fashion. Ogden sent the general new shirts and ties, the one he "invariably wore" having "simply snapped" because it had become so "attenuated."[42]

Armstrong depended upon Ogden for more than friendship and wardrobe. He trusted him to supply uniforms for his male students and to contact potential donors to whom he—Armstrong—did not have direct access. Upon the death of Gen. John Marshall, longtime treasurer of Hampton Institute, Armstrong even proposed that Ogden fill that position and ultimately succeed him as principal. Ogden declined but remained on the Board of Trustees and became its president in the years after Armstrong's death.[43]

Samuel Armstrong's successful restructuring of his trustee board, which occurred concurrently with the rapid expansion of the institute, was a great personal triumph. But there also were drawbacks. The rich men now on his board actually could exercise some control over him. The more numerous small donors upon whom Armstrong originally had depended could give less money than a few wealthy ones, but they were allowed a correspondingly smaller voice in school policy. These new, wealthy trustees and benefactors, on the other hand, could exert enormous influence. In restructuring his Board of Trustees, Armstrong provided a model which would be employed to control the goals and curricula of many black normal schools and colleges in the early twentieth century. Armstrong did not anticipate this outcome; but, as will be seen below, such unintended effects of his strategy began to be felt even before his death.[44]

In its report of "Donations Received" for 1872, the institute reported contributions from more than two hundred patrons. Of these, only seven gifts were of one thousand dollars or more. The largest was four thousand dollars, from the Homer Treat Fund, in the form of railroad bonds. Most contributions were from individuals who sent fifty or one hundred dollars. Some donations were as small as two or five dollars.[45]

These small donations demanded no accountability, and their donors allowed Armstrong to use them as he saw fit. For example, in exchange for a one-hundred-dollar donation to furnish an Indian student's room, Armstrong offered contributors a photograph of that room. On file at Hampton are still over a dozen postcard photos of the identical dormitory room. Apparently this photo was sent to any such donor, while in fact the contribution actually went into the general fund to help keep the school going.[46]

Beginning in the 1880s, small contributions from individuals and religious groups began to decline, just at a time when Hampton's expenses were increasing exponentially. Many of these small donors had been abolitionists, missionaries, and former freedmen's aid workers who began to die

Student dormitory room, c. 1885. Copies of this photograph were sent to donors who sent contributions to Hampton Institute's building fund. Courtesy of Hampton University Archives.

in that decade. Armstrong became increasingly dependent upon donors who had not hundreds, but tens of thousands of dollars to give. With these larger donations came greater specificity about how the funds should be used. A missionary lady in Boston might be satisfied with a duplicate postcard of a room she supposedly furnished. But when Collis Huntington, president of the Central Pacific and the Chesapeake & Ohio railroads gave over thirty-one thousand dollars to build the "Huntington Industrial Works," he expected to see that edifice when he visited Hampton's campus.[47]

Men like Huntington were very much a part of a new interregional coalition that saw industrial education—as conceived of in the antebellum pauper schools—as the appropriate model for black economic and social containment in the coming century. These men became great admirers of both the style and the goals of Washington's Tuskegee Institute. They tended to think of Hampton in the same light. As a biographer explained, Huntington believed that "training the Negro could be a benefit only if it were kept within narrow limits. The brightest of them . . . could safely learn trades and thereby have a means of lifting themselves out of the ranks of unskilled labor. To attempt to go further, to give them even the beginnings of a formal education, was pernicious folly. Would someone please tell him what in the hell the Negro was expected to do with his 'education' after he had it?"[48]

These were the men of whom Samuel Armstrong had to "ask aright;" men who thought first of "narrow limits" and of "safety" when they considered support for Negro education. The general shamelessly catered to Huntington's prejudice in his correspondence with him. He mentioned only the industrial side of Hampton's education and concluded, "I hope you can help us. It will help to give the darky a fair chance." Privately Armstrong complained to his treasurer, John Marshall, that the Industrial Works failed to pay their way and diverted students from necessary academic pursuits, but he said nothing in public.[49]

The general subordinated his educational goals to the practical necessity of keeping Hampton solvent. He found it expedient to defer to men like Huntington. Although the Normal School component remained the heart of Hampton's curriculum, in his publications Armstrong increasingly emphasized the ancillary trade programs. Since wealthy donors were more willing to give money for such things, Armstrong, in his fundraising campaigns, exaggerated their centrality. But, to paraphrase an old saying, the cart was beginning to lead the horse—a reality of which Armstrong feigned unawareness. In his 1890 "Principal's Report," the general acknowledged that "about one-third" of the students were in the "Normal" program; the others worked "more or less" full-time and were in the Night School or trade programs. This was not the design that Armstrong had proposed in 1868. Learning manual skills had been intended as a means toward an end, not an end in itself.[50]

Armstrong had become imprisoned by his own success. Money received had to be spent in the manner specified by the donor, and apparently the general refused to admit to himself that this might direct his institute away from his initial vision. At least in his own thinking, his goals for the students remained the same. He wrote, "The aim of this institution is to prepare them for self-support, to graduate men and women able to at once earn a livelihood, accumulate property, and, by so doing, become a part of the conservative element of the country." But the end result seemed more modest than it had been in 1868 or even in 1881, when he had spoken of the South as the black man's "empire." A year later, Armstrong would argue, "The Negro and Indian races are especially in need of mechanical education *to fit them for the sphere they shall occupy.*"[51]

There was a clear disparity between Armstrong's vision and that of a man like Huntington. Sadly, Armstrong's notions, shaped as they were by an entirely different experience with a very different racial group, obscured that difference. When Armstrong spoke of a "sphere" for African Americans and Native Americans, he meant "for the present." When Collis Huntington spoke, he meant "forever." Whether through self-deception or expediency, Armstrong failed to acknowledge such distinctions. Indeed, the ideas expressed in some of his correspondence seem closely to parallel the beliefs of men like Huntington. Armstrong's strategy helped to fund the institute and brought him great acclaim, but it left the school he had created unequipped to respond to changing currents of race relations and to emerging black educational demands in the years after his death.

Samuel Armstrong ignored the economic and pedagogical consequences of his board restructuring, avoided the implications of his refusal to support the Civil Rights Bill, and prevaricated about the Blair Bill. In exercising a remarkable talent for mendacity, he followed the habits of his native Hawaiian countrymen. In Hawaiian culture, certain things were inconvenient to reflect upon and therefore were best ignored. That relatively innocent self-deception was no match for the mean-spirited and conscious agenda pursued by so many of the men whom Armstrong desired as his peers. They might celebrate him as the best among them, and the general clearly basked in their accolades. But what each wanted—the reasons they were engaged in a mutual enterprise—differed dramatically. An attitude like Armstrong's, which envisioned the South as blacks' "future empire," simply was incompatible with one like Huntington's, which presumed that blacks never would need more than the rudiments of reading and writing.

The missionary's son, unhappily, chose not to see the contradiction. He campaigned to fund Hampton until physical weakness forced him to pause. Many years before, he had told Emma that Boston was not his "home"; rather it was his "battleground." It was there, he claimed only partly in jest, that he went "to beg."[52]

It was on that Boston battlefield, while begging, that General Armstrong first was felled. He had done a magnificent job. He had made Hampton Institute and his philosophy of "education for backward races" a model for enlightened Americans and for Europeans who wanted to advance the benighted people under their colonial rule.[53] The nonwhite peoples subjected to this paternalism, of course, never were consulted on such matters. It would be at least another generation before they were able to force recognition of *their* goals for education.

Samuel Chapman Armstrong perceived himself to be "saving backward races." In truth, he inadvertently was articulating a benign rationale for their continued containment and repression. Moreover, in the process he was working himself to death. He traveled too much and rested too little. His intention became "to stay the course." Too seldom did he question his apostasy on matters of principle, when practicality pointed to another route. Too seldom did he reflect upon why he so frantically sought celebration of himself and his school. His heart could not sustain its owner's pace. At a Boston fundraiser in 1886, he collapsed with a heart attack. Collis Huntington sent a special rail car; and, once again, the general returned home to Hampton.[54]

13

FINAL VOYAGES

Home to Hawaii and Home to Hampton

A work that requires no sacrifice does not count much in fulfilling God's plans. . . . He who makes no such sacrifice is most to be pitied. He is a heathen, because he knows nothing of God.

—*Samuel C. Armstrong, 1892*

Shortly after the New Year, in 1893, Samuel Chapman Armstrong and his family dined with an old college friend, John Denison, in Mansion House at Hampton. After pronouncing the grace, Armstrong paused and burst into laughter, "I hope that worked!" he chuckled, "I couldn't shut but one eye!" General Armstrong was a cripple. A stroke in 1891 had left him paralyzed on one side. His third attack, in May 1893, killed him. Nevertheless, he remained—to the end—the joking and grinning adventurer, still viewing life with wonder from "the front door of that missionary house."[1] In his final years, the general gave new order to his own life and tried to insure the permanence of his life's most significant achievement—Hampton Institute. He accomplished both and thereby may have hastened his demise.

When Armstrong was stricken in 1886, Hampton's Board of Trustees recognized the seriousness of his illness. It issued an appeal for funds in tribute to Armstrong's work. "He cannot be spared," the circular proclaimed. "The nation needs his wisdom on the great questions touching the Negro and the Indian. The Hampton Institute needs his guidance to a more perfect development. Society needs the inspiration of his noble life." The institute needed an endowment that would put it "beyond the contingency of a single life." The trustees' goal was five hundred thousand dollars. Endorsements poured in from Armstrong's friends and patrons; John Greenleaf Whittier dedicated his *St. Gregory's Guest and Recent Poems* to Armstrong. Former United States President Rutherford B. Hayes once again felt compelled to equate Armstrong with a great American icon. He wrote, "So far as I can judge[,] General Armstrong stands next to Lincoln in effective work for the negro. His work, like Lincoln's[,] is for the whole country also, and for all mankind. It hits the nail on the head. It solves the whole negro problem."[2] Northern educational institutions celebrated the general and his work by conferring honorary degrees upon him. His alma mater, Williams, did so in 1887; Harvard followed in 1889.[3]

The trustees were wise to mount an intensive fundraising campaign in the wake of Armstrong's illness. At first, Armstrong uncharacteristically followed doctors' orders and sought total rest. He was bedridden for six weeks following that 1886 attack. Friends like Archibald Hopkins and Robert Ogden offered to come and keep him company. He spent many of those hours of enforced passivity thinking of his first home and of those who still remained there. Even as a convalescent, Armstrong would not yield his self-defined role of advisor and guide to nonwhite peoples. He began a letter to the Cousins' Society on a personal note:

> I am in the longest illness of my life, rapidly recovering from heart trouble, which has kept me on my back for several weeks; and many pleasant visions of the islands have come back, not only while on my bed, but more while sitting on my front piazza of late, watching the exquisite view from it, of sea, and sky and shore, and breathing the soft and delicious breezes from across Hampton Roads. . . . A certain quality in the air here, at times, is identical with . . . the very delicious trade winds that so often fanned us while riding along Kahului shore to Haiku. It will make you better men and women if you let it. . . . There is no breaking away from early associations, especially such as we had in Hawaii. Its influence is both strong and constructive. .

The general quickly shifted, however, from the stance of a homesick boy to that of a didactic educator. He continued: "The Cousins' Society has a peculiar and special relation to the human problem[,] especially to the Polynesian and Chinamen. The latter seem to me to be rising in importance. The future is full of possibilities. No one yet fully understands the significance of Hawaii."[4]

Armstrong sensed the seriousness of his illness. He seemed to conclude, however, that he could best utilize whatever time he had left by doing more rather than less. In 1887, his good friend, Robert Ogden, well aware of Samuel's impetuous habits, tried to counsel him: "I want very much to have a leisurely conference with you, free from all pressure or hurry. . . . I wish you to come to Philadelphia and stay a few days on your way to New York, quietly at my house. I never was more convinced in my life that you need the careful attention of the dilettante loafer. . . . Are you not speaking more eloquently [now] for the causes to which your life has been given than when you are on the warpath?"[5]

Such advice was to no avail. Armstrong resumed his northern fundraising efforts. He augmented that travel with annual tours of Virginia and other southern states to observe his former students' progress as teachers.[6] Worse still, he added to his schedule yearly trips to the western states to recruit Indian students. Clearly, part of his purpose was to employ his personal charm to diffuse continuing criticism from western missionaries about the coeducation of Native American and African Americans at Hampton.[7]

Even as he traveled extensively, Samuel Armstrong kept close watch over his creation, Hampton Institute. Perhaps in an effort to prepare the school for his inevitable departure through retirement or death, he systematized reporting procedures for all of Hampton's departments.[8] Nor did Armstrong give up his central instructional role at the institute. He continued to teach his course for the senior class and speak at chapel each weekend when he was on campus.[9]

It was during this brief period between 1886 and his renewed illness in 1891 that Samuel Armstrong faced a dramatic test of his principles. At first the issue seemed a small matter, but in fact it illustrates very well the contradictory successes and limitations that surfaced at Armstrong's institute in the last decade of the nineteenth century. The general long had argued that African Americans would have to depend primarily upon themselves for their elevation; that Hampton was training leaders who would carry out that mission; and that, while generations would be required to change the conditions and culture of the black masses, a small minority of blacks could improve much more rapidly.

Armstrong had acted upon these beliefs at his own school and beyond. He had been gracious in accepting criticism from students and alumni. When he traveled with groups like the Hampton Singers, he insisted that he and his white staff dine and sleep in the same accommodations afforded the black students.[10] He had supported Hampton's best black graduates, such as Booker T. Washington, for positions originally envisioned for whites. Most important, he had begun to incorporate his most able graduates into the staff of Hampton Institute. He also recommended them for the Virginia Board of Curators, which oversaw use of the state's Land Grant funds allocated to Hampton (although, significantly, not for the school's Board of Trustees).[11]

By 1889, more than a dozen Hampton alumni were employees of the school in all areas except academic faculty. In most ways they were treated equally, but they and the white teachers ate in separate dining rooms, ostensibly because the total number of black and white staff and faculty could not be accommodated in any of the available dining halls. The graduates took exception to this arrangement and protested in a petition to Armstrong. The general seemed shocked by the complaint. He responded: "My dear friends: I think much of the race problem before us and feel that frank expressions between us, by creating a better understanding will do good. . . . Would it add to your pleasure . . . to exchange with one of the teachers' tables which should go into the room you occupy and you go into the teachers' dining room as a table? I would not object to changing with you my table. What would you think of being scattered among the teachers instead of being as you are at a table by yourselves?"[12]

Armstrong then polled the white teachers to see if they objected to such proposed changes. Given the tone of his own letter to the graduates, the general was surely startled by their anonymously written responses. All except one expressed, with different degrees of vehemence, opposition to the integration of the teachers' dining room. Reasons given ranged from personal distaste for dining with the graduates—especially if they were seated at the same tables—to concern that the graduates would abuse the traditional custom of having weekend dinner guests from the local community. While they claimed to have no objection to eating with the graduates, these respondents feared that the graduates would invite "uncouth colored people" on such occasions. Only one teacher from New Hampshire wholeheartedly supported the idea. "How can we teach them to be equal and deny them common civility?" she fumed.[13]

Here, at his own school, in circumstances of his own making, Samuel Chapman Armstrong finally had to confront the contradictions of his own vision, his own background, and late-nineteenth-century racial reality. He had succeeded in preparing the best of his graduates for equality. He had hired them at his own school. But most of his white teachers, almost all of whom hailed from New England—the region he thought of as the most enlightened in the nation—refused to dine with their former pupils. In 1889, Armstrong clearly was out of step with the racial mores of his white contemporaries. At the same time, he could not fully perceive his black graduates' resentment. He had paternalistically concluded his letter to those protesters, "A sense of complaint having come to me for a long time and feeling [there] is a highly communicable spirit among your race, I think it a good time to ask these questions."[14] In truth, it was the worst of times. The general seemed befuddled. He no longer was willing (or, perhaps, physically and mentally able) to impose his will upon his white faculty. There is no evidence that the issue was resolved. Records indicate that segregation of black and white staff in dining continued at Hampton into the twentieth century.[15]

For Armstrong, internal strife at the school had to be contained so that the institution's public image might remain pristine. Perhaps that was what he had in mind in his final "Memoranda." In it he admonished his successors, "In the School, the great thing is not to quarrel; to pull together; to refrain from hasty, unwise words and action, to unselfishly and wisely seek the best good of all; and to get rid of workers whose temperaments are unfortunate—whose heads are not level; no matter how much knowledge or culture they may have. Cantankerousness is worse than hetero-doxy."[16] That statement, in its ambiguity, was quintessential Armstrong. Was it staff members advocating racial equality or those opposed to it whom Armstrong was condemning? In being opaque, the general almost guaranteed that the latter would triumph in the short run.

Perhaps it actually had become easier to proclaim Hampton's promise than to see to its realization on campus. Certainly Armstrong redoubled his efforts to fund Hampton's future. In Boston, New York, and Philadelphia, he was celebrated rather than tested. He was acclaimed as carrying on the work of Garrison and Lincoln. In the South, black school leaders and southern white moderates heralded his work as a model for their own.[17]

At this juncture, Armstrong made an unpredictable change in his personal life. He decided to marry again. He proposed to Mary Alice Ford, one of his teachers at the institute, and she accepted.[18] As his second wife, Samuel Armstrong chose a woman whose background was almost identical to that of his first wife, Emma, and that of his mother. She came from New Hampshire, not Massachusetts, but she too had attended a normal school in New England. She joined Hampton's staff in 1884. In 1890, she was only twenty-six, and the general was fifty-one. But their brief marriage was a happy one, during which Mary Alice and Samuel became parents of

Samuel Chapman Armstrong with second wife, Mary Ford Armstrong, c. 1891. Courtesy of Hampton University Archives.

two children—a daughter, Margaret Marshall Armstrong; and a son, Daniel William Armstrong. Mary Ford Armstrong outlived her husband by sixty-five years and died in 1958.[19]

Armstrong's second marriage energized him, perhaps to his detriment.[20] Against the advice of his friends Archibald Hopkins and Robert Ogden, Samuel chose to make a cross-country and trans-Pacific voyage in 1891. He went home to Hawaii, accompanied by his two older daughters. (The new Mrs. Armstrong remained behind to care for the couple's infant daughter.) This time, he had the use of Collis Huntington's transcontinental rail link. On the way, he stopped to visit his aged mother, who now lived in San Jose, California, close to her daughters. It was the last time he saw her. In another of those tragic ironies that punctuated Armstrong's life, Clarissa Armstrong died on 20 July 1891, while Armstrong and his girls were visiting his first home on Maui.[21]

The occasion for Armstrong's Hawaiian homecoming was the fiftieth anniversary celebration of his first alma mater, the Punahou School, at which he delivered the keynote address. Armstrong's speech resonated with his belief that struggle, whether by black or white, ennobled the struggler: "The friction and fuss in God's army does much to defeat it. . . . God helps those who help themselves. Your Hawaiian problem is a hard one, but it is good for you. Would you have this Paradise without your own effort if you could? I sometimes think that Adam and Eve didn't have half a chance in the Garden of Eden, because too much was done for them. For our human nature the conditions of Plymouth Rock were better."

Of his own work at Hampton, Armstrong said, "All agree that education is [of] paramount importance[,] but no one-sided education will answer. After trying for many years the plan of training the hand, head and heart with negroes and Indians in America I find myself believing in it more than ever, and a wonderful growth of public sentiment in its favor. Educate the whole man is the idea; fit the pupil for the life he is likely to lead."[22]

Characteristically, Armstrong chose his words so as to offend no one. Left unsaid, however, was who would determine the kind of life a given student was "likely to lead." The clear implication was that it would be "enlightened men" like the general himself and the upper-class whites in his audience.

Armstrong's speech was much acclaimed and widely circulated in America; but the journey had been too much for him. Still, he refused to slow his pace. On Thanksgiving Day, 1891, during a speech in Stoneham, Massachusetts, Armstrong suffered a stroke and collapsed, his right side paralyzed. Long-time friends and allies arranged to pay for Armstrong's month-long convalescence at Parker House in Boston, before he was able to travel. They also rallied at a benefit meeting at Old South Hall in Boston to celebrate Armstrong and raise money for his school. Speakers included Rev. Edward Everett Hale;

Samuel Elliot of the Boston School Community; Rev. Samuel Barrows, editor of the *Christian Register*; and Booker T. Washington of Tuskegee. It was an assembly of the kinds of men Armstrong had been able to bring together around his vision. "New England deacon," "Boston millionaire," and "Quaker philanthropist" (as John Denison would note in his eulogy)[23] were joined by a black man who had been a former slave.[24] Once again Collis Huntington sent a special rail car, and once again Armstrong went home to Hampton, this time accompanied by his young wife, two of his daughters, and a nurse.[25]

Although he would remain crippled physically for the rest of his life, Armstrong's mind and spirit recovered with remarkable alacrity. He was no longer able to travel extensively, but he read, tried to keep up with the daily management of the institute, and corresponded with friends. He wrote to Archibald Hopkins, "I wish you could run down here for a Sunday or any day and go out boating with me. It is good to be near the water. I go to dine and visit shops, etc., in roller chair."[26] The daily operations of the school were conducted by Vice Principal and Chaplain H. B. Frissell, as were fundraising expeditions to the North.[27]

Despite his high spirits, Armstrong's physical condition continued to decline. It is clear that by May 1892 Armstrong could no longer write his own letters. They were no longer in his hand, and his signature was followed by the initials MFA, undoubtedly those of his wife, Mary Ford Armstrong.[28] General Armstrong finally was forced to acknowledge the rapid deterioration of his health. He wrote to the Board of Trustees, "For the first time since the school opened in 1868, I have been unable to regularly meet and talk to students and instruct the Senior Class through the winter months. This failure has been my greatest disappointment and trial, for daily touch with pupils . . . has been my constant inspiration and comfort." Armstrong was prepared to face the inevitable: "I am ready to resign and retire whenever it is best for the School and its work that I should do so. The change must come before very long and the School is more ready for it than you think. For years I have been preparing for it."[29]

In the spring of 1893, Armstrong spent two months with his protégé, Booker T. Washington, at Tuskegee. Even though the general arrived after midnight on 18 February, Washington had assembled the entire staff and student body of his institute to greet their guest with a torchlight parade, specially composed songs and poems of praise, and music by the full institute cadet band. The reception was typical of the fanfare that Washington showered upon his white benefactors, but it also undoubtedly was a heartfelt welcome to the man who had been most important in Booker Washington's life. The general occasionally was able to make addresses to the Tuskegee students at chapel. As noted above, a special wheelchair was constructed to enable Armstrong to move about the campus, pushed by the stronger male students.[30]

Armstrong was much missed at his own school. The girls of Hampton's senior class celebrated his return in a letter to him: "Dear General, We . . . feel it a great pleasure to have you with us again. . . . We enjoyed your talk of Sunday evening very much indeed. It was the greatest text of the term. We also enjoyed the books which you sent us [at] Xmas and wish to express our gratitude to you for them. We feel that it is through your great perseverance and interest in us that we have been able to reach this, the highest point at Hampton."[31]

Armstrong's spirit was indomitable, but it was clear to all that he was failing rapidly. The general threw his final energies into planning Hampton's twenty-fifth anniversary celebration, at Commencement on 25 May 1893. He also prepared a "Memoranda" to his Hampton family and his supporters, to be read "immediately upon my death." He wrote:

> I wish to be buried in the School graveyard, among the students, where one of them would have been put had he died next. I wish no monument or fuss whatever over my grave; only a simple headstone. . . . I wish the simplest funeral services, without sermon or attempt at oratory—a soldier's funeral.
>
> I wish no effort at a biography of myself made. Good friends might get up a pretty good story, but it would not be the whole truth. The truth of a life usually lies deep down—we hardly know ourselves—God only does. I trust His mercy. It pays to follow one's best lights—to put God and country first; ourselves afterward.
>
> Taps has just sounded.[32]

On May 11, 1893, two weeks before Hampton's twenty-fifth anniversary celebration, Samuel Chapman Armstrong died in his sleep. His wishes, of course, were disregarded. The celebration became a memorial service for the general. Eulogies from friends, benefactors, and former students poured in to his widow and the school. With much ceremony and recitation of poetry, Armstrong was given a funeral with full military honors, orchestrated by the commandant of the adjacent Soldiers' Home. His casket was carried to the burial site by an honor guard of five black and five Indian cadet company commanders. He was interred in the center of the student cemetery. Three years later, a large lava stone from the base of Moiliili volcano in Hawaii was sent to mark his grave. Succession passed smoothly to Hollis B. Frissell.[33]

Samuel Chapman Armstrong would have been served best by those who followed—especially his admirers—if they had heeded one request in his final "Memoranda." He wanted "no effort at a biography." He knew that "good friends might get up a pretty good story, but it would not be the whole truth."[34]

Armstrong grave site in Hampton Institute cemetery, c. 1910. Courtesy of Hampton University Archives.

Soon numerous laudatory biographies began to appear. In 1894, the faculty and officers of Hampton Institute formed themselves into an "Armstrong League of Hampton Workers," to raise scholarships and perpetuate Armstrong's legacy. Branches of the League were created throughout the North.[35] Armstrong was elevated to the status of a minor deity. His arguments in support of industrial education became a part of the formula for repression and humiliation of African Americans at the end of the nineteenth century and in the first decades of the twentieth. No longer able to temper his words and illuminate his positive intent with action, Armstrong the demigod, together with his prize pupil Booker T. Washington, quite properly became a prime target for vitriolic condemnation by those who demanded quality education for black people and an end to white paternalism.

In all the disputation, the complex, many-faceted man who was Samuel Chapman Armstrong was lost. "The truth of a life usually lies deep down—we hardly know ourselves," Armstrong had cautioned near the end of his life. He was right. During his lifetime, he fashioned out of missionary instincts, education, and military experience a particular vision of race and society that he pursued for the rest of his life. In the process, Armstrong created a school for freedmen that uniquely met their particular needs at that particular time. As times changed, Armstrong's students evolved much more quickly than his school was able to do. During his era, his tolerance and his support for their initiative distinguished his life and Hampton Institute. His true legacy, and therefore the ultimate measures of his life's impact, are his alumni and their descendants.

Armstrong had proclaimed Hampton Institute to them as a place "where you can come . . . as you are and become the man and woman you wish to become." The general, as he pursued financial and political security for his school and personal glory for himself, sometimes may have lost sight of that guiding principle. His students did not. They took what Hampton and its principal offered and in many ways made it suit their own needs. Racist and paternalistic though much of early Hampton's program may have been, it represented a way up and out of poverty and ignorance. It offered, at the least, access to a larger world.

From the beginning, Hampton's students probably understood this world in the South better than the well-meaning white folk who ran Hampton. (Remember Booker Washington's admonition to Armstrong about white Alabamans: "We have to lead them along gently.") Armstrong's graduates took what his school had to offer and used it to shape for themselves lives that undeniably were more meaningful and comfortable than they otherwise would have been. These graduates did not—could not—solve the abiding problem of American society's racism. It was not a problem of their creation, nor one susceptible of solution through their actions alone. When Hampton's graduates announced, "We are here; we are ready," white America, including even Armstrong, blinked; it, and he, refused to see.

One hundred years later, Americans of European descent seem still to have motes in their eyes. Because of men like Samuel Armstrong, the vision of African Americans may be a bit clearer. It is altogether appropriate, therefore, that Samuel Chapman Armstrong is buried amid those who knew and loved him best: his students and their teachers. It is the shared burden of his descendants and theirs to realize fully Armstrong's vision and Hampton's promise.

Notes

Frequently Used Abbreviations

AMA   American Missionary Association

ARCIA   *Annual Report of the Commissioners of Indian Affairs* (Washington, D.C.: Government Printing Office)

BRFAL   Bureau of Refugees, Freedmen and Abandoned Lands, Virginia, Record Group 14, National Archives, Washington, D.C.

HIRA   Records of Alumni and Former Students, Hampton Institute, in Hampton University Archives, Hampton, Virginia

HMCSL   Hawaiian Missionary Children's Society Library, Hawaiian Historical Society, Honolulu, Hawaii

HNAI   Hampton Normal and Agricultural Institute, Hampton, Virginia

HUA   Hampton University Archives, Hampton, Virginia

LMS   Helen Ludlow, ed., "Personal Memories and Letters of General Samuel C. Armstrong," 1898, unpublished manuscript in Hampton University Archives, Hampton, Virginia

MALC   Mary Anna Longstreth Collection, Historical Society of Pennsylvania, Philadephia

SCA   Samuel Chapman Armstrong

WCWC   Armstrong Family Papers, Williamsiana Collection, Williams College, Williamstown, Massachusetts

Preface

1. See Suzanne Carson Lovitt, "SCA, Missionary to the South" (Ph.D. diss., Johns Hopkins Univ., 1952); Robert F. Schneider, "SCA and the Founding of Hampton Institute" (Senior thesis, Williams College, 1973); Booker T. Washington, *Up from Slavery* (New York, 1901), Francis Peabody, *Education*

for Life (New York, 1918); and Edith Armstrong Talbot, *SCA: A Biographical Study* (New York, 1904).

2. W. E. B. DuBois, *Souls of Black Folk* (Chicago, 1903), esp. the chapter "Of Mr. Booker T. Washington and Others."

3. See Donald Spivey, *Education for the New Slavery: Black Industrial Education, 1868–1915* (Westport, Conn.: Greenwood Press, 1978); August Meier, *Negro Thought in America* (Ann Arbor: Univ. of Michigan Press, 1963); Robert Francis Engs, *Freedom's First Generation: Black Hampton, Virginia, 1861–1890* (Philadelphia: Univ. of Pennsylvania Press, 1979); and James D. Anderson, *The Education of Blacks in the South, 1860–1935* (Chapel Hill: Univ. of North Carolina Press, 1988).

4. George M. Fredrickson, *The Inner Civil War* (New York: Harper and Row, 1965).

5. James M. McPherson, *Abolitionist Legacy* (Princeton, N.J.: Princeton Univ. Press, 1975).

INTRODUCTION

1. SCA to Archibald Hopkins, 16 June 1868, in WCWC.

CHAPTER 1. THE ARMSTRONG LEGACY: RICHARD ARMSTRONG AND HIS HAWAIIAN MISSION

1. LMS, p. 5. This manuscript, prepared by one of SCA's devoted faculty members at Hampton Institute, is an uncritical celebration of his life. Letters reproduced therein have been edited so that no fault may be found with any of the Armstrong clan or with Hampton Institute. This author has attempted to find originals of the letters quoted and, whenever possible, uses those originals.

2. Ibid., 6.

3. Mary Frances Armstrong, "Richard Armstrong," in WCWC.

4 Ibid.

5. SCA Scrapbook, WCWC.

6. LMS, 7.

7. Bertram Wyatt-Brown, *Lewis Tappan and the Evangelical War Against Slavery* (New York: Atheneum, 1971), 28.

8. M. F. Armstrong, "Richard Armstrong."

9 Ibid.

10. Helen Ludlow, "Clarissa Chapman Armstrong," in WCWC. This memorial to Clarissa Armstrong is unpaginated.

11. LMS, 9.

12. LMS, 10.

13. LMS, 11.

14. LMS, 11, 19.

15. LMS, 12; Ludlow, "Clarissa C. Armstrong."

16. Richard Armstrong was a compulsive "list-maker." Along with all the goods
    that the missionary group had taken on board, he also recorded the names,
    ages, and weights of all his missionary colleagues. Since many of their de-
    scendants became powerful families in Hawaiian society, it is worth noting
    their names here. Besides Richard and Clarissa Armstrong, the couples were:
    William P. and Mary Ann McKinney Alexander, Alonzo and Mary Ann
    Jenny Chapin, John S. and Ursula Newell Emerson, Cochran and Rebecca
    Smith Forbes, Harvey A. and Rebecca Howard Hitchcock, David B. and
    Sarah Joiner Lyman, Lorenzo and Betsy Curtis Lyons, Ephraim and Julia
    Brooks Spaulding. The one unattached male was Edmund Rodgers, who may
    have been returning from a visit home to the United States. The record is
    unclear. Richard Armstrong Papers, WCWC.
17. Richard Armstrong, "Journal Kept on My Voyage to the Sandwich Islands,"
    in WCWC.
18 Ibid.
19 Ibid.
20 Ibid.
21. LMS, 12.
22. Richard Armstrong, "Journal Kept."
23 Ibid.
24 Ibid.
25 Ibid.
26 Ibid.
27. Richard Armstrong Diary, 20 Nov. 1832, in WCWC.
28. Richard Armstrong, "Journal Kept." Armstrong refers to these islands as both
    the "Washington Islands" and the "Marquesas Islands." The modern spell-
    ing is used here.
29. LMS, 27.
30. LMS, 29–32.
31. LMS, 29.
32. LMS, 29, 34.
33 Ibid.
34. There is some confusion about the number of children Richard and Clarissa
    Armstrong had. There were ten in all, eight of whom lived to adulthood.
    This first William N. died shortly after the Armstrongs' return to Hawaii.
    As was the custom in many families of that period, his name was given to
    his infant brother. One other Armstrong son, Reuben, died in infancy in
    1843. Armstrong Genealogy File, HUA.
35 Ibid.
36. LMS, 37–42.
37. SCA, *Lessons from the Hawaiian Islands* (Hampton, Va.: Normal School
    Printing Office, 1884), in HUA. There are many useful and entertaining
    books on this period of Hawaiian history, including Hiram Bingham, *A Resi-
    dence of Twenty-One Years in the Sandwich Islands* (Hartford, Conn., 1849);
    Harold W. Bradley, *The American Frontier in Hawaii* (Stanford, Calif.: Stanford
    Univ. Press, 1942); Gavan Daws, *Shoals of Time: A History of the Hawaiian Is-*

lands (New York: Macmillan, 1968); Manley Hopkins, *Hawaii: The Past, Present and Future of Its Island Kingdom* (London, 1862); Edward Joesting, *Hawaii: An Uncommon History* (New York: Norton, 1972). These works were consulted in preparing the brief summary of Hawaiian history that follows.

38. SCA, *Lessons from the Hawaiian Islands*, 206–8.
39. SCA Scrapbook, HUA.
40. Richard Armstrong, "Journal Kept," 24 Mar. 1838.
41 Ibid.
42. SCA, *Lessons from the Hawaiian Islands*, 210–11; Benjamin O. Wist, *A Century of Public Education in Hawaii* (Honolulu, 1940), 66–67; Rich Budnick, *Stolen Kingdom: An American Conspiracy* (Honolulu: Aloha Press, 1992), 13.
43. Ludlow, "Clarissa C. Armstrong."
44 Ibid.
45. M. F. Armstrong, "Richard Armstrong."
46. Richard Armstrong, "Journal Kept," 18 Nov. 1838.
47. Ibid., 20 Nov. 1832.
48. Ibid., undated entry, 1837.
49. Ibid., 24 Mar. 1838. As will be seen, SCA adopted similar views about varying classes of white men in the American South.
50. Ludlow, "Clarissa C. Armstrong."
51. M. F. Armstrong, "Richard Armstrong."
52. Arthur P. Dudden, *The American Pacific: From the Old China Trade to the Present* (New York: Oxford Univ. Press, 1992), 59.
53. M. F. Armstrong, "Richard Armstrong." This combination of land acquisition and training in how to use it was a central part of SCA's early design for Hampton Institute.
54. Dudden, *American Pacific*, 57; Wist, *A Century*, 63.
55. Budnick, *Stolen Kingdom*, 16–17; M. F. Armstrong, "Richard Armstrong." Richard's intensified dedication to temperance undoubtedly reflected his experience with alcoholism in the native Hawaiian nobility.
56. Budnick, *Stolen Kingdom*, 37.
57. SCA, "Reminiscences," in WCWC.
58 William N. Armstrong, as quoted in ibid.
59. Dudden, *American Pacific*, 56.
60. SCA, "Reminiscences." Italics in original.
61. Wist, *A Century*, 54–59.
62 Ibid.
63 Ibid.
64. SCA, "Jubilee of Oahu College, June 25, 1891," in HMCSL.
65. Ibid.; Wist, *A Century*, 63–71.

CHAPTER 2. SAMUEL CHAPMAN ARMSTRONG: COMING OF AGE IN HAWAII

1. Armstrong Genealogy File, HUA. After the move to Honolulu, Richard and Clarissa had two more daughters, Clara (1840) and Amelia (1845), who would survive to adulthood. Another son, Reuben (1842), died in infancy.

2. John Denison, "Address in Memory of SCA, January, 1894," in *Classbook for 1862,* reunion book, in WCWC.
3. Ibid.
4. Henry B. Restarick, "Hawaii and General Armstrong," in WCWC; Talbot, *SCA,* 14; SCA Scrapbook, WCWC.
5. Talbot, *SCA,* 15–16; M. F. Armstrong, "Richard Armstrong."
6. Talbot, *SCA,* 16.
7. By the 1850s, the descendants of the original missionaries had formed the Hawaiian Missionary Childrens' Society, also known as the "Cousins' Society," which continues to exist in Hawaii.
8. Talbot, *SCA,* 16.
9. Ibid., 15.
10. Ibid., 11.
11. Ellen Armstrong [Weaver] to Bishop Henry B. Restarick, n.d., in Armstrong Family Papers, WCWC. It is instructive about Armstrong that, even in his mature years, he never viewed as wrong this desecration of the graves of a people of a different race and religion.
12. Ellen Armstrong Weaver to Bishop Restarick, n.d., in Armstrong Family Papers, WCWC.
13. SCA, "Reminiscences."
14. SCA, "Journal, 1858," as quoted in LMS, 64. These explorations were major undertakings for teenagers, requiring them to sail dozens of miles across open seas from one island to another.
15. Ibid., 78. *Telemachus* was a model boat that Sam constructed for one of the younger missionary boys.
16. Ibid. (Nov. 30, 1858), 79.
17. Ibid. (Jan. 9, 1858), 90.
18. SCA, "Jubilee," HMCSL.
19. LMS, 29.
20. LMS, 44.
21. LMS, 44, 71. Ludlow defines a *lomi-lomi* as "the wonderful native massage which takes all the aches out of tired bones." Caucasians came to delight in it.
22. Talbot, *SCA,* 30–31.
23. Ibid., 34–35.
24. SCA, "Journal, 1858" (1 Jan. 1858), as quoted in LMS, 89.
25. Ibid., 53.
26. Denison, "Address in Memory."
27. SCA, "Address Delivered at Kawaiahao Church, June 25, 1891," supplement to *Daily P.C. Advertiser,* 26 June 1891, in HMCSL.
28. LMS, 62.
29. W. R. Castle, "Armstrong and Hawaii," in "Exercises for the Dedication of the Armstrong Memorial, 30 Jan. 1913," 14.
30. SCA, *Lessons from the Hawaiian Islands,* 219–20.
31. Ibid., 220.
32. Ibid., 214.
33. Standard encyclopedias give an adequate and more objective account of this

period, but for the views of participants and their advocates, see SCA, *Lessons from the Hawaiian Islands;* and Sylvester K. Stevens, *American Expansion in Hawaii, 1842–1898* (Harrisburg, Pa.: Archives Publishing Co., 1945), 46–159.

34. SCA to Jennie (Mary Jane) Armstrong, 29 Jan. 1860, in WCWC.
35. LMS, 46–47.
36. SCA to Ellen Armstrong [Weaver], 22 Sept. 1861, in WCWC.

CHAPTER 3. ACCULTURATION AND MATURATION: A HAWAIIAN IN AMERICA

1. Hawaiian informants advise me that SCA may have romanticized this description. The Huaana Road cannot be seen from the harbor.
2. LMS, 98.
3. Ibid.
4. LMS, 102.
5. LMS, 103.
6. SCA to Clarissa Armstrong, 13 Nov. 1860, quoted in LMS, 107.
7. SCA to Richard Baxter Armstrong, Nov. 30, 1860, in LMS, 108.
8. Ibid., 109. It is notable that SCA never spoke of Hawaiians, African Americans, or native Americans with such contempt as he did the natives of Central America. There is no evidence that he later sought to include Central Americans in his polyglot student body at Hampton Institute.
9. Ibid., 111.
10 Ibid.
11. Ibid., 112.
12 Ibid.
13. Ibid., 118.
14. Ibid., 120.
15. Ibid., 120.
16. SCA, "Journal" (Aug. 1860), HUA.
17. SCA to Clara Armstrong, 12 Dec. 1860, in LMS, 114.
18. Talbot, *SCA,* 48; SCA to Clara Armstrong, 5 Jan. 1862, in LMS, 214.
19. *Williams College Catalogue,* 1988–89 (Williamstown, Mass.: Williams College, 1988).
20. In this, Williams succeeded. Even 200 years later, Williams College is a very difficult place to get to when approached from eastern Massachusetts. Unhappy faculty and students, who could abide the isolation no longer, trekked eastward over the mountains in 1821 to found Amherst College in a less remote location.
21. Frederick Rudolph, *Mark Hopkins and the Log* (New Haven, Conn.: Yale Univ. Press, 1956), 91.
22. Ibid., 52–53.
23. Ibid., 60–61.
24. SCA to Ellen Armstrong [Weaver], 9 May 1862, WCWC.
25. Rudolph, *Mark Hopkins,* 26.
26. Denison, "Address in Memory"; SCA Scrapbook, WCWC.
27. SCA to Cousins' Society, 4 Jan. 1862, in WCWC.
28. SCA to Ellen Armstrong [Weaver], 24 Feb. 1861, in WCWC.

29. Rudolph, *Mark Hopkins,* 61.
30 Ibid.
31. Rudolph, *Mark Hopkins,* 227. As quoted from James Garfield to John Bascomb, professor of rhetoric at Williams College, Jan. 1872, in James Garfield Papers, Library of Congress, Washington, D.C.
32. SCA to Clarissa Armstrong, 10 Jan. 1861, in LMS, 126; SCA to Amelia Armstrong, 2 Feb. 1861, in LMS, 127.
33. SCA to Clara Armstrong, 5 Jan. 1862, in LMS, 214.
34. SCA to Clara Armstrong, 16 Jan. 1862, in LMS, 214.
35. LMS, 96.
36. Mark Hopkins, "The Living House; or, God's Method of Social Unity: A Baccalaureate Sermon," 3 Aug. 1862, in WCWC.
37. Denison, "Address in Memory."
38. Ibid. "Plumb survigorness" is apparently 19th-century slang for a man of exceptional energy, strength, and good health.
39. SCA to Clarissa Armstrong, 10 Jan. 1861, in LMS, 126–27.
40 Ibid.
41. Denison, "Address in Memory."
42. Henry Pitt Warren, "Founder's Day Address, Hampton Institute, 1913," in WCWC.
43. Frank Carter, "Founder's Day Address, Hampton Institute, 1902," in WCWC.
44. SCA, "At Williams College" (apparently excerpts from a diary Armstrong kept while at Williams), manuscript in HUA.
45. SCA to Archibald Hopkins, 20 Apr. 1861, in WCWC.
46. SCA to Clarissa Armstrong, 10 Jan. 1861, in LMS, 128.
47. SCA to Baxter Armstrong, 17 May 1861, in LMS, 128.
48. SCA to *Williams Quarterly* 9, no. 1 (Aug. 1861), in WCWC.
49. SCA to Ellen Armstrong [Weaver], 5 June 1861, in WCWC.
50. SCA, "At Williams College," and SCA to Ellen Armstrong [Weaver], 22 Sept. 1861, both in WCWC.
51. SCA to Baxter Armstrong, 21 Apr. 1861, in LMS, 144–45.
52. SCA to Cousins' Society, 2 Jan. and 28 Mar. 1862, both in HMCSL; SCA to Ellen Armstrong [Weaver], 5 June 1861, in WCWC.
53. SCA to Clara Armstrong, 5 Jan. 1862, in LMS, 214.
54. SCA to Cousins' Society, 2 Jan. 1862, in HMCSL, 206; SCA to Clarissa Armstrong, 15 Apr. 1862, in LMS, 219–20.
55. SCA to Clara Armstrong, 30 Mar. 1861, in LMS, 218.
56. SCA, "College Days," in HUA.
57. SCA to Clara Armstrong, 2 Apr. 1861, in LMS, 138.

Chapter 4. "To Save the Union": Samuel Chapman Armstrong and America's Civil War

1. SCA to Clarissa Armstrong, 20 Dec. 1862, in LMS, 292–93.
2. SCA to Amelia Armstrong, 27 Dec. 1863, in LMS, 356.

3. SCA to Amelia Armstrong, 30 Dec. 1860, in WCWC.
4. SCA to Baxter Armstrong, 17 May 1861, in WCWC.
5. Ibid.
6. SCA to Baxter Armstrong, 21 Apr. 1861, in WCWC.
7. SCA to Clara Armstrong, 25 Jan. 1862, in LMS, 219.
8. SCA to Clarissa Armstrong, 16 July 1862, in LMS, 223.
9. Ibid., 225–26.
10. Ibid., 227–28.
11. Ibid.
12. This *ad hoc* system, in which prominent citizens organized volunteer units which then were incorporated into the national army, was employed widely by both North and South in the early years of the war. See James M. McPherson, *Ordeal by Fire* (New York: Knopf, 1982), 169.
13. SCA to Clarissa Armstrong, 9 Aug. 1862, in LMS, 234–35; "Reminiscence" [of William Armstrong], in LMS, 231.
14. SCA to Clarissa Armstrong, 9 Aug. 1862, in LMS, 236.
15. Ibid., 235.
16. Ibid., 236.
17. SCA to Clarissa Armstrong, 17 Sept. 1862, in LMS, 248.
18. Ibid., 254.
19. "Reminiscence" [of William Armstrong], LMS, 232.
20. SCA, "War Journal," 1862, in LMS, 266.
21. Ibid., 252–53.
22. Ibid., 259–64.
23. Ibid., 265. *Parole* meant agreement not to fight. In this instance, the paroles never were finalized, and the 125th remained on parole for little more than a month. For an excellent brief description of the battles at Harpers Ferry and Antietam, see McPherson, *Ordeal by Fire,* 280–88.
24. SCA, "War Journal," in LMS, 265.
25. SCA to Clara Armstrong, 5 Oct. 1862, in LMS, 245–46.
26. SCA to Ellen Armstrong [Weaver], 21 Nov. 1862, in LMS, 275. It should also be noted that Northern families, equally unfamiliar with military discipline, often would ask their soldiers to come home, to help on the farm or simply to rest, since camp life often led to illness, and seemed to impede recovery. See James M. McPherson, *Battle Cry of Freedom* (New York: Oxford Univ. Press, 1988), 326–30.
27. SCA, "War Journal," in LMS, 271. SCA was proud that his Company D experienced few desertions and was one of the few companies that continued to drill. He attributed his men's obedience to the care he had given to them previously. Ibid., 267.
28. SCA to Clara Armstrong, 5 Oct. 1862, in LMS, 247.
29. SCA, "War Journal," in LMS, 273.
30. SCA to Ellen Armstrong [Weaver], 21 Nov. 1862, in LMS, 274. To Armstrong's delight, this time the regiment was transported in "elegant passenger cars" rather than boxcars. The difference seemed to buoy the spirits of the troops greatly.
31. SCA to Clarissa Armstrong, 5 Dec. 1862, in LMS, 276–79.

32. SCA to Cousins' Society, 22 Feb. 1863, in HMCSL.
33. Ibid.
34. SCA to Clarissa Armstrong, 2 Jan. 1863, in LMS, 292.
35. SCA to A. Hopkins, 15 and 25 Jan. 1863, in LMS, 297–99.
36. SCA to Baxter Armstrong, 8 Dec. 1862, in LMS, 285.
37. SCA to A. Hopkins, 8 Dec. 1862, LMS, 283.
38. SCA to Clarissa Armstrong, 20 Dec. 1862, in LMS, 287–88.
39. SCA to Clarissa Armstrong, 3 Jan. 1863, in LMS, 294.
40. SCA to Clarissa Armstrong, 14 Apr. 1863, in LMS, 306. In a letter to "Albany, New York, Democrats," 12 June 1863, Abraham Lincoln, defending his suppression of the press, despaired, "Must I shoot a simple-minded soldier boy who deserts, while I must not touch a hair of a wily agitator who induces him to desert?" Quoted in *The Living Lincoln,* ed. Paul M. Angle and Earl Schenck Miers (New York: Barnes & Noble, 1992), 551.
41. LMS, 305.
42. LMS, 303.
43. SCA to Clara Armstrong, 7 June 1863, in LMS, 312.
44. SCA to Clara Armstrong, 15 June 1863, in LMS, 316; SCA to Clarissa Armstrong, 5 July 1863, in LMS, 317.
45. SCA to Clara Armstrong, 15 June 1863, in LMS, 317.
46. Ibid., 318–20.
47. SCA to Clara Armstrong, 17 July 1863; SCA to Clarissa Armstrong, 5 July 1863, For a brief account of the Battle of Gettysburg and the role played by the Second Corps, see McPherson, *Battle Cry,* 326–33.
48. SCA Scrapbook, WCWC.
49. SCA to Clarissa Armstrong, 5 July 1863, in LMS, 321; "Chaplain Simmon's Account," in LMS, 340.
50. SCA to Armstrong Baxter, n.d. [Aug. 1863?], in LMS, 341.
51. For an excellent account of the New York Draft Riot, see Iver Bernstein, *The New York City Draft Riot* (New York: Oxford Univ. Press, 1990).

CHAPTER 5. "TO MAKE MEN FREE": COMMANDER OF BLACK TROOPS

About the epigraph: "The Negro Battle Hymn" is contained in LMS, 508.

1. For a moving portrait of this aspect of the American Civil War, see Warren Wilkinson, *Mother May You Never See the Sights I Have Seen* (New York: William Morrow, 1990).
2. McPherson, *Battle Cry,* 608–11, 684.
3. For the most recent treatment of Lincoln's decision to enlist black troops, see David Donald, *Lincoln* (New York: Simon & Schuster, 1995), 367, 430–31. Also see Joseph T. Glatthaar, *Forged in Battle: The Civil War Alliance of Black Soldiers and White Officers* (New York: Free Press, 1990), esp. 1–33.
4. Ira Berlin, Barbara J. Fields, Steven F. Miller, Joseph R. Reidy, and Leslie S. Rowland, *Slaves No More: Three Essays on Emancipation and the Civil War* (New York: Cambridge Univ. Press, 1992), 187–233; Dudley Cornish, *The Sable Arm* (New York: W. W. Norton, 1966), 135–36; Glatthaar, *Forged in*

Battle, 32. The 54th Massachusetts was the subject of the 1989 film, *Glory!* The Freedmen and Southern Society Project has produced the most comprehensive work on African American soldiers in the Civil War: *The Black Military Experience,* ed. Ira Berlin, Joseph R. Reidy, and Leslie S. Rowland (New York: Cambridge Univ. Press, 1992).

5. Cornish, *Sable Arm,* 79–93.
6. Andrew Evans to Samuel Evans, 2 and 18 May 1863, and Samuel Evans to Andrew Evans, 17 May 1863, all in Evans Family Papers, Ohio Historical Society, Columbus, Ohio.
7. SCA to A. Hopkins, 29 Sept. 1863, in WCWC.
8. SCA to Clarissa Armstrong, 17 Nov. 1863, in WCWC.
9. SCA to "Cousins," 22 Feb. 1863, in HMCSL; SCA, *Lessons from the Hawaiian Islands.*
10. SCA to Clarissa Armstrong, 17 Nov. 1863, in WCWC.
11. Ibid.
12. SCA to A. Hopkins, 17 Dec. 1863, in LMS, 354.
13. SCA to Clarissa Armstrong, 30 Aug. 1864, in WCWC.
14. SCA to A. Hopkins, 17 Dec. 1863, in LMS, 355.
15. Ibid.
16. SCA to "Cousins," 26 Nov. 1863, in HMCSL.
17. SCA to Clarissa Armstrong, 4 Mar. 1864, in LMS, 366. For summary histories of Armstrong's black regiments, the 9th and 8th USCT, see Frederick H. Dyer, *A Compendium of the War of the Rebellion* (New York: T. Yoseloff, 1959), 3:1725.
18. SCA to Clarissa Armstrong, 8 Mar. 1864, in LMS, 367–68.
19. SCA to Clarissa Armstrong, 27 Apr. 1864, in LMS, 379, SCA to Baxter Armstrong, 11 Oct. 1864, in LMS, 403–4.
20. For an insightful and groundbreaking study of this period and region, see Willie Lee Rose, *Rehearsal for Reconstruction: The Port Royal Experiment* (New York: Oxford Univ. Press, 1964). On the northern plantation managers, see Lawrence Powell, *New Masters: Northern Planters During the Civil War and Reconstruction* (New Haven, Conn.: Yale Univ. Press, 1980). For the response of the new freedmen to these northerners, from the perspective of a black missionary teacher, see *The Journal of Charlotte Forten: A Free Negro in the Slave Era,* ed. Ray Billington (New York: Norton, 1953).
21. SCA to Clara Armstrong, 29 Mar. 1864, in LMS, 375.
22. SCA to Clarissa Armstrong, 27 Apr. 1864, in LMS, 378.
23. SCA to Baxter Armstrong, 8 Feb. 1864, in LMS, 363–64.
24. SCA to Clarissa Armstrong, 12 May 1864, in LMS, 383.
25. SCA to Clarissa Armstrong, 30 Aug. 1864, in LMS, 397.
26. SCA to Clarissa Armstrong, 18 Aug. 1864, in LMS, 387. For short accounts of the final Virginia campaign, see McPherson, *Ordeal by Fire,* 410–28, 478–82.
27. SCA to Clarissa Armstrong, 18 Aug. 1864, in LMS, 389.
28. SCA to A. Hopkins, Oct. 1864, in LMS, 399; SCA to Baxter Armstrong, 11 Oct. 1864, in LMS, 402.
29. SCA to Clarissa Armstrong, 24 Nov. 1864, in LMS, 417. For an account of

the AMA's work in southeastern Virginia during the war, see Engs, *Freedom's First Generation.*

30. SCA to A. Hopkins, Oct. 1864, in LMS, 399–400.
31. SCA to Clarissa Armstrong, 14 Mar. 1865, in WCWC.
32. Ibid.
33. Ibid.
34. SCA to Clarissa Armstrong, 9 Apr. 1865, in WCWC.
35. Ibid.
36. Continuation of ibid., dated 24 Apr. 1865. Armstrong's injury was not seriously debilitating to him but made his handwriting after 1865 almost impossible to decipher.
37. Ibid.
38. Berlin et al., *Slaves No More,* 232–33; Glatthaar, *Forged in Battle,* 209–10.
39. As quoted in Glatthaar, *Forged in Battle,* 218.
40. SCA to Clarissa Armstrong, 30 May 1865, in LMS, 445–48; SCA to A. Hopkins, 26 June 1865, in LMS, 450; Glatthaar, *Forged in Battle,* 218–22.
41. SCA to Clarissa Armstrong, 30 May 1865, in LMS, 445–48; Donald, *Lincoln,* 367–68.
42. SCA to Clarissa Armstrong, 10 Aug. 1865, in LMS, 456–58.
43. Ibid., 462.
44. SCA to Clara Armstrong, 23 Aug. 1865, in WCWC.
45. Ibid.
46. SCA to Baxter Armstrong, Sept. 1865, in LMS, 484.
47. SCA to Clarissa Armstrong, 20 Oct. 1865, in WCWC; Dyer, *Compendium of the War,* 3:1725.
48. SCA to Clarissa Armstrong, 20 Oct. 1865, in WCWC. Large numbers of Freedmen's Bureau agents were former officers of the USCT. See Glatthaar, *Forged in Battle,* 210–12; and William McFeely, *Yankee Stepfather* (New Haven, Conn.: Yale Univ. Press, 1968), 65–83.
49. Achievement of citizenship was not a primary goal in Armstrong's decision to serve. This likely was the case with many other foreign soldiers who fought for the Union. Ella Lonn, *Foreigners in the Union Army and Navy* (New York: Greenwood Press, 1959), 72.

Chapter 6. To Realize Freedom's Promise: Freedmen's Bureau Agent, 1866–1868

About the epigraph: From O. O. Howard, "Anniversary Address, Hampton Institute, 1889," in LMS, 518.

1. This black agenda was first articulated in the words of AMA missionaries to the Sea Islands of South Carolina: "Farmhouse, schoolhouse, courthouse, and church house." See Rose, *Rehearsal for Reconstruction.* Attempts to realize this agenda are documented in Engs, *Freedom's First Generation,* passim. The most comprehensive documentation of the emancipation experience is in the volumes of the Freedmen and Southern Society Project. For an overview of these volumes, see Ira Berlin et al., *Slaves No More.*

2. Eric Foner, *Reconstruction: America's Unfinished Revolution, 1863–1877* (New York: Harper and Row, 1988), 159–64; on Virginia, see also Engs, *Freedom's First Generation,* 99–119.

3. Foner, *Reconstruction,* 271–316, 524–601, and passim.

4. Official titles for district officers of the Freedmen's Bureau varied considerably, although the position and responsibilities did not. A man in Armstrong's position might be referred to as "sub-assistant-commissioner," "assistant subcommissioner," "agent," or "superintendent." In this study, Armstrong will be referred to as "superintendent" or "agent," the two titles he most often used.

5. SCA to Jennie Armstrong, 22 Nov. 1866, in WCWC.

6. "Reminiscence" [of William Armstrong], LMS, 525–26.

7. Virginia's eastern coast along the Chesapeake Bay usually is divided into: Upper Peninsula, Middle Peninsula, and Lower Peninsula. The last usually is referred to simply as the Peninsula. That will be the usage here.

8. For a more extensive description of Hampton Roads and conditions there during the Civil War, see Engs, *Freedom's First Generation,* esp. 25–43 and 85–97.

9. C. B. Wilder to Orlando Brown, 18 Jan. 1866, in BRFAL.

10. SCA to A. Hopkins, 12 Sept. and 9 Oct. 1866, and 8 Mar. 1867, all in WCWC. SCA to Jennie Armstrong, 22 Nov. 1866, in WCWC.

11. SCA to A. Hopkins, 5 July 1867, in LMS, 593.

12. SCA to Baxter Armstrong, 3 Mar. 1865, in WCWC.

13. McFeely, *Yankee Stepfather,* 131–32.

14. For a full discussion of the failure of land redistribution schemes during Reconstruction, see Eric Foner, *Reconstruction,* 153–70; on specific events in southeastern Virginia, see Engs, *Freedom's First Generation,* 99–111.

15. McFeely, *Yankee Stepfather,* 103–34.

16. C. B. Wilder to Orlando Brown, 17 Nov. 1865, in BRFAL.

17. Reminiscences of Albert Howe, in LMS, 532. H. B. Scott to C. B. Wilder, 1 Nov. 1865; and C. B. Wilder to Orlando Brown, 27 Sept. and 16 Nov. 1865, and 5 Jan. 1866, all in BRFAL.

18. Circular Order, 4 Nov. 1865, BRFAL.

19. Ibid.

20. C. B. Wilder to AMA, 15 Jan. 1866, in AMA Archives, Amistad Research Center, Tulane Univ., New Orleans, La.

21. SCA to Clarissa Armstrong and Ellen Armstrong [Weaver], 15 Mar. 1866, in WCWC.

22. SCA to Clarissa Armstrong, 14 Mar. 1865, in WCWC.

23. *True Southerner,* 15 Mar. 1866, in HUA.

24. SCA to Orlando Brown, "Semi-Annual Report," 30 June 1866, BRFAL. SCA to Clarissa Armstrong, 15 Mar. 1867, in LMS, 558–60.

25. SCA to Clarissa Armstrong, 15 Mar. 1867, in LMS, 560.

26. SCA to Jennie Armstrong, 22 Nov. 1866, in LMS, 570.

27. SCA to Lt. Massey, 16 May 1866, in BRFAL.

28. Engs, *Freedom's First Generation,* 131. Thornton and Taylor became leading ministers in Hampton during Reconstruction. They and Norton also became powerful political leaders once blacks achieved the franchise.

29. SCA to Orlando Brown, "Semi-Annual Report," 30 June 1866, BRFAL.
30. SCA to Clarissa Armstrong, 30 Apr. 1867, in LMS, 585.
31. SCA to Orlando Brown, 28 Mar. 1866, in BRFAL; SCA to Asst. Superintendents, Circular Order no. 10, 24 May 1866; SCA to Orlando Brown, 28 Apr. 1866; all in BRFAL. These policies were especially offensive and unfair to the hundreds of Peninsula blacks who had been free before the war. The Freedmen's Bureau saw only color and made no distinctions based upon a black's antebellum status.
32. SCA to Orlando Brown, 28 Mar. 1866, in BRFAL; SCA to Lt. Col. Donnell, 9th Regiment, 12 Sept. 1866, in HUA.
33. SCA, "Letter of Appeal," in LMS, 545–47.
34. Oliver P. St. John to J. B. Kinsman, 19 Nov. 1864; St. John to SCA, 27 June 1866; and SCA to St. John, 5 July 1866, all in BRFAL. Mrs. L. A. Grimes to SCA, 5 July 1866, and SCA to B. L. Stearns, 13 July 1866, both in HUA.
35. SCA to Jennie Armstrong, 20 Jan. 1867, in WCWC.
36. SCA to Orlando Brown, 12 Jan. 1867, in BRFAL; Bureau of the Census, *9th U.S. Census* (1870).
37. SCA to Orlando Brown, "Semi-Annual Report," 30 June 1866, BRFAL. SCA to Clarissa Armstrong, 15 Mar. 1867, in LMS, 580–81.
38. SCA to Orlando Brown, "Semi-Annual Report," 30 June 1866, BRFAL. SCA to Clarissa Armstrong, 30 Apr. 1867, in LMS, 586.
39. SCA to Orlando Brown, "Quarterly Report," 30 June 1868, BRFAL.
40. SCA to Emma Walker [Armstrong], n.d. [Spring 1868?], in WCWC.
41. SCA to Jennie Armstrong, 7 Mar. 1867, in LMS, 576.
42. SCA to Orlando Brown, "Quarterly Report," 1 Nov. 1868, BRFAL.
43. SCA to A. Hopkins, 15 Mar. 1867, in WCWC.
44. SCA to Francis Judd, 23 Mar. 1867; SCA to Clara Armstrong, 13 Sept. 1867; and SCA to Jennie Armstrong, 22 Nov. 1866, all in WCWC. Also see Joesting, *Hawaii*, 174–82. Whatever SCA's opinion of his homeland was, his Civil War Service and later creation of Hampton Institute made him something of a national hero there.
45. SCA to Baxter Armstrong, 16 July 1868, in LMS, 689.
46. SCA to Jennie Armstrong, 1868, in LMS, 678.
47. SCA to Jennie Armstrong, 22 Nov. 1866, in WCWC.
48. SCA to Clara Armstrong, 13 Sept. 1867, in LMS, 600–601.
49. SCA to A. Hopkins, 1 Oct. 1867, in LMS, 603. The transcript of this letter in LMS may be a merging of two letters. As it is presented, SCA appears to have begun the letter while it was anticipated that E. P. Parsons would be the new principal, but to have concluded it upon receipt of news that Parsons had declined the position.

CHAPTER 7. "TO TEACH AND TO LEAD": FOUNDING HAMPTON INSTITUTE

About the epigraph: From SCA, "A Paper Read at the Anniversary Meeting of the AMA" (hereafter "Address to AMA"), Syracuse, N.Y., 24 Oct. 1877, in HUA.

1. Foner, *Reconstruction*, 159–64, 217–316. Also see Engs, *Freedom's First Generation*, 99–119.

2. Joe M. Richardson, *Christian Reconstruction: The American Missionary Association and Southern Blacks, 1861–1890* (Athens: Univ. of Georgia Press, 1986), vii–viii.

3. Robert C. Morris, *Reading, 'Riting, and Reconstruction: The Education of Freedmen in the South, 1861–1870* (Chicago: Univ. of Chicago Press, 1976), 149–73.

4. For a discussion of this process of disillusionment at one missionary site, see Engs, *Freedom's First Generation,* 67–83.

5. *American Missionary Magazine* 9 (1865): 3.

6. *American Missionary Magazine* 11 (1867): 108.

7. For examples of the AMA's agonizing debate over its proper direction, see *American Missionary Magazine* 9 (1865): 3; 11 (1867): 108; 12 (1868): 223; 14 (1870): 266.

8. *American Missionary Magazine* 11 (1867): 108.

9. Foner, *Reconstruction,* 99–100; Ronald Butchart, *Northern Schools, Southern Blacks, and Reconstruction: Freedmen's Education, 1862–1875* (Westport, Conn.: Greenwood Press, 1980), 174–75; Anderson, *Education of Blacks,* 28; V. P. Franklin, *Black Self-Determination: A Cultural History of African-American Resistance* (New York: Lawrence Hill Books, 1992), 167–68; and William A. Link, *A Hard Country and a Lonely Place: Schooling, Society, and Reform in Rural Virginia, 1870–1920* (Chapel Hill: Univ. of North Carolina Press, 1986), 42–43. It is interesting to note that the Ford Foundation, in cooperation with Harvard University's Graduate School of Education, in the 1960s and 1970s, undertook a somewhat similar mission to train the leadership of historically black colleges.

10. Anderson, *Education of Blacks,* 239–40.

11. Richardson, *Christian Reconstruction,* 109–19.

12. Ibid., 123–35. Fisk opened in 1866 with the financial assistance of the AMA and was called "The Fisk School." The school was reorganized as an institute of higher learning in a two-year period starting in 1867. See Joe M. Richardson, *A History of Fisk University, 1865–1946* (University, Ala.: Univ. of Alabama Press, 1980).

13. Foner, *Reconstruction,* 144–45. Frequently it was the freedmen themselves who started these schools, before the arrival of the Freedmen's Bureau and northern teachers. Ibid., 96–98; Engs, *Freedom's First Generation,* 13; Jacqueline Jones, *Soldiers of Light and Love: Northern Teachers and Georgia Blacks, 1865–1873* (Chapel Hill: Univ. of North Carolina Press, 1980), 69–70.

14. "Letter of Appeal," 16 Apr. 1866, in LMS, 547–48.

15. Philip Whitewell Wilson, *An Unofficial Statesman—Robert C. Ogden* (New York: Doubleday, Page and Co., 1924), 126.

16. Richardson, *Christian Reconstruction,* 81; LMS, 604–12.

17. SCA to Whipple, 15 May, 6 and 18 July, and 18 Sept. 1866; and SCA to E. P. Smith, 9 Oct. 1867; all in AMA Archives.

18. SCA, *Lessons from the Hawaiian Islands.*

19. SCA, "Address Delivered at Kawaiahao Church, June 25, 1891."

20. SCA, "Address to AMA, Syracuse, N.Y.," 24 Oct. 1877, in HUA.

21. *Principal's Report* (1881), HUA. SCA, in *Southern Workman,* July 1876, in HMCSL.

22. SCA to A. Hopkins, 6 Dec. 187[3?], in WCWC.

23. SCA to Emma Walker [Armstrong], 1878, in WCWC.

24. SCA to Emma Walker [Armstrong], 1869, in WCWC.

25. Link, *A Hard Country,* 181; Ogretta McNeil, "Social Discipline: The Strike of 1927," paper presented at the President's Forum, University of Pennsylvania, Philadelphia, Apr. 1986, University of Pennsylvania Archives. The student strike of 1927 and several earlier instances of student dissatisfaction centered on the mandated singing of spirituals for white visitors. Problems of this sort began to surface primarily after Armstrong's death in 1893.

26. *Catalogue of HNAI* (1870–71), in HUA.

27. SCA, "Normal School Work Among the Freedmen" (Address to the National Education Association of Boston, 6 Aug. 1872), in HUA.

28. *Principal's Report* (1875–76), HUA. SCA, "Normal School Work Among the Freedmen."

29. SCA, as quoted in F. Peabody, *Education for Life,* 118–19.

30. SCA, in *Southern Workman* (July 1876).

31. *Annual Report* (1880), HUA.

32. Charles A. Bennett, *History of Manual and Industrial Education Up to 1870* (Peoria, Ill., 1926), 242.

33. Theodore Dwight Weld, *First Annual Report of the Society for Promoting Manual Labor in Literary Institutions, Including the Report of Their General Agent* (New York, 1833), 56–64.

34. Robert S. Fletcher, *A History of Oberlin College* (Oberlin, Ohio, 1943), 1:347, 1:349–50, 2:634, 2:644–45; James Boykin, "Physical Training," chap. 13 in *Report of the Commissioner of Education, 1891–92* (Washington, D.C., 1894), 509; Morris Bishop, *A History of Cornell* (Ithaca, N.Y.: Cornell Univ. Press, 1962), 56–57.

35. See Bennett, *History of Manual School Education;* Boykin, "Physical Training"; Spivey, *Education for the New Slavery, passim*; Anderson, *Education of Blacks,* esp. 33–78. Also see James D. Anderson, "Philanthropic Control Over Private Black Higher Education," in *Philanthropy and Cultural Imperialism: The Foundations at Home and Abroad,* ed. Robert F. Arnove (Boston: G. K. Hall, 1980), 149–58. Professor Anderson draws a sharp distinction between the attitudes and goals of missionaries and those of supporters of industrial education. An examination of SCA's interactions with both does not support such a sharp distinction. An important chronological dimension also must be considered. Understanding of the purpose of industrial education evolved and changed during Armstrong's 25 years at Hampton. The direction of those changes became most obvious after Armstrong's death in 1893.

36. Engs, *Freedom's First Generation,* 148–49.

37. SCA, "Jubilee of Oahu College, June 25, 1891," in HMCSL. On Lahainaluna Seminary, see chap. 1 above.

38. SCA, "From the Beginning," as quoted in LMS, 619.

39. See Robert F. Engs, "The Hampton Connection, 1874–76: Hampton Graduates and the Alumni Support Network," *Hampton Institute Journal of Ethnic Studies* 11, no. 1 (May 1984): passim.

40. SCA to Emma Walker [Armstrong], n.d. [Spring, 1868?], in WCWC.

41. SCA to A. Hopkins, 1 Oct. 1867, in LMS, 603.

42. Rayford Logan, *Howard University, 1867–1967* (New York: New York Univ. Press, 1969), 52, 100.

43. *Catalogue of HNAI* (1870–71), HUA.

44. Richardson, *Christian Reconstruction,* 252–53.

45. SCA to Emma Walker [Armstrong], 3 Feb. 1868 and 24 Aug. 1870, both in WCWC.

46. SCA to Clarissa Armstrong, 20 Oct. 1865, in WCWC; Logan, *Howard University,* 12–15, 20–25.

47. LMS, 604–12.

48. *The Courant,* 10 June 1875, in Clippings File, HUA.

49. *Norfolk (Va.) Journal,* 9 June 1871, in Bacon Papers, Yale Univ.

50. SCA to Ellen Armstrong [Weaver], 21 Jan. 1865, in WCWC.

51. SCA to A. Hopkins, 21 Feb. 186[8?], in WCWC.

52. W. N. Ruffner to SCA, 5 Nov. 1873, in HUA; SCA to Emma Walker Armstrong, [Nov. or Dec.] 1872, in WCWC.

53. SCA to Emma Walker Armstrong, [Nov. or Dec.] 1872, in WCWC. Engs, *Freedom's First Generation,* 151, mistakenly presents this quotation as a comment by Armstrong on disciplinary problems at Hampton. The mistake was due, in part, to Armstrong's horrid handwriting. Rereading the original letter and taking note of the context of the letter—he was in Richmond raising funds—it is clear that he was talking about the *politics* of raising money for black schools, not about the black character.

54. Jack P. Maddex, Jr., *The Virginia Conservatives, 1867–1879* (Chapel Hill: Univ. of North Carolina Press, 1970), 215–16; Alrutheus A. Taylor, *The Negro in the Reconstruction of Virginia* (Washington, D.C., 1926), 168–70.

55. Engs, *Freedmen's First Generation,* 153.

56. SCA to Emma W. Armstrong, 28 Aug. 1870 and [Nov. or Dec.] 1872, both in WCWC. Henry Whittlesey to SCA, 19 Feb. 1870; R. A. Chapman to SCA, 2 Mar. 1870; and SCA to Whipple, 2 Mar. 1870, all in HUA; Richard B. Drake, "The American Missionary Association and the Southern Negro, 1861–1888" (Ph.D. diss., Emory Univ., 1957), 180.

57. Denison, "Address in Memory."

58. Engs, *Freedom's First Generation,* 139–43; SCA, "Address to AMA, Syracuse, N.Y.," 24 Oct. 1877.

59. *Catalogue of HNAI* (1871–72).

60. SCA to Clarissa Armstrong, 17 Aug. 1868, in LMS, 691.

CHAPTER 8. A MORE PERSONAL ARMSTRONG: SAM, EMMA, AND THE MISSIONARY LADIES, 1868–1878

1. *Annual Report* (various years, 1868–78), HUA; F. Peabody, *Education for Life,* 102–4; Rebecca Bacon to Leonard Bacon, 17 Mar. 1869, in Bacon Papers; SCA to Clarissa Armstrong, 19 Aug. 1869, in LMS, 711.

2. "Remembrance of Lucy Washburn," 10 Apr. 1918, in Mackie File, HUA.

3. "Remembrance of Albert Howe," n.d., in Mackie File, HUA.

4. "Remembrance of George Davis, Class of 1874," n.d., in Mackie File, HUA.

5. "Remembrance of Frank Banks, Class of 1876," n.d., in Mackie File, HUA.

6. Audiotaped interviews by Robert F. Engs, transcripts in collection of Engs: Mrs. Lillian Weaden Kemp, 9 Aug. 1974; Mrs. Hattie McGrew, 31 July 1973; Mrs. Phoencie Armstead Tull, 7 Aug. 1973. Alice Bacon file, HUA. At the time when I discovered this historical footnote, the city of Hampton was selecting a name for its new hospital. Those who wanted to retain the name "Dixie" were most displeased to learn the name's actual origin.

7. SCA to Martha Waldron, 7 Dec. 1880, and Waldron to SCA, 5 Jan. 1881, both in HUA.

8. SCA to Miss Peabody, 20 Sept. 1880, in HUA.

9. Richardson, *Christian Reconstruction,* 76; Rebecca Bacon to Leonard Bacon, 4 Oct. 1870 and 13 June 1871, both in Bacon Papers.

10. SCA to Emma W. Armstrong, 11 Sept. 1870, in WCWC.

11. *Annual Report* (1871–72), HUA. For interesting accounts of other "lady missionaries," see J. Jones, *Soldiers of Light and Love;* Henry L. Swint, ed., *Dear Ones at Home* (Nashville, Tenn.: Vanderbilt Univ. Press, 1966); and Rose, *Rehearsal for Reconstruction.* For the perspective of a middle-class northern black woman teaching with these white females, see *The Journal of Charlotte Forten,* ed. Billington; also see Linda M. Perkins, "The Black Female American Missionary Association Teacher in the South, 1861–1870," in *Black Women in United States History,* ed. Darlene Clark Hine (New York: Carlson Publishers, 1990), vol. 3: 1049–63.

12. SCA to A. Hopkins, 19 Mar. 1867, in LMS, 581; SCA to A. Hopkins, Nov. 1867, in WCWC.

13. "Chronology of Emma Dean Walker [Armstrong]," in HUA.

14. SCA to Clarissa Armstrong, 17 Aug. 1868, in LMS, 591.

15. See, as examples of these letters, SCA to Emma W. Armstrong, 1, 6, 7, 8, and 9 Jan. and 3 Feb. 1869, all in WCWC.

16. SCA to Emma W. Armstrong, 14 Nov. 1867, in WCWC.

17. SCA to A. Hopkins, 6 Apr. 1868; and SCA to Emma W. Armstrong, 7 Jan. and 9 Feb. 1869; all in WCWC.

18. SCA to Emma W. Armstrong, 14 Nov. 1867, in WCWC.

19. SCA to Clarissa Armstrong, 17 Aug. 1868, in LMS, 591.

20. SCA to Emma W. Armstrong, n.d. [Spring, 1869], in WCWC. Tragically, Emma's doubts proved well founded.

21. SCA to Clarissa Armstrong, 17 Aug. 1868, in LMS, 590.

22. SCA to Mark Hopkins, 21 Sept. 1869; and SCA to Emma W. Armstrong, n.d. [Fall, 1869?]; both in WCWC.

23. LMS, 643.

24. "Chronology of Emma Walker [Armstrong]," HUA. The baby was named after Louise Hopkins, daughter of Mark Hopkins and a close friend of both Armstrongs.

25. SCA to Emma W. Armstrong, 29 Aug. 1870, in WCWC.

26. Ibid.; SCA to Emma W. Armstrong, 10 Sept. 1870; and Emma W. Armstrong to Clarissa Armstrong, as a postscript to SCA to Clarissa Armstrong, 24 Dec. 1871; all in WCWC.

27. Emma W. Armstrong to Frances Walker, 12 Apr. 1871, in WCWC; "Chro-

nology of Emma Walker [Armstrong]," HUA. Several women colleagues have suggested that Emma probably was experiencing a severe postpartum depression, an illness not recognized by 19th-century doctors.

28. Emma W. Armstrong to Mary Anna Longstreth, Jan. 1875, in MALC.
29. Emma W. Armstrong to Longstreth, 5 and 6 Nov. 1874, in MALC.
30. Mary Mackie to Longstreth, 8 Nov. 1874, in MALC.
31. See, e.g., SCA to Emma W. Armstrong, 5 Dec. 1872 and 13 Dec. 187[7]?, both in WCWC.
32. Emma W. Armstrong to Longstreth, 16 Apr. 1875; and SCA to Longstreth, 7 and 13 Sept. 1875, all in MALC; "Chronology of Emma Walker [Armstrong]," HUA.
33. Clara Fields to Longstreth, 19 Dec. 1877; and Longstreth Journal (11 Jan. 1878); both in MALC.
34. Clara Fields to Longstreth, 19 Dec. 1877; Longstreth to SCA, 20 Jan. and 3 and 29 May 1878, all in WCWC; SCA to Emma W. Armstrong, Dec. 1877, in WCWC.
35. Longstreth to SCA, 20 Jan. and 3 May 1878, in WCWC.
36. Mrs. J. B. F. Marshall to Longstreth, 17 Aug. 1878, in MALC.
37. SCA to Longstreth, 21 May 1878, in MALC.
38. M. C. Reinertsen (Emma's nurse and companion) to Longstreth, 31 July, 5 Aug., and 4 and 10 Sept. 1878, all in MALC.
39. SCA to Longstreth, 11 Aug. 1878, in MALC.
40. Reinertsen to Longstreth, 11 Oct. 1878, and SCA to Longstreth, both in MALC.
41. SCA to Ellen Armstrong [Weaver], 31 July 1871, in LMS, 728; SCA to Longstreth, 1 Dec. 1878, in MALC; Longstreth to SCA, 10 Dec. 1878, in HUA.
42. SCA to Longstreth, 1 Dec. 1878; Helen Ludlow to Longstreth, 22 Dec. 1878; and SCA to Longstreth, 10 Apr. 1879; all in MALC.

Chapter 9. "Education for Life": Early Years of Hampton Institute, 1868–1878

About the epigraph: Quoted in F. Peabody, *Education for Life,* 97.
1. Gilbert Royals to SCA, 7 June 1868; William Foulkes to SCA, 24 Jan. 1868; C. L. Mead to SCA, 1 Jan. 1868; all in HUA.
2. E. F. W. Baker to SCA, 13 June 1878, in HUA.
3. P. Henkel to SCA, 1 Feb. 1890, in HUA.
4. Engs, *Freedom's First Generation,* 147; Arthur P. Davis, "William Roscoe Davis and his Descendants," *Negro History Bulletin* 13 (1950): 75–81.
5. *Annual Report* (1871–72), HUA.
6. Booker T. Washington, *Up from Slavery* (New York, 1901), 35–36. In Booker T. Washington, *The Story of My Life and Work* (Toronto, Ont., Canada, 1900), 157–58, he tells a more realistic story, in which he is fed and given rest before that "test" is taken.
7. Helen Ludlow, ed., *Twenty-Two Years' Work of the Hampton Normal and*

Agricultural Institute (Hampton, Va., 1893); Hampton Student Registration Records (1887), HUA.

8. Louis Harlan, *Booker T. Washington: The Making of a Black Leader* (New York: Oxford Univ. Press, 1972), vol. 1: 56–57; *Annual Report* (1872–73), HUA.
9. *Principal's Report* (1879), HUA.
10. *Principal's Report* (1871–72), HUA.
11. SCA, "Normal School Work Among the Freedmen."
12. *Principal's Report* (1876–77), HUA.
13. SCA to Philadelphia Friends, 4 Nov. 1878; and SCA to Miss Welch, 4 Mar. 1876; both in HUA. Hampton Admissions Flyer, 1870, HUA.
14. SCA, "From the Beginning," in LMS, 614–19.
15. Ibid., 149; *Annual Report* (1870), HUA; "Trade School Course" (1879), HUA.
16. Engs, *Freedom's First Generation,* 148–49; Ludlow, *Twenty-Two Years,* 57 and passim.
17. The literature on racial interaction and the resurgence of racism in the decades after Reconstruction is constantly evolving. C. Vann Woodward began the modern debate with *The Strange Career of Jim Crow,* 3d rev. ed. (New York: Oxford Univ. Press, 1974). Updates include Howard N. Rabinowitz, "More Than the Woodward Thesis: Assessing the Strange Career of Jim Crow," *Journal of American History* 75, no. 4 (Mar. 1989): 1156–78. Also see Joel Williamson, *The Crucible of Race: Black-White Relations in the American South Since Emancipation* (New York: Oxford Univ. Press, 1984); and Edward L. Ayers, *The Promise of the New South: Life After Reconstruction* (New York: Oxford Univ. Press, 1992), 132–59. For more of the African American perspective, see Franklin, *Black Self-Determination,* passim.
18. Engs, *Freedom's First Generation,* 149–50; *Annual Report* (1872–73), HUA.
19. *Annual Report* (1872–73), HUA.
20. "Disciplinary Records" (1875–76, 1877–78), HUA.
21. SCA to Dr. J. T. Boutelle, 8 Dec. 1879, and SCA to Capt. P. T. Woodfin, 10 Dec. 1879, both in HUA. Engs, *Freedom's First Generation,* 151.
22. Engs, *Freedom's First Generation,* 151. The quotation from Armstrong which follows these examples in the cited text is inaccurate and taken out of context. It refers to the *political* problems of getting aid for black schools, not to disciplinary issues.
23. "Disciplinary Records" (1884–85), HUA.
24. SCA to Emma W. Armstrong, 8 June 1872, in WCWC.
25. SCA to Emma W. Armstrong, 5 June 1872 and 8 Jan. 1878; SCA to W. J. Blackburn, 21 Oct. 1873 and 19 Jan. 1874; J. B. Towe to SCA, 2 Oct. 1877; and Tolitha Turner to SCA, 5 Nov. 1877; all in WCWC. "Disciplinary Records" (1876–77), HUA.
26. J. M. Moody to SCA, 3, 29, and 30 Apr. 1876, all in HUA.
27. E. A. White, E. A. Byrd, R. Kelser, A. W. Calvin, R. B. Jackson, W. T. Williams, C. Voorhees, W. Logan, W. M. Ivy, W. R. Unthank, W. M. Reid, R. H. Matthews, E. Harrison, A. Moore, W. S. Forsythe, B. Bradley, R. Smoat, F. D. Banks, P. W. Oliver, B. T. Washington, J. C. Robbins, and T. S. D. Berger to SCA, [Winter?] 1875, in HUA.

28. Engs, *Freedom's First Generation,* 155–56.
29. SCA to Emma W. Armstrong, 15 Sept. [no year], in HUA; Wilson, *Ogden,* 132–33.
30. L. B. Phillips to SCA, May 1877, in HUA; SCA to W. E. Cameron, governor of Virginia, 1 Feb. 1882, in HUA.
31. Engs, *Freedom's First Generation,* 158. See chap. 8 above.
32. For evidence of SCA's meticulous attention to the smallest details, see SCA, Letterbooks, 1870–90, HUA.
33. *American Missionary Magazine* 16, no. 4 (Apr. 1872): 84; SCA to William Thornton, 3 May 1878, in HUA; SCA to Editors of School Newspapers, 7 Nov. 1877, in HUA.
34. SCA to Emma W. Armstrong, [Nov. or Dec.] 1872, in WCWC. Several undated letters to Emma exist in WCWC. Context indicates they were written in November or December 1872, while Armstrong was recruiting singers in and around Richmond.
35. *New York Weekly Review,* 22 Mar. 1873; and *Rochester (N.Y.) Democrat,* 31 Mar. 1873, both clippings in HUA. SCA to Emma W. Armstrong, n.d. [Nov. 1872], in WCWC.
36. SCA to Emma W. Armstrong, Feb. 1873, in WCWC. This story about Grant is what SCA wrote to Emma; I have been unable to confirm it from other sources.
37. *Southern Workman* (Nov. 1880).
38. *American Missionary Magazine* 15, no. 5 (May 1871). William Lloyd Garrison to SCA, 4 June 1874; and William Still to SCA, 5 June 1874; both in HUA. Charles Williams, *Diary and Letters of Rutherford B. Hayes* (Columbus, Ohio, 1924–26), 3:482. The Dr. Franklin to whom Hayes refers is Benjamin Franklin, who founded an orphan's school in Philadelphia—it evolved to become the Univ. of Pennsylvania—on principles very similar to those of Armstrong's Hampton. Ironically, today, Penn still is criticized by its Ivy League peers as "too vocational."
39. Longstreth Journal (May 23, 1878), MALC.
40. Ibid.
41. SCA to A. Hopkins, 6 Dec. 187[3]?, in WCWC.
42. Anderson, *Education of Blacks,* 63; Hampton Institute Commencement Program, 1876, HUA.
43. Anderson, *Education of Blacks,* 63; see Hampton curriculum tables above.
44. SCA to Emma W. Armstrong, 5 June 1872, in WCWC.

Chapter 10. "Education for Backward Races": Teaching Two Races

About the epigraph: From SCA to Emma W. Armstrong, 13 Apr. 1878, in WCWC. Portions of this chapter are taken from Robert F. Engs, "Red, Black and White: A Study in Intellectual Inequality," in *Region, Race, and Reconstruction,* ed. J. Morgan Kousser and James M. McPherson, (New York: Oxford Univ. Press, 1986), 241–65. For the best recent study of the Indian Program at Hampton, see Mary Lou Hultgren and Paulette Fairbanks Molin, "To Lead and to Serve: Catalogue Essay and Chronology," in *To Lead and to Serve: American Indian Education at Hampton Institute, 1878–1923,* by Hultgren and Molin (Virginia Beach: Virginia Foundation for the Humanities and Public Policy, for the Hampton Univ. Museum, 1989). Extraordinary photographs accompany and enrich the text. The history of Indian education, and particularly the experiment at Hampton, remains a hotly debated subject. See, e.g., Donal Lindsay, *Indians at Hampton Institute, 1877–1923* (Champaign-Urbana: Univ. of Illinois Press, 1995), a sharply critical interpretation of the Indian Program. Lindsay failed to employ many of the sources used by Engs and by Hultgren and Molkin.

1. Margaret R. Muir, "Indian Education at Hampton Institute and Federal Policy" (Master's thesis, Brown Univ., 1970), 20–21.
2. Ibid.
3. Ibid., 57–59; Hultgren and Molin, "To Lead," 17–18.
4. For a useful capsule summary of the 19th-century consensus (shared even by many black leaders) on the meaning of civilization and the process by which it was attained, see: Wilson J. Moses, *Alexander Crummell: A Study of Civilization and Discontent* (New York: Oxford Univ. Press, 1989), 7. Because "civilization implied a historical process," white Americans, including SCA, assumed that darker-skinned peoples—who had started the process later—never could catch up, no matter what help they were given.
5. *Catalogue of HNAI* (1870), HUA.
6. SCA to Emma W. Armstrong, 19 Apr. 1878, in WCWC.
7. Hultgren and Molin, "To Lead," 51–55.
8. Everett A. Gilcreast, "Richard Henry Pratt and American Indian Policy, 1877–1906: A Study of the Assimilation Movement" (Ph.D. diss., Yale Univ., 1967), 1–7, 17, 24.
9. Ibid., 25–30.
10. Joseph W. Tingey, "Indians and Blacks Together: An Experiment in Biracial Education at Hampton Institute (1878–1923)" (Ed.D. diss., Teachers College, Columbia Univ., 1978), 148–49.
11. SCA to Emma W. Armstrong, 13 and 15 Apr. 1878, in WCWC.
12. The famed "before and after" photographs of Indian students—the "before" in Indian attire and the "after" in "citizens' dress"—clearly were public relations devices. Most Native American students arrived at Hampton in European style clothing.
13. Gilcreast, "Richard Henry Pratt," 12–14; F. Peabody, *Education for Life,* 156; Muir, "Indian Education," 80.
14. Hultgren and Molin, "To Lead," 37.
15. Ibid., 18; Gilcreast, "Richard Henry Pratt," 25; *Ten Years' Work for Indians at Hampton Institute* (Hampton, Va., 1888), 12.
16. *Ten Years' Work,* 31–38.
17. ARCIA (1878), 174. The bulk of Hampton's Indian students in the years 1878–88 were Dakota Sioux from the Yankton, Crow Creek, Lower Burie, Standing Rock, and Cheyenne River agencies.
18. Ibid., 73; *Ten Years' Work,* 11; ARCIA (1882), 73.

19. ARCIA (1879), 20–22, 30–33.
20. ARCIA (1882), 181; *Ten Years' Work,* 31; Miss Hobbs to Longstreth, 14 Apr. 1878, in MALC.
21. *Ten Years' Work,* 30. It should be noted that, in the final years of the Indian School program, after Armstrong's death, that students arrived better prepared and were able to enter the Normal Program.
22. Ibid., 25, 30; *Catalogue of HNAI* (1884), HUA.
23. Muir, "Indian Education," 43. (It is not clear if women students received a similar gift upon their departure.)
24. *Annual Report* (1880), HUA, pp. 6, 12–16.
25. Ibid.; *Ten Years' Work,* 13; SCA, *Indian Education at Hampton* (New York, 1881), 6.
26. F. Peabody, *Education for Life,* 154; *Ten Years' Work,* 33; Eleanor Gilman, retired staff member of Hampton Institute, audiotape interview by Robert F. Engs, 11 Mar. 1968, in author's files.
27. *Ten Years' Work,* 32–33.
28. Ibid., 25; ARCIA (1882), 184.
29. Tingey, "Indians and Blacks Together," 274; *Ten Years' Work,* 19–24; M. F. Armstrong, Helen Ludlow, and Elaine Goodale, *Hampton Institute, 1868–1885: Its Work for Two Races* (Hampton, Va., 1885), 23, HUA. By 1900, the separate dining hall for Indians had been replaced by separate tables for Indians in the regular dining area.
30. *Annual Report* (1884), HUA, p. 54.
31. *Ten Years' Work,* 34; Tingey, "Indians and Blacks Together," 179; SCA to E. Whittlesey and A. K. Smiley, Board of Indian Commissioners, 15 Mar. 1888, in HUA.
32. Hultgren and Molin disagree with my conclusion that the two programs were as separate as described. They are correct that the programs became more integrated in the years following Armstrong's death and as later Indian students came to Hampton much better prepared than their predecessors. Hultgren and Molin, "To Lead," 21–22.
33. Ibid., 19; Tingey, "Indians and Blacks Together," 198–200; Minutes of Meetings of Wigwam Council, 1890–91, HUA.
34. *Annual Report* (1884), HUA.
35. *Ten Years' Work,* 14.
36. Ibid., 15, 58.
37. Hultgren and Molin, "To Lead," 31–35.
38. Ibid., 31; Engs, *Freedom's First Generation,* 156–59.
39. Ultimately, the younger age of most Indian students and the curriculum provided for them made the married couples program impractical. Hultgren and Molin, "To Lead," 39.
40. *Catalogue of HNAI* (1884), 5.
41. M. F. Armstrong, Ludlow, and Goodale, *Hampton Institute,* 22.
42. *Ten Years' Work,* 14.
43. M. F. Armstrong, Ludlow, and Goodale, *Hampton Institute,* 15, 19.
44. Martha Waldron probably is referring to *phthisis,* a 19th-century term for

tuberculosis. The speculation that color shade, or "blood" mixture, some-how could determine susceptibility to this disease reflects the woeful state of medical knowledge and racial mythology among those who treated Hampton students. Armstrong, Ludlow, and Goodale, *Hampton Institute*, 19.

45. Armstrong, Ludlow, and Goodale, *Hampton Institute*, 23.

46. *Ten Years' Work*, 30; SCA, *Indian Education at Hampton*, 4; ARCIA (1883), 165.

47. *Annual Report* (1881), HUA, p. 7.

48. Ibid. It is not entirely clear whether, in these statements, Armstrong was speaking his mind or pandering to his northern and southern white bene-factors. His private correspondence suggests that his views about blacks were more positive and that his comments about Indians represented a conscious, optimistic distortion of his actual opinions, for fundraising purposes. See Engs, *Freedom's First Generation*, 139–60; SCA, Letterbooks, HUA.

49. SCA, *Indian Education at Hampton*, 5.

50. Ibid., 12.

51. SCA to Longstreth, 22 Sept. 1878, in MALC. In addition to the several books and pamphlets by Hampton faculty cited above, the institute frequently printed smaller promotional leaflets and pamphlets. In all of them Indian education was stressed heavily, and in some the black students on campus were mentioned only in noting that, on infrequent occasions, the Indian students met with them. Dozens of such publications are in the HUA files.

52. Helen Ludlow, *Are the Eastern Industrial Schools for Indian Children a Fail-ure?* (Philadelphia, 1886), 4–6; copy in HUA.

53. ARCIA (1888), 13.

54. SCA to Whittlesey and Smiley, 15 Mar. 1888, in HUA.

55. ARCIA (1888), 11 and 13.

56. *Southern Workman* 41 (Oct. 1912): 547; F. Peabody, *Education for Life*, 167–68. As of this writing, Hampton has reinstated a program for Indian stu-dents. Now Indian students are fully integrated with the regular, predomi-nantly African American, student body.

CHAPTER 11. "GATHERED TO SCATTER": LIVES AND WORK OF HAMPTON'S ALUMNI

1. See Spivey, *Education for the New Slavery;* Anderson, *Education of Blacks;* Engs, *Freedom's First Generation*.

2. Emily Austin to SCA, 5 Sept. 1878, and SCA to Austin, 18 Sept. 1878, both in HUA.

3. See *Ten Years' Work;* Ludlow, *Twenty-Two Years*.

4. HIRA. These records include data on every class that attended Hampton. Al-though some alumni records have been misplaced or damaged over the past 100 years, Hampton, of all the historically black colleges, possesses the most complete collection of alumni correspondence. It is a source that scholars have barely begun to tap. I use these records, rather than student letters published in the *Southern Workman*, because the latter letters were edited heavily to fit

points Armstrong and his staff wished to make publicly. Some of the letters which reveal the more liberating and academic aspects of Hampton's educational environment never were published in the *Southern Workman.*

5. SCA, *Indian Education at Hampton,* 13.

6. *Ten Years' Work,* 49.

7. Ludlow, *Eastern Industrial Schools,* 7; M. F. Armstrong, Ludlow, and Goodale, *Hampton Institute,* 17–18; Ludlow, *Twenty-Two Years,* 295–96, 317–18, 487.

8. Ludlow, *Twenty-Two Years,* 203.

9. U.S. Dept. of the Interior, *Hampton Normal and Agricultural Institute, Bureau of Education Bulletin* no. 27 (Washington, D.C., 1923), 91.

10. Susan LaFlesche File and Anna Dawson File, both in HIRA.

11. Thomas Sloan File and William Jones File, both in HIRA; Tingey, "Indians and Blacks Together," 213–16.

12. F. Peabody, *Education for Life,* 118.

13. HIRA.

14. Ibid. Fields's descendants continued to practice law in Hampton as late as 1988.

15. HIRA.

16. Ibid, 1874, 1875, 1876.

17. Frank T. Hyman File, HIRA. Frank's father was John B. Heyman, first black congressman from North Carolina.

18. Ibid.; Engs, *Freedom's First Generation,* 156.

19. Mary Melvin to Hampton Institute, 11 Nov. 1911, in HIRA.

20. William H. Adams to SCA, 18 Mar. 1878, in HIRA.

21. Included in mailing from Mary Melvin to Hampton Institute, 11 Nov. 1911, in HIRA.

22. John Newsome File, HIRA.

23. John Pool File, HIRA.

24. Sarah Hemmings to Hampton Institute, 21 May 1877, in HIRA. Also see Georgie Grey File, Lucy Morse File, and John Collins File, all in HIRA.

25. Joseph Mebane to SCA, 8 Aug. 1876, in HIRA.

26. M. J. Sherman to Alumni, Dec. 1908, in HIRA.

27. Lorenzo Ivy to Miss Tileston, 14 Dec. 1885, in HIRA.

28. HIRA.

29. Thomas Scott File, HIRA.

30. Anekthey Holland to M. J. Sherman, 26 Jan. 1909, in HIRA.

31. Joseph Mebane File, HIRA.

32. William Alexander Forsythe File, HIRA.

33. SCA to J. J. Bryant, 2 Jan. 1880; SCA to W. Ruffner, 2 Jan. 1880; George Thomas to SCA, 3 Sept. 1877; SCA to N.C. Schools Examiner, 26 Oct. 1879; SCA to N.J. Supt. of Public Schools, 10 Feb. 1879; SCA to Strieby, 7 and 18 Jan. 1878; T. S. Boliver to SCA, 16 Dec. 1889 and 21 Jan. 1890; Wallace V. Adams to SCA, 15 Nov. 1892; SCA to Adams, 29 Nov. 1892; all in HIRA.

34. William M. Skinner, Jr., to SCA, 3 Aug. 1889; SCA to Blanche K. Bruce, 31 Oct. 1879; J. Marshall to A. A. Bobson, 19 Feb. 1884; and Gabriel Whitehurst to SCA, 29 May 1878; all in HIRA.

35. Luther P. Jackson, *Negro Officeholders in Virginia* (Norfolk, Va.: Guide Quality Press, 1945), 1, 7, 36, 59, 63, 64, 67; Foner, *Reconstruction,* 592.

36. For a thorough and insightful analysis of the early Armstrong-Washington relationship, see Harlan, *Washington,* esp. 1:52–77.
37. Ibid., 79, 100; SCA to B. T. Washington, 10 Feb. 1879, HUA.
38. Harlan, *Washington,* 1:100. Harlan correctly notes that integration did not mean equality. A clear distinction between "teachers" (white) and "graduates" (black) remained into the 20th century.
39. Booker T. Washington File, HIRA. There are thousands of items in this file, including many clippings concerning Washington's achievements, compiled by his proud former teachers.
40. Harlan, *Washington,* 1:100–110.
41. B. T. Washington to SCA, 21 June 1881, 3 Feb. 1882, 19 Jan. 1885, 12 Aug. 1889; and J. Marshall to B. T. Washington, 9 May 1883; all in Booker T. Washington File, HIRA. It is remarkable that Washington apparently did not know these rudiments of bookkeeping after two years of operating Tuskegee.
42. B. T. Washington to SCA, 21 June and 26 Dec. 1881, in Booker T. Washington File, HIRA.
43. B. T. Washington to SCA, 18 Feb. 1884, 19 Jan. 1885, and 2 July 1890, all in Booker T. Washington File, HIRA.
44. These letters are too numerous to catalogue here, but as examples, see: B. T. Washington to SCA, 19 June and 18 Nov. 1885, 7 June 1886, 4 June 1887, 14 Apr. 1889, 26 Jan. and 7 June 1890, and 16 May 1891, all in Booker T. Washington File, HIRA.
45. B. T. Washington to SCA, 4 Feb. and 29 Apr. 1884, 4 Apr. and 13 Dec. 1889, and 19 Sept. and 27 Oct. 1891 (italics in original letter), all in Booker T. Washington File, HIRA.
46. B. T. Washington to SCA, 2 Aug. 1882, in Booker T. Washington File, HIRA. Harlan, *Washington,* 1:151, 1:201–3.
47. Undated program with notation, "We should do something of the kind," in Cora M. Folsom File, HUA.
48. Ibid.
49. Harlan, *Washington,* 1:203.

CHAPTER 12. EDUCATIONAL PROPAGANDIST AND ENTREPRENEUR, 1874–1886

About the epigraph: From Francis Peabody, "Founder's Day Address," 30 Jan. 1898, in HUA.
1. Engs, *Freedom's First Generation,* 154.
2. Edward S. Joyner to SCA, 1 June 1874; and William Wyson to SCA, 5 Mar. 1878; both in HUA.
3. Harlan, *Washington,* 1:66 and n. 27, p. 355; SCA, *Principal's Report* (1888 and 1890), HUA.
4. *Principal's Report* (1871), HUA.
5. *Principal's Report* (1881), HUA.
6. SCA, *Principal's Report* (1889), HUA.
7. *Principal's Report* (1891), HUA.
8. Ibid.

9. *Principal's Report* (1890), HUA.
10. *Principal's Report* (1891), HUA.
11. The rise of the Southern Farmers' Alliances and the minimal role played by black farmers are discussed in Ayers, *Promise of the New South,* 214–48.
12. *Principal's Report* (1887), HUA.
13. Ayers, *Promise of the New South,* 322.
14. Link, *A Hard Country,* 13, 21, 175–76.
15. *Principal's Report* (1889 and 1890), HUA.
16. William H. Ruffner to SCA, 1 June 1874, in HUA.
17. Joyner to SCA, 1 June 1874, in HUA.
18. SCA to James Garfield, 16 Feb. 1874, in HUA.
19. SCA to Ruffner, 1 Nov. 1879; and SCA to William Mahone, 5 Dec. 1881; both in HUA.
20. SCA to Peter Carter, 22 Feb. 1879, in HUA.
21. SCA to Ruffner, 1 Nov. 1879, in HUA.
22. Link, *A Hard Country,* 17–20.
23. For a discussion of the seriousness with which southerners viewed the Blair Bill, see C. Vann Woodward, *Origins of the New South* (Baton Rouge: Louisiana State Univ. Press, 1971), 63–64; and Williamson, *Crucible of Race,* 113.
24. SCA to Capt. Thompson, 1 Nov. 1879, in HUA.
25. Ibid.
26. *Annual Report* (1877), HUA.
27. Ayers, *Promise of the New South,* 46–47; SCA, *Principal's Report* (1883), HUA.
28. SCA, *Principal's Report* (1883), HUA. *Congressional Record,* 50th Cong., 1st Sess., 274. SCA on the Blair Bill, n.d., in SCA Scrapbook, HUA.
29. SCA to Emma W. Armstrong, 25 Nov. 1873[?], in WCWC.
30. SCA to the Class of '62, Williams College, 30 Sept. 1874, in LMS, 3:752–53.
31. SCA to Thomas Fenner, 9 Feb. 1887, in HUA.
32. George Brown to SCA, 19, 20, and 23 May 1882; SCA to H. Price, 17 and 20 May 1883; SCA to Whittlesey, 19 May 1883; SCA to Robert Lincoln (Secretary of War), 17 Jan. 1884; all in HUA.
33. Engs, *Freedom's First Generation,* 148.
34. "Trustee List, 1869–93," in Trustees File, HUA.
35. SCA to Emma W. Armstrong, 7 Sept. 1870, in WCWC. SCA to Whipple, 18 and 29 Sept. 1874; H. W. Hubbard to T. K. Fessenden, 17 Dec. 1879; and SCA to Strieby, 30 Jan. 1880; all in HUA. *Annual Report* (1876–77), HUA. It is worth noting that, to this day, Hampton University remains aloof from collaborative fundraising ventures for black higher education, such as the United Negro College Fund.
36. SCA to Henry Potter, 2 Jan. 1879, in HUA.
37. "Trustee List, 1869–93," HUA.
38. Ibid. Hampton's listing of early trustees is curious but helpful, because members are listed not in alphabetical order, but in order of longevity on the board, offering a graphic depiction of how the board changed over time.
39. Wilson, *Ogden,* 125.
40. Ogden to SCA, 26 May 1877, in HUA; SCA to Ogden, 14 June 1878, in Robert C. Ogden Papers, Library of Congress, Washington, D.C.

41. Wilson, *Ogden,* 126–27.
42. Ibid., 127–28.
43. Ibid., 156; Ogden to SCA, 28 Dec. 1883, in HUA.
44. Anderson, "Philanthropy," 149, 153–54.
45. "Report of Donations Received," in *Annual Report* (1871–72), HUA.
46. "Helping Educate Indians," n.d.; SCA Scrapbook; and Picture Files for 1880s; all three in HUA.
47. Cerinda W. Evans, *Collis Porter Huntington* (Newport News, Va.: Mariner's Museum, 1954), ii, 666.
48. Oscar Lewis, *The Big Four: The Story of Huntington, Stanford, Hopkins, and Crocker, and the Building of the Central Pacific* (New York, 1938), 263–64.
49. SCA to Huntington, 19 Oct. 1879; and SCA to J. F. B. Marshall, 27 Oct. 1890; both in HUA. One of the ironies of the Huntington-Hampton connection is that the Huntington Industrial Works soon disappeared from the campus, while the Collis P. Huntington Memorial Library served the school from 1903 until 1992, when it became the home of the Hampton University Museum and Archives.
50. *Principal's Report* (1890), HUA.
51. SCA to Joseph P. Gardner and SCA to Frederick F. Frelinghuysen, both 10 Nov. 1882, in HUA (italics added).
52. SCA to Emma W. Armstrong, 18 Dec. 1877, in WCWC.
53. See Kilpatrick Sales, *The Highest Stage of White Supremacy: The Origins of Segregation in South Africa and the American South* (New York: Cambridge Univ. Press, 1982), 54; George M. Fredrickson, *Black Liberation: A Comparative History of Black Ideologies in the United States and South Africa* (New York: Oxford Univ. Press, 1995), 119. The "Armstrong model" was adopted in the early 20th century, largely through the work of Booker T. Washington, rather than as a result of Armstrong's own efforts.
54. Interviews with anonymous Hampton staff contained in "[Samuel C.] Armstrong Chronology File," HUA.

CHAPTER 13. FINAL VOYAGES: HOME TO HAWAII AND HOME TO HAMPTON

About the epigraph: From SCA, "Memoranda," 1892, in "The Armstrong Symbol," Ogden Papers.
1. Denison, "Address in Memory."
2. Elbert B. Monroe, President of the Board of Trustees, "Important Statement Regarding General SCA," Sept. 1886; Rev. Phillip Brooks to H. B. Frissell, 11 Sept. 1886; Rev. Edward Everett Hale to Frissell, 8 Sept. 1886; and John G. Whittier to J. F. B. Marshall, 8 Sept. 1886; all in HUA. Rutherford B. Hayes to Edward Everett Hale, 5 Jan. 1892, in Rutherford B. Hayes Papers.
3. "SCA Chronology," HUA.
4. SCA to "Cousins," 26 Sept. 1886, in HUA.
5. Wilson, *Ogden,* 137, 138.
6. As observed in chap. 10, many former Hampton students entered teaching even though they had not completed the school's program. They, too, were

considered "Hampton's children"; they, too, were supported and evaluated by Armstrong and his touring faculty.

7. For reports of these journeys, sent back to Hampton by Armstrong, see LMS, 1009–26 and passim. Edited versions also appeared in the *Southern Workman,* 1887–88.

8. "Department Reports" (1893), HUA. For an example of Armstrong's attention to detail, see J. W. H. Pryor (student) to SCA, 9 Jan. 1893, in HUA. Pryor complained about the lack of fire and running water at the school farm, "Shellbanks." Armstrong appended a note to the letter suggesting to the farm manager: "Could not the boys have fire without too much risk? [A]nd water be brought in [by] pipes instead of buckets?"

9. Draft of *Principal's Report* (1892), HUA; Senior Girls to SCA, 22 Mar. 1893, in HUA.

10. R. R. Moton, "A Sketch of the Life and Work of Gen. Armstrong," *Howard Univ. Quarterly* 1, no. 3 (July 1893), clipping in SCA Scrapbook, HUA.

11. SCA to Rev. W. G. Alexander, 26 May 1887, in HUA.

12. SCA to "The Misses Georgie Washington, Sarah Peake, [illegible] . . . at Graduate Table," 13 Apr. 1889, in "Dining Table" File, HUA.

13. Anonymous teachers' letters, c. Apr. 1889, HUA. Although the letter is anonymous, the only teacher from New Hampshire appears to be Mary Alice Ford, soon to become the second Mrs. Armstrong.

14. SCA to " . . . Graduate Table," 13 Apr. 1889, HUA.

15. Hampton's archivists continue to search their records in an effort to clarify the conclusion of this incident. It is worth noting, however, that other facilities at Hampton Institute, including its chapel and auditorium, remained integrated until 1906, when the Massenburg Law outlawed such gatherings in Virginia. The statute was aimed specifically at the institute but also brought Virginia into line with statutes mandating segregation in other southern states.

16. SCA "Memoranda," HUA.

17. LMS, 1148–49.

18. Margaret Armstrong Howe to Eleanor Gilman, 19 Mar. 1959, in HUA.

19. Ibid.

20. There are enduring legends at Hampton, impossible to substantiate, that Armstrong, after being crippled by his second stroke, was able to maintain conjugal relations with the help of a manservant who—at a signal, the general banging his cane—would carry him to and from Mrs. Armstrong's bedchamber. Armstrong, after all, became father of a son only two months before his death. That son, David, spent much of his life assisting blacks at Hampton and in the U.S. Navy. Ironically, he died at exactly the same age as his father, 54, in 1947, while playing tennis. "SCA Chronology," HUA.

21. LMS, 1140–41.

22. SCA, "Address Delivered at Kawaiahao Church, June 25, 1891."

23. Denison, "Address in Memory."

24. LMS, 1149.

25. Ibid., 1155; Mary Alice Armstrong to H. B. Frissell, 24 Dec. 1891, in HUA.

26. SCA to A. Hopkins, 8 Apr. and 17 May 1892, both in WCWC.

27. LMS, 1156–63. Hollis Frissell was designated Armstrong's successor by the trustees in 1886. He served as principal from 1893 until his death in 1917. During his years as principal, Hampton's devotion to industrial education at the expense of its academic component became most fully articulated. Wilma King-Hunter, "Coming of Age: Hollis B. Frissell and the Emergence of Hampton Institute," Ph.D. diss., Indiana University of Pennsylvania, 1982; "Hollis B. Frissell Chronology," HUA. The collection of Frissell papers at HUA is even more extensive than the Armstrong collection. Professor King-Hunter is the first modern scholar to make extensive use of them.

28. SCA, Letterbook no. 8 (1892), HUA.

29. SCA, *Principal's Report* (1892), HUA.

30. Harlan, *Washington,* 1:201–2; Booker T. Washington to Hampton Institute, and Rev. Bedford (Tuskegee Trustee) to Hampton Institute, n.d. [Feb. 1893?], both as quoted in LMS, 1185–87.

31. Senior Girls to SCA, 22 Mar. 1893, in HUA.

32. SCA, "Memoranda," in Ogden Papers.

33. By 3 May 1893, Frissell was signing school correspondence as "Acting Principal." By 9 June, he signed them simply as "Principal." SCA, Letterbooks, Box 8, HUA.

34. SCA, "Memoranda," in Ogden Papers.

35. See "Eulogies" File; esp. moving items are a telegram from Booker T. Washington and an obituary by Robert Russa Moton, two of Armstrong's most illustrious pupils. *The Advertiser* [Honolulu, Hawaii], 11 Oct. 1956; *Principal's Report* (1894), HUA.

Selected Sources

Manuscripts and Archival Collections

Alumni Records. Hampton University Archives, Hampton, Virginia.

American Missionary Association Archives. Amistad Research Center, Tulane University, New Orleans, Louisiana.

Armstrong, Samuel Chapman. File. Hampton University Archives, Hampton, Virginia.

Armstrong Family Papers. Williamsiana Collection, Williams College, Williamstown, Massachusetts.

Bureau of Refugees, Freedmen and Abandoned Lands. Papers. National Archives, Washington, D.C.

Disciplinary Files. Hampton University Archives, Hampton, Virginia.

Garfield, James. Papers. Library of Congress, Washington, D.C.

Hawaiian Missionary Children's Society Library, Hawaiian Historical Society, Honolulu, Hawaii.

Hayes, Rutherford B. Papers. Rutherford B. Hayes Memorial Library, Columbus, Ohio.

Longstreth, Mary Alice. Collection. Historical Society of Pennsylvania, Philadelphia.

Ludlow, Helen W., ed. "Personal Memories and Letters of General Samuel C. Armstrong." Unpublished manuscript, 1898, in Hampton University Archives, Hampton, Virginia.

Ogden, Robert C. Papers. Library of Congress, Washington, D.C.

Photography Collection. Hampton University Archives, Hampton, Virginia.

Principal's Letterbooks. Hampton University Archives, Hampton, Virginia.

Trustees Files. Hampton University Archives, Hampton, Virginia.

Periodicals

American Missionary Magazine
Southern Workman
True Southerner

Books and Articles

Anderson, James. *The Education of Blacks in the South, 1860–1935.* Chapel Hill: Univ. of North Carolina Press, 1988.

Ayers, Edward L. *The Promise of the New South: Life After Reconstruction.* New York: Oxford Univ. Press, 1992.

Berlin, Ira; Barbara J. Fields; Steven F. Miller; Joseph P. Reidy; and Leslie S. Rowland. *Slaves No More: Three Essays on Emancipation and the Civil War.* New York: Cambridge Univ. Press, 1992.

Berlin, Ira; Joseph P. Reidy; and Leslie S. Rowland, eds. *The Black Military Experience.* New York: Cambridge Univ. Press, 1982.

Butchart, Ronald E. *Northern Schools, Southern Blacks, and Reconstruction: Freedmen's Education, 1862–1875.* Westport, Conn.: Greenwood Press, 1980.

Cornish, Dudley. *The Sable Arm.* Lawrence: Univ. Press of Kansas, 1987.

Daws, Gavan. *Shoals of Time: A History of the Hawaiian Islands.* New York: Macmillan, 1968.

Donald, David. *Lincoln.* New York: Simon and Schuster, 1995.

Dudden, Arthur P. *The American Pacific from the Old China Trade to the Present.* New York: Oxford Univ. Press, 1992.

Dyer, Frederick H. *A Compendium of the War of the Rebellion.* New York: T. Yoseloff, 1959.

Engs, Robert Francis. *Freedom's First Generation: Black Hampton, Virginia, 1861–1890.* Philadelphia: Univ. of Pennsylvania Press, 1979.

Evans, Cerinda W. *Collis Porter Huntington.* 2 vols. Newport News, Va.: Mariner's Museum, 1954.

Foner, Eric. *Reconstruction: America's Unfinished Revolution, 1863–1877.* New York: Harper and Row, 1988.

Franklin, V. P. *Black Self-Determination: A Cultural History of African-American Resistance.* New York: Lawrence Hill Books, 1992.

Fredrickson, George M. *Black Liberation: A Comparative History of Black Ideologies in the United States and South Africa.* New York: Oxford Univ. Press, 1995.

Glatthaar, Joseph T. *Forged in Battle: The Civil War Alliance of Black Soldiers and White Officers.* New York: Free Press, 1990.

Hultgren, Mary Lou, and Paulette Fairbanks Molin. *To Lead and to Serve: American Indian Education at Hampton Institute, 1979–1923.* Virginia Beach: Virginia Foundation for the Humanities, 1989.

Jones, Jacqueline. *Soldiers of Light and Love: Northern Teachers and Georgia Blacks, 1865–1873.* Chapel Hill: Univ. of North Carolina Press, 1980.

Harlan, Louis. *Booker T. Washington.* 2 vols. New York: Oxford Univ. Press, 1972; rev. ed., 1983.

Jackson, Luther P. *Negro Officeholders in Virginia, 1865–1895.* Norfolk, Va.: Guide Quality Press, 1945.

Joesting, Edward. *Hawaii: An Uncommon History.* New York: Norton, 1972.

Link, William A. *A Hard Country and a Lonely Place: Schooling, Society, and Reform in Rural Virginia, 1870–1920.* Chapel Hill: Univ. of North Carolina Press, 1986.

Lindsay, Donal. *Indians at Hampton Institute, 1877–1923.* Champaign-Urbana: Univ. of Illinois Press, 1995.

Logan, Rayford. *Howard University, 1867–1967.* New York: New York Univ. Press, 1969.

McFeely, William. *Yankee Stepfather.* New Haven, Conn.: Yale Univ. Press, 1968.

Maddex, Jack P., Jr. *The Virginia Conservatives, 1867–1879.* Chapel Hill: Univ. of North Carolina Press, 1970.

McPherson, James M. *Battle Cry of Freedom.* New York: Oxford Univ. Press, 1988.

————. *Ordeal by Fire.* New York: Alfred A. Knopf, 1982.

Morris, Robert C. *Reading, 'Riting, and Reconstruction: The Education of Freedmen in the South, 1861–1870.* Chicago: Univ. of Chicago Press, 1976.

Powell, Lawrence. *New Masters: Northern Planters During the Civil War and Reconstruction.* New Haven, Conn.: Yale Univ. Press, 1980.

Peabody, Francis Greenwood. *Education for Life: The Story of Hampton Institute.* New York: Doubleday, Page and Company, 1918.

Rabinowitz, Howard N. "More Than the Woodward Thesis: Assessing the Strange Career of Jim Crow." *Journal of American History* 75, no. 4 (Mar. 1989): 1156–78.

Richardson, Joe M. *Christian Reconstruction: The American Missionary Association and Southern Blacks, 1861–1890.* Athens: Univ. of Georgia Press, 1986.

Rudolph, Frederick. *Mark Hopkins and the Log.* New Haven, Conn.: Yale Univ. Press, 1956.

Rose, Willie Lee. *Rehearsal for Reconstruction: The Port Royal Experiment.* New York: Bobbs-Merrill Company, 1964.

Spivey, Donald. *Education for the New Slavery.* Westport, Conn.: Greenwood Press, 1978.

Taylor, Alrutheus Ambush. *The Negro in the Reconstruction of Virginia.* Washington, D.C.: Association for the Study of Negro Life and History, 1926.

Williamson, Joel. *The Crucible of Race: Black-White Relations in the American South Since Emancipation.* New York: Oxford Univ. Press, 1984.

Wilson, Philip Whitewell. *An Unofficial Statesman—Robert C. Ogden.* New York: Doubleday, Page and Company, 1924.

Woodward, C. Vann. *Origins of the New South.* Baton Rouge: Louisiana State Univ. Press, 1971.

————. *The Strange Career of Jim Crow.* 3rd rev. ed. New York: Oxford Univ. Press, 1974.

Wyatt-Brown, Bertram. *Lewis Tappan and the Evangelical War Against Slavery.* New York: Atheneum, 1971.

DISSERTATIONS AND THESES

Drake, Richard Bryant. "The American Missionary Association and the Southern Negro, 1861–1888." Ph.D. diss., Emory Univ., 1957.

Gilcreast, Everett Arthur. "Richard Henry Pratt and American Indian Policy, 1877–1906: A Study of the Assimilation Movement." Ph.D. diss., Yale Univ., 1967.

Lovitt, Suzanne Carson. "Samuel Chapman Armstrong, Missionary to the South." Ph.D. diss., Johns Hopkins Univ., 1952.

Schneider, Robert F. "Samuel Chapman Armstrong and the Founding of Hampton Institute." Senior thesis, Williams College, 1973.

Tingey, Joseph Williard. "Indians and Blacks Together: An Experiment in Biracial Education at Hampton Institute (1878–1923)." Ed.D. diss., Teachers' College, Columbia Univ., 1978.

INDEX

Adams, William (Hampton student), 135
African Americans: agenda and needs of freed slaves, 57–62; Armstrong's vision for, xi, xiii; education goals of freed, 71–72; effect of Hampton-style education on, 84–85; idea of former slaves as soldiers, 45–46; industrial and manual labor education for, 79–80; post–Civil War service in USCT (1865), 52–55; preparation at Hampton Institute, xv; under Reconstruction policies, 58–70; residents of Sea Islands (Gullahs), 49; SCA's agenda related to, 48; SCA's comparison to Hawaiians, 74, 76; SCA's perception of needs and culture of, 76–79; SCA's postwar concerns for and treatment of, 60–65, 84; service in Union Army, 47–50
African American students: devotion of alumni to Hampton, 134–36; funding for Hampton from alumni, 138–39; postgraduate careers of, 133–36
Alexander, Archibald, 2
Alford, Thomas "Wildcat" (Hampton student), 131
AMA. *See* American Missionary Association (AMA)
American Baptist Home Mission Society schools, 72–73
American Missionary Association (AMA), 49; founding of teacher-training schools, 73; goals of, 71; Hampton trustees as members of, 153; intent to found normal school in Hampton, 69; loses control of Hampton, 84; purchases Little Scotland plantation, 81

Anderson, James, xii
Armstrong, Caroline Jane (sister of SCA), 5, 12, 23
Armstrong, Clarissa Chapman (mother of SCA), 2–5, 13–14, 22, 86–87, 164
Armstrong, Daniel William (son of SCA), 164
Armstrong, Edith Hull (daughter of SCA), 93, 97
Armstrong, Eleanor Pollack (grand-mother of SCA), 1
Armstrong, Emma Walker (first wife of SCA), 67, 76, 89–96
Armstrong, James (grandfather of SCA), 1
Armstrong, James (uncle of SCA), 25
Armstrong, Louise Hopkins (daughter of SCA), 93, 97, 98
Armstrong, Margaret Marshall (daughter of SCA), 164
Armstrong, Mary Alice Ford (second wife of SCA), 97, 163–65
Armstrong, Mary Jane (sister of SCA), 9, 12
Armstrong, Richard Baxter (brother of SCA), 9, 12, 22, 97
Armstrong, Richard (father of SCA): activities in Hawaiian politics, 9–10; death of (1860), 22, 25; early life and education, 1–2; fight for land reform in Hawaii, 10; goals for education in Hawaii, 11; Hawaiian minister of public instruction, 10–11, 13, 20; manual labor concept of, 9, 11; missionary in Hawaii, 2–4, 6–8, 11; missionary in Marquesas Islands, 5–6; as pastor of Kawaiahao church, 9–10; strategies as missionary in Hawaii, xix–xx, 8–9

Educating the Disfranchised and Disinherited was designed and typeset on
a Macintosh computer system using PageMaker software. The text and titles
are set in Adobe Garamond. This book was designed by Todd Duren, composed by Kimberly Scarbrough, and manufactured by Thomson-Shore, Inc.
The recycled paper used in this book is designed for an effective life of at
least three hundred years.